FAITH IS...

JOSEPH AMAEZE

DARUDAN PUBLISHING

First published in 2022
by Darudan Publishing

Milton Keynes, Buckinghamshire, U.K

www.darudanpublishing.com

ISBN: 978-0-9935860-4-0

Printed in Great Britain by Lightning Source UK Ltd

Cover design: Vikncharlie

Image used with kind permission of © Gerd Altmann.

CONTENTS

Foreword

23. Investing in something regardless of the returns.
24. Having no plan B.
25. Crying with expectation.
26. Travelling on a journey where only you know the destination.
27. Taking a risk when the odds are against you.
28. Appearing to plant in the wrong season in the wrong soil.
29. Making a fool of yourself.
30. Doing and saying crazy stuff.
31. Believing in something you can't prove.
32. Seeing an impossible outcome.
33. Parking your five senses.
34. Trusting in one you have never seen.
35. Believing that water can come out of a rock.
36. Seeing riches when everyone else sees poverty.
37. Being pitied or avoided.
38. Investing without due diligence.
39. Not dwelling in the past.
40. Becoming pregnant with invisible seed.
41. Telling a story nobody believes.
42. Wrestling with doubt and boxing with unbelief.
43. Reaching up with conviction.
44. Focusing on God's integrity.
45. Not keeping up with the joneses.
46. Not following the majority.
47. Not feeding your appetites.
48. Being patient.
49. Seeing light in the midst of darkness.
50. Celebrating before the event.
51. A scary assurance.
52. Obeying an instruction to go somewhere you have never been.
53. Ignoring all the warning signs.

54. Walking in love with those you want to hate.
55. Speaking about things no eye has seen.
56. Leaving your comfort zone.
57. Jumping without a parachute.
58. Not assessing circumstances from the facts.
59. Diligence in spite of results.
60. Craving what no man can provide.
61. Being encouraged in the midst of discouragement.
62. Setting goals not based on ability.
63. Wanting to quit but showing up anyway.
64. Sowing all you have.
65. Walking in authority regardless of earthly status.
66. Believing things will change.
67. An eternal mindset.
68. Thanksgiving at a graveside.
69. Taking a step.
70. Calling out the result before the game.
71. Sleeping in a storm.
72. Remaining upbeat even when there's a cloud over your head.
73. Shutting down negative input.
74. Recognising and accepting closed doors.
75. Being still when everything is mobile
76. Believing that the seen was created by the unseen.
77. Submitting to the unknown.

Final Word

To Isoken, my wife and fellow traveller on this seemingly indefinite journey.

FOREWORD

What is faith? Some of us may be quick to say that *"faith is the substance of things hoped for, the evidence of things not seen"* [Hebrews 11:1]. Scripturally, that would be correct. However, think about that question in the context of your life experience and your walk with Christ. I therefore ask again – what is faith?

As one who has agonised over this question, I have searched the scriptures, hungrily seeking a set menu on the subject I could devour. I have heard hundreds of messages and sermons preached, as well as read many books and articles all proclaiming the same theme assuring me that faith cometh by hearing and hearing by the word [Romans 10:17 KJV]. However, quoting that scripture and experiencing results are two different things. Therein lies the frustration for many of us because the Bible makes clear that without faith it is impossible to please God [Hebrews 11:6]. Think about that. If we need faith to receive anything from God, and despite our best efforts we seem to come up short in this department, then we have a crisis.

This book was birthed along my daily commute by train when, armed with an enquiring mind, and a smartphone, I began to write. I considered faith from its most pragmatic roots and compiled my thoughts into meaningful prose. What I presumed would end up being seven or eight divinely inspired statements on the subject mushroomed, so that by the time I got to work they had morphed into over seventy. As is natural for me, I instantly saw a book with each of these faith statements forming a short chapter. The statements may only have been accumulated in a couple of hours or so, but in reality they are the culmination of many years contemplating the issue as I lurched from one challenge to another in the wilderness of God's development.

I recall a time in my life when answers to prayers came rapidly, but as I matured through exposure to God's word, like many others, I experienced friction. Prayers were still answered but the waiting times were longer. Anyone been there? It got to the point where the old faith became insufficient. I needed a new brand of faith to confront my challenges. At the heart of this faith would be a strong conviction which no grade of adversity could dislodge. In the midst of a crisis my grasp of faith led me to write an article in a Christian magazine titled "Faith Requires Mountains". The idea being that without mountains one cannot grow in faith.

I am still scaling mountains in a bid to grow my faith. But the experience has enriched my appreciation of God in more ways than a mind driven by five senses could ever comprehend. What you are about to read are seventy-seven articles on the subject of faith derived from the statements I referred to earlier. The thoughts in each one derive from my rock-climbing experience in the wilderness of faith, and I pray that they resonate with you as you tackle yours.

Joseph Amaeze
Milton Keynes
United Kingdom

15 November 2021

1

Sticking to the path regardless

Faith is sticking to the path we are on regardless of what comes our way. One moment we are confidently striding along a paved pathway armed with the misplaced presumption that it will be a short trek to a place of rest, only to discover the terrain becoming harsher the further we progress until we find ourselves in a wilderness. In this circumstance would you stick to the path regardless?

For some of us it may be a relationship that starts off well but along the way hits a bump in the road. In our pain, we jump ship driven by the discomfort of the environment rather than the leading of God's Holy Spirit. For others, it might be a job that begins on a high note with enviable terms and conditions and a role that seems tailor made for us until a new boss shows up who doesn't rate us and nitpicks at our work. For many faced with these situations when prayer fails to illuminate or produce the desired relief and all efforts to reverse the tide seem futile, it seems as if our divine GPS has misdirected us. In that season some of us question God's veracity if not openly, in our hearts. Others amongst us succumb to despair as our prayers to God for relief seem to go unanswered. What once seemed like a blessing now appears to be a curse. How many of us have jumped ship because we misread the situation based either on our instincts or the bad counsel of others?

Faith is sticking to the path we find ourselves along regardless of what hardships we encounter along the way. When we set off it looked like a piece of cake but as our surroundings transformed, with each step, we soon realise that we had been misled by our five senses.

Now I dare say that some of us would opine strong views on being misled and seek to retrace our steps, naturally. Why would we continue to trek along a route to a place of rest when the journey is anything but convenient? This was the dilemma facing the Children of Israel when they left Egypt. Loaded with high expectation on the back of what they had just seen God do, they had no premonition of the difficulties that lay ahead. As the old expression goes – *it was smooth sailing* up to a point. The reaction of the Children of Israel was anger and panic. They felt betrayed by those assigned to lead them to their place of rest and more significantly they felt betrayed and let down by God. Is that how we feel when our expectations are subjected to brutal contradictions?

We prayed for life, but death occurred; we prayed for wealth, but poverty endured. These are the contradictions of life that confront many a believing Christian, and sadly it is at the doorstep of this opposition that some of us make a U-turn and head the other way. Admittedly there are a stoic minority amongst us who will brave the harsh elements and put-up strong resistance. These hardy souls, fuelled by their own strength and resilience, forge ahead oblivious to the challenges. For them, it is all about survival of the fittest and the well-worn mantra of *God helps those who help themselves*. However, stoicism is not the evidence of faith.

It reminds me of the Children of Israel who after receiving God's judgment requiring them to wander around in the wilderness for forty years as punishment for disbelieving Him, sought to progress with earthly courage to the place of rest. Though it was only a short distance away they were killed in the process. Why? God was not in the equation [Numbers 14:40-45]. They lacked faith in God but wanted to obtain what He had promised without relying on Him to get it.

In another context, sticking to the path could be all about refusing to disobey God regardless of the temptation to do so. Examples abound through scripture of men like Joseph who despite the betrayal of his brothers and the injustice of Egypt refused to take the easy way out when confronted with temptation because he did not wish to offend God. Other men like Daniel and his friends who refused to eat meat sacrificed to idols because they did not wish to lose their purity or transfer their allegiance from the God of Israel. Who can forget Job who refused to curse God or speak out against Him after suffering such loss and torment in the hands of Satan? Job was eventually rewarded for his faithfulness. All these men had something in common; they had made God a priority in their lives and so regardless of what they encountered along the way they were able to stick to the path. They had no idea if or when He would show up to deliver them. Their commitment to the path was not dependent on their five senses.

Sticking to the path regardless of what challenges are encountered along the way is evidence of faith in God's word but is not something He expects us to do in our own strength. His strength is made perfect in our weakness [2 Corinthians 12:9]. Our assurance is that when we trust Him, He will be with us no matter what circumstances we confront along the way [Isaiah 43:2].

2

Not having any or all the answers

Faith does not need all the facts before it takes a step. It is not reckless or impulsive but courageous. Faith often kicks in when we do not have any or all the answers to the issues we confront in life.

No matter how intelligent or experienced we are, we will never have all the answers. In many areas of life people often have no answers. An easy example is the universe around us. This is the subject of speculation and presumption based on questionable science where planets are downgraded every generation and what was previously considered to be settled is discredited by later research e.g., Darwin's Theories. As Humanity reinvents itself and readjusts its marking scheme, Christians know that only the omniscient God has all the answers. When we know what to do, we tend not to rely on faith but when we come up against a brick wall, we need to look beyond ourselves to God. I would argue that even when we have an idea of what to do, and have all the information we need, there is still a strong ground for exercising faith in God rather than ourselves.

The man credited by the Bible as being the wisest man in the world (knowledge-wise) was King Solomon and even he urges us to trust in the Lord with all our hearts and not to lean on our own understanding. In all our ways we are encouraged to acknowledge Him (seek His counsel), and He will direct our paths [Proverbs 3:5-6]. Faith, therefore, reveals itself when we don't have all the answers and need direction. When we have in effect come to the end of ourselves and are basically clueless;

this is the point at which our faith has its best opportunity to reveal itself and spread its wings.

The Bible is full of people who had no answers to their problems and yet triumphed over every challenge. One who comes to mind is Abraham otherwise known as the Father of Faith. At the age of almost a hundred, when he was infertile and impotent, and married to a wife who was barren and almost ninety years old, he had no clue as to whether or not they would ever become biological parents of a child. He already had a child by his wife's Egyptian maid but when God made it clear that this child could not be his heir, Abraham was thrust into an unenviable situation where he had to hope against hope [Romans 4:18]. In other words, when his situation was hopeless, Abraham hoped. Against all hope Abraham believed that he would become a father because God promised him that his descendants would be numerous like the stars of the sky. This is remarkable because Abraham was as good as dead, and his aged wife was barren. Barrenness in old age is a double whammy. Yet, both believed God. As a result Sarah, Abraham's wife, received the strength to conceive and give birth to a son named Isaac [Hebrews 11:11]. In the natural, Abraham and Sarah had no answer to their predicament and what they desired was humanly impossible to obtain. This was the point at which their faith was demonstrated.

Faith cannot grow when we have all the answers. When we have all the answers we trust in our own judgment and boldly make decisions. Faith never shows up where there is an overflow of knowledge. It probably explains why some highly intelligent people with extremely high IQs refuse to seek or even believe in the existence of God. It is not their fault. They are blindsided by their own genius and the adulation and accolades that it attracts. It is why in the Bible the wise man – Ahithophel, who was a King's counsel, committed suicide when his counsel was ignored by the king in favour of that proffered by Hushai a man of lower intellectual merit [2 Samuel 17]. His pride was deeply hurt by the fact that his wise counsel was ignored. However, as we learn from Apostle Paul, God often uses the foolish things of this world to put to shame the wise [1 Corinthians 1:27]. God used the counsel of Hushai to obtain the result He wanted and thereby restored King David to his throne. David's faith in God in this critical hour resulted in deliverance and restoration.

Many of us know the life of David, and so there is no need to narrate the details of his journey. Suffice it to say that he was a man who frequently consulted God on every matter refusing to rely on his own judgment. Who can forget his reaction to the sacking of his community at Ziklag by the Amalekites and how he consulted God before deciding what action to take rather than just setting-off in pursuit of the invaders [1 Samuel 30]? He did not have all the answers and knew that reacting in the way his men expected would potentially result in even greater tragedy. On the few occasions where he relied on his own counsel, he ended up causing tragedy around him – transporting the Ark of the Covenant in complete disregard for Moses' directions; his indiscretion with Bathsheba; the murder of her husband; and his ill-advised census.

For the Christian, therefore, faith should show up when we do not have any or all the answers to the situations confronting us, as this is the most opportune moment for God to be glorified.

3

Being propelled by the word not the world

Yes, faith is being propelled by the word and not the world. You may have heard the scripture that teaches that faith comes by hearing the word of God [Romans 10:17]. This means that meditating on the word of God is at the root of faith. The more we hear and digest the word the more we grow in faith and, the more we grow in faith, the more we distance ourselves from the lifestyle and choices of the world around us.

This is essentially living a life governed by the word of God rather than the dictates of the society around. It is living in the world but not operating according to its rules. This kind of lifestyle is impossible to achieve without faith. The Bible cautions us against *friendship* with the world – finding affinity with the things of the world such as its mode of operation and the things it glorifies. We are told not to love the world or the things of the world [1 John 2:15]. If any man loves the world the bible confirms that the love of the Father [God] is not in them. We are also told that friendship with the world is enmity with God and that anyone who chooses to be a friend of the world becomes an enemy of God [James 4:4].

Planning that runs contrary to worldly trends is doomed to fail in the normal scheme of things because the world is structured to suffocate and quench anything within it that opposes it. Whilst it is possible to live a radical lifestyle and be deemed eccentric, to operate against the prevailing wisdom of the day is termed suicidal. Let me expatiate. A radical lifestyle in spiritual terms is actually another variant of worldliness, as it is earthly in origin and driven by choice. The evidence is seen in the many so-called radical lifestyles that soon become all the rage and spawn a new trend or fashion. Some have given up the trappings of wealth to dwell in rural settings living frugally like monks and consider themselves radical. There are others who eschew modern amenities like TV and mobile phones and pride themselves on being radical. Some believe that dressing in a particular way marks them out as radical. But time has shown that most radicalism is no better than a fad.

What about religion? There are multiple religions in the world each vying to convert the same audience with a 'new' message that has never been heard before and promising radical experiences to those who are bold enough to join them. However, religion has become integrated into our societies particularly in the West where the artificial policies of diversity and inclusiveness are preached. Religion is now mainstream and acceptable as an alternative lifestyle. And the occult? Well that's just another dark religion shrouded in thinly fabricated secrecy but practised quite openly by many in search of a new experience. Religious messages permeate every part of modern life and in the case of the occult dominate our media and entertainment.

Being propelled in life by God's word as captured in the Bible is not radical in the earthly religious sense, because it involves putting one's trust in a God whom no man has ever seen and believing in a book that professes a culture and lifestyle so much at odds with that promoted by the world. Religion doesn't put its trust in God's word even if it professes allegiance to a deity. The brand of radicalism we are talking about here is one rooted in the lifestyle and choices of a man named Jesus Christ. Every aspect of the Bible is about this man, and it is the primary tool by which the Holy Spirit enlightens those seeking to know Him more. Over two thousand years ago, Jesus was crucified near Jerusalem by the Roman occupiers simply because He claimed to be the son of God and advocated a lifestyle that was offensive to the religious order of the day. Jesus was a template of divinity in human form. Those who follow His example today and carefully adhere to the instructions in the book about His life (the Bible) are known as *Disciples of Christ*.

Disciples aren't those who assemble in churches on Sunday for a couple of hours or more, but they are the Monday to Sunday radicals who have received the gift of eternal life which Jesus offered in exchange for His gruesome death. These radicals live a life of faith based on what He taught and what other prophets taught about Him. Those who live this radical life are known as His disciples. Their aspiration is to know Him more and become like Him whilst in their current human form. In an age when the name 'Jesus' has become a cuss word by a society riddled with ignorance, it takes real faith to not only boldly proclaim this name with pride but to identify with His lifestyle and message. Religion can attempt to live the Ten Commandments, but it cannot love in the face of hate, or forgive trespasses that hurt it.

This life of faith adheres to the Sermon on the Mount – possibly Jesus' most radical message and one which many still marvel at today. Let's look at some examples. So Jesus taught in Matthew 5 that God judges the meditations of the heart when weighing sin. Therefore adultery can be committed merely by looking at another with lustful thoughts. This is a lifestyle where we are called to love our enemies and pray for those who persecute us because this is how children of God behave (Matthew 5:44-48). It is a life where we are commanded not to worry even if we are economically defeated because by trusting God and making His purpose a priority, He will provide us with everything we need (Matt 6:31-33). We are given the example of the birds and the flowers which are fed and clothed by God respectively, as a caution against worrying over our circumstances. Even though many of us know this scripture and can quote it, many of us aren't living it. The reason is probably a trust issue and was why many of the Children of Israel did not make it to the Promised Land. When we are motivated by God's word (the Bible) we acquire boldness and walk on water. But when we examine the elements and let them intimidate us, we give in to fear like Peter (Matthew 14:28). Peter is one of only two human beings to ever walk on water and he achieved this feat because his eyes were on Jesus. To live like this takes faith in God.

4

An assurance you cannot explain outside God's word

An assurance you cannot explain outside God's word is faith. You cannot explain why you feel such assurance, all you do is experience it. It is not linked to anything around you that can be perceived with the natural eyes. It has nothing to do with your upbringing; social status; economic standing; domicile; circumstances of birth; race; tribe or nationality. All hell is breaking loose, but you are at ease. You may express concern, but there is stillness in your heart. It is the quiet assurance you receive whenever you take God at His word. This is the sort of assurance that reflects the God brand of faith.

By assurance we are not speaking about the world's brand of confidence which is often misplaced. The world around us is in turmoil and all sorts of fear-based conditions and phobias are rife amongst society. Mental health problems are among the most endemic in the western world despite the preponderance of stuff accumulated by people, with many talented and highly skilled people consulting Psychiatrists in a bid to get help. A recent UK study highlighted the scale of the problem when it revealed that two out of every five young people are suffering from one form of mental illness. This is a worrying statistic. Admittedly not all of them are due to a fearful heart but most have agonised over life and become insecure. Their insecurity flows into their choices, and they start to believe the lie that God has deserted them. Once a Christian believes they have been abandoned or jettisoned by God, it's open season for all manner of fears, and anxieties to secrete themselves into that person's life.

Paul reminds us that if God is for us no one dare be against us [Romans 8:31]. Satan however seeks to block this knowledge by lies and deception that filter into our minds as we face various challenges – real and imagined. He engages in all manner of subterfuge designed to derail our senses and get us distracted from the truth. The believer who walks by sight [five senses] and not by faith is exposed to Satan's contradictions and is ill-equipped to dislodge the mindset that is established as a result of exposure to lies. A lack of assurance is evidence of an unhealthy mind. Such unhealthy minds breed fear and insecurity. Fear and insecurity in turn breed negativity, bitterness, envy, rage, hatred, and other such poisonous thought patterns that are responsible for all the crimes we witness or hear about in our society.

The first murder recorded in history began as a result of a poor self-image and insecurity. Cain murdered his younger brother because of his own insecurity. Cain did not feel accepted by God because he observed Abel enjoying God's favour [Genesis 4:4-5]. How many times have we observed a person envy another because of that person's success? This is a classic case of insecurity or lack of assurance. God describes his countenance as downcast (discouraged or disheartened) but assures him that if he improved his relationship with God, he would likewise experience favour. However, rather than repairing his relationship with God he opted to give in to the mindset plaguing him which resulted in murder.

If this seems obvious to the believer, it is not so obvious to the unbeliever (or potential believer as I like to term non-Christians). Physicians all over the world are trying to tackle mental disease as an illness without recognising its root. Cain's insecurity resulted from his lack of faith in God. That lack of faith can be traced back to his parents' sin against God when they disobeyed Him and fell out of His grace, resulting in a fearful disposition. Fear in Adam destroyed the assurance that once existed in humanity and with it a Pandora box was opened that unleashed all manner of dark mindsets including the insecurity that produced the first murder. Does this mean that Christians never suffer lack of assurance? Absolutely not! There are many who battle with insecurity and all manner of psychological problems not directly linked to anything they have done wrong. Even those who actively seek a close relationship with God through Jesus Christ also experience dark moments. But we cannot ignore the root of such illness in the sinfulness that entered the world as a result of Adam's disobedience. Apostle Paul confirms the above hypothesis when he clarifies that sin entered the world through Adam and produced death which spread to everyone making all men sinners [Romans 5:12].

The Bible promises that God will keep in perfect peace anyone whose mind is focussed on Him because that person trusts Him. [Isaiah 26:3]. This perfect peace is the foundation of the assurance which those who trust in Him enjoy. When the Bible says that a righteous person shall be as bold as a lion [Proverbs 28:1] it speaks of the assurance that Christians who trust in Him enjoy. There will be moments of doubt and times of weakening but in the general scheme of things these should not last. A Christian's steady state should be assurance. The Bible confirms that a righteous man is not afraid of evil tidings as his heart is fixed (or steadfast) trusting in the Lord [Psalm 112:7]. This trust derives from the quality of their relationship with God through meditation on his word.

It does not matter what is happening around a righteous man — as long as his eyes are on God's Holy Word, he will be divinely rooted and unshakeable.

5

Holding on to something that cannot be perceived with the five senses

In a previous statement, I referred to the well-known scripture on faith – Faith is the substance of things hoped for the evidence of things not seen [Hebrews 11:1]. When we hold on to something that cannot be perceived with the five senses, we have entered into the dimension known as *faith*. Let me clarify.

A promise is intangible. It cannot be perceived with the five senses. The object of a promise on the other hand can be seen. For instance, if I promised to give you my car next year, whilst the promise I made is intangible, my car which is the object of that promise is tangible and can be seen. Your expectation presumably based on my character and integrity is that I will give you the car at the appointed time. Most people would then remain expectant that at the appointed time next year they will become the owner of my car and the more prestigious the car the greater the joy and anticipation. This is a straightforward example of faith. Even though you have not yet received the car you have faith that you will. You could even begin to make plans for stuff you want to do with the car based on my promise. If only it were that simple in reality, we would all exhibit faith.

The statement, however, envisages something slightly more complex. To illustrate, I will refer to the story of a woman called Hannah who was the mother of a prophet known as Samuel [see 1 Samuel 1:1-20]. Hannah was the first wife of a man named Elkanah and she was barren. Elkanah had another wife named Peninnah who had borne him children. Hannah's heart ached for a child but despite her many prayers she remained childless, and this was the root of her sorrow. To crown Hannah's pain, Peninnah poked fun at her condition because God had shut her womb. Hold it one moment! God had shut Hannah's womb. Yes, it is recorded in the Bible [verse 6]. However, barrenness is a contradiction because, at the start of creation, God blessed Adam and Eve and commanded them to be fruitful. Barrenness only arrived in the earth because of sin. I believe that this means God *permitted* Hannah to be barren by not intervening to deliver her from something that had entered her family line because of sin in the earth. However, God causes all situations (good and bad) to work together for the good of those who love Him and who are called in accordance with His purpose [Romans 8:28]. I thought I ought to make this point for clarity.

On a particular pilgrimage to the Holy City of Shiloh, Hannah was so overwhelmed by her situation that she began to pray without any words actually coming out of her mouth. Her lips were forming the words, but no sound was emitted. Hannah was praying within her soul. As she prayed from the bitterness of her soul, with tears, she vowed that if God had mercy on her and delivered her from the barrenness by giving her a male child, she would in turn give that child back to God to serve Him all his days. She also added that the child would be a Nazarene (one separated unto God just like Samson). When Eli the Priest observed her lips, he thought she was drunk, but she clarified that she was only praying from her heavy-heartedness and the weight of her burden. Satisfied that she was not drunk, the priest asked her to go in peace and prayed that God would grant her the petition she asked of Him. The Bible records that Hannah left the temple and went to find food and her countenance was no longer sorrowful. Had she become pregnant at this stage? No. But she had received a promise in her soul that she would be pregnant. How was that promise delivered? By Eli the Priest who stood in the place of God in the temple. Eli had spoken but Hannah had heard God. The evidence that Hannah had received a promise was that she was no longer sad. This is faith. She was not physically pregnant, but she had received the promise of a pregnancy. This is what it means to hold on to something that cannot be perceived with the five senses.

The Bible subsequently records that after Hannah returned home and slept with her husband, God remembered her. How did God remember her? Did He remember her tears, or her wordless prayers, or her vow? I believe he remembered all these, but I believe that above all he remembered her transformed countenance after she received His promise spoken through the lips of Eli the priest. God remembered her faith.

As a result of God's remembrance, Hannah conceived and in due season gave birth to a son whom she named Samuel (meaning *I asked him of the Lord.*) We all pray and weep and make vows to God about what we will do for Him if He answers our prayers but many times, we do not receive anything because it is possible that we might not have received His promise. I firmly believe that the starting point of faith is a promise – a promise from God. Abraham received a promise from God, and he believed God even though his situation was hopeless. Likewise, God is looking to us to seek a promise from Him and then receive it by faith just like Hannah did.

6

Trust that seems insane

Have you ever held fast to a belief with a level of trust that seems insane? If so, this is the evidence of faith. Trust is a core element of faith because you must have confidence in the source of what you are expectant for. Such trust may seem insane to the mainstream because it goes against the grain of what society believes. You may be branded with derogatory names for your stubborn grip, but the evidence of your faith is that you never lose that steadfastness. Faith is about gripping until the manifestation of your expectation.

This brand of trust gets results even though it does appear insane to the casual observer. Several examples come to mind. The first example is that of the Hebrew boys Hananiah, Mishael, and Azariah (renamed Shadrach, Meshach, and Abednego in Babylon). The Bible records an incident that aptly showcases the insane brand of trust that we are talking about.

The three young men were senior administrators in the Babylonian Empire under the reign of the narcissistic and brutal King Nebuchadnezzar [Daniel 1:6-7]. They were Hebrews (Jews) who had been brought into Babylon as captives of war following the invasion of their country by the vicious king's armed forces. It is believed that they were made eunuchs (because they were kept under the care of a man named Ashpenaz the master of the king's eunuchs) and selected because of their pleasant appearance, knowledge, skills, and aptitude to be trained up as administrators. During their tenure as senior administrators, they refused to obey an edict of the king to bow to an image of gold erected by him [Daniel 3].

Now everybody in the kingdom, including governors, captains in the army, judges, the treasurers (accountants), rulers of provinces, bowed down and worshipped the golden image when the musical prompt was issued. It was a law in Babylon, that everyone should worship the golden image and the penalty for disobedience was death by burning in a fiery furnace.

However, it was reported to the king that three of his administrators were defying his edict and refusing to worship the golden image. The whistleblowers claimed that Shadrach, Meshach, and Abednego had no regard for the king and did not serve his gods or the golden image which he had erected. The king reportedly flew into a rage and commanded for them to be brought to him. Before we consider the rest of the account it is important to get a sense of what the three men were up against.

They were up against the most powerful, influential, and ruthless person in the world at that time. In fact, King Nebuchadnezzar was the most powerful and accomplished ruler in the world, overseeing the largest and most prominent nation across the earth. He had a track record of impressive military victories against other great nations of the time which he reduced to rubble and the survivors were taken into captivity. He was vain and narcissistic, with a penchant for inscribing his name on walls and pillars of his ancient city. The very construction of a golden image reveals his arrogance whilst the furnace he created to roast rebels reveals his ruthlessness.

When the three Jewish administrators were brought before the king, they stood no chance on paper of remaining defiant and holding on to their lives. The king was known for having his way and there was no rule of law at the time to afford them a fair hearing or chance of appeal if found guilty. The king was their judge, jury, and executioner. It is possible that they experienced a degree of apprehension in his fearsome presence but there is no record of this. He was undoubtedly intimidating but the Bible does not record any evidence of intimidation on their part. When they are commanded to obey the edict, they respond in a manner that reveals their brand of insane trust.

In the face of his tyrannical presence and the threat of instant but excruciating death, if only for the few minutes it took for them to melt from the intense heat, they boldly stood their ground placing their trust in God. Nebuchadnezzar made his position clear. The three Jewish men were to either bow down and worship the image and live or be cast alive into the burning fiery furnace he had created for rebels. He however made the mistake of adding, "and who is that God that shall deliver you out of my hands." [Daniel 3:15]. This was a direct challenge to the God of Israel. One can almost imagine Hananiah, Mishael, and Azariah stirring from their docile but stubborn state to a place of robust defiance. In effect they informed the king that: (i) they would not be careful with their response to his request; (ii) God whom they served was able to deliver them from the burning fiery furnace; (iii) God would deliver them out of the king's hand; and (iv) even if God did not deliver them, they would not serve the king's gods nor worship the golden image which he had erected.

There must have been stunned silence across the place as the three men finished speaking and a hushed silence would have fallen like a giant shroud over the crowd. In the eyes of all observers, they had just signed their death warrant. Nobody spoke to King Nebuchadnezzar that way and lived to share the experience. However, in the eyes of God, the three men had demonstrated an insane level of trust in Him. In the face of certain death, they remained defiant in their loyalty to a God whom they accepted might not intervene to save them. Well, I am sure most of us know the rest of the story but for those who do not I urge you to read the third chapter of the Book of Daniel in the Bible. The three men were thrown into the furnace and God intervened to rescue them miraculously. They survived the flames and there was no evidence of burn marks on either their bodies or clothes.

We may never face a threat like King Nebuchadnezzar but in our own experience we often come up against situations where the sort of insane brand of trust is required. In those situations, there is a risk that God will not come through for us. Many Christian disciples have displayed similar courage in the face of persecution for their faith and took a similar stance resulting in the loss of their lives. Their courageous refusal to denounce Jesus Christ cost them their lives but is still recorded by God as faith. In His sovereignty God decides what He does without consulting us but there is a great reward for those martyrs of the faith who refused to bow to the intimidation. Like Apostle Paul they have fought a good fight, finished their course, and kept the faith (2 Timothy 4:7).

7

Being afflicted by doubt but never caving-in to it

Faith is being afflicted by doubt but never caving-in to it. This may sound contradictory, but you need to read that statement again. Faith is not the total absence of doubt. Doubt is always present in some form, but it never has dominion. Doubt may afflict your mind but when you're walking by faith you never cave-in to its demands.

The picture of a person walking by faith with zero doubt is not a true reflection of most of us. Yes, there are some who have been given a gift of faith for the purpose of fulfilling an audacious agenda for the Kingdom, but they are not in the majority. There is no basis for feeling guilty if you experience a degree of doubt. Having a degree of doubt means that it has not yet dominated your thoughts. It is lingering in the background of your mind but is not in control. In other words, faith and doubt are co-habiting in your mind. Provided faith has the upper hand, the presence of doubt will not prevent a person receiving from God what He has promised to give.

The presence of doubt comes because we occupy a human body and have a soul. Our soul is programmed by whatever it feeds on and part of the time (most of the time in some cases) it is fed from the five senses. The reason for this is because we are human, and we live in a fallen world where humanity has lost the ability to walk by faith 24/7 like Adam used to do before the fall. Our fallen nature which the Bible refers to as the 'flesh' compels us to gravitate after earthly things (things that originate from the earth but lack the capacity to access divinity.) Governed by our five senses we typically believe what we can perceive through these senses and doubt what they cannot perceive. Doubt therefore arises when we are told something that makes no sense to our fleshly nature. Even when a part of us wants to believe what we have been told, we struggle because we cannot visualise it.

When God called forth a cowardly young man and informed him that he was going to liberate his nation from the oppression of a more powerful nation that had an army more than five times larger in size, it is easy to see why the young man's mind would be plagued by niggling doubt. Gideon was a young man overcome with fear and possessing a poor self-image [Judges 6-8]. When God approached him and called him *a mighty man of valour*, he was not convinced that he was the person being referred to. Because of his doubt, he kept putting God to the test, but God patiently engaged with him until Gideon summoned up the courage to obey. Initially Gideon's doubt was great, but God saw within him a suppressed courage. That suppressed courage was the residue of his faith. By getting Gideon to confront and overcome his fears, God got him to a place where his faith far exceeded his doubt.

However, a degree of doubt is different from being full of doubt. The expression, "being full of doubt" describes a situation where there is no room for faith in a person's mind. This is a fatal mindset. When doubt lingers on without anything counteracting it, it grows. As it grows it starts to dominate. As it dominates it creates a mindset until it ultimately becomes a state of unbelief.

Unbelief is the absence of belief. This is fatal to any Christian because we are called to walk by faith. The

Bible makes clear that unbelief prevents anyone from receiving God's promises [Hebrews 3:17-19 and 4:1-6]. Unbelief is evidence of the absence of faith and without faith the Bible tells us that it is impossible to please God [Hebrews 11:6]. If we cannot please God, we cannot receive anything from Him. To get a sense of how damaging unbelief is you need to see what the Bible says about it. The bible speaks about an evil heart of unbelief [Hebrews 3:12]. An evil heart? This means unbelief is a sin. To completely doubt God is a sin.

When doubts afflict a human mind, they are like armour piercing darts aimed at a helmet. Satan is the archer, and his objective is to steal, kill, and destroy anything that remotely resembles Jesus Christ. He targets a person's mind with doubts as a way of derailing their destiny. It is how he caused man to fall. He made Eve doubt what God had said and then sauntered through the open doorway of her mind to program her against Adam and cause the fall of humanity. The only thing that stands in the way of these fiery darts is a shield of faith.

When James says that those lacking wisdom should seek it from God, he cautions that when asking they should not waver (doubt) because the one who wavers is like a wave of the sea tossed and driven by the wind. He clarifies that such a person is schizophrenic and will never receive anything from God because of that instability [James 1:5-8]. This refers to one who asks God for something but does so with no expectation of receiving. This is a state of mind where doubt outweighs faith. There is a pendulum swing between belief and doubt, but the weight lingers longer at the side of doubt. Such a person is usually religious – having a form of godliness but denying the power inherent in it, because they invest more in their flesh than their spirit. Those who invest more in the flesh are more prone to doubt.

A person afflicted by doubt can still receive the manifestation of the Lord's promises to them provided they do not cave-in to such doubt or give it the upper hand. Doubt can be present but only as a bystander with no influence. No matter how intently Satan afflicts our minds, doubt must never be allowed to grow. This is because like weeds they have a tendency to take over. The ultimate objective is to dislodge even the most benign doubts because these stunt our growth.

The one afflicted by doubts but who does not cave-in to them will have what Christ called 'mustard seed faith'. Mustard seeds are small, but they have the potential to grow. Mustard seed faith is little faith, but it has the potential to grow into strong faith. The key to growth is prayer and meditation during which the promises of God flood a person's spirit. Fasting also has a way of energising our prayers enabling us to effectively dislodge doubt [Matthew 17:21]. By dwelling on the promises of God as captured in his word, a person with mustard seed faith grows in faith. As the person grows in faith, they dislodge those niggling doubts. This is where we must all get to.

8

Wearing out adversity

Faith is wearing out adversity. When you are more resilient than what you are up against, you have the potential to outlast and outlive it. In effect, faith is vividly on display when you exhaust the stuff that's been sent to exhaust you. Now you may argue that this is not something unique to the Christian faith in that many stoic and resilient people who have no faith in God have successfully worn out the adversity in their lives and triumphed over it. For instance, you may point to survivors of various debilitating diseases as an example of those who wage a psychological war against those deadly diseases and beat them. Whilst one admires their stoic and robust attitude in the face of a life and death situation, the reality is that for everyone who successfully *beats* a disease, there are a hundred others who don't, despite their best endeavours. Some things in life cannot be overcome by a stoic and defiant stance.

I coined this statement, 'wearing out adversity' during a particularly difficult period in my life where everything seemed to be against me, and stagnation was prevalent. I sensed that I was in an adverse situation but couldn't figure a way out despite my prayers and meditation on scripture. I began to realise after a while that in some situations there are no shortcuts. If God has permitted the situation, it means that He wants us to stay the course. In the heat of the moment, I vowed to wear out the adversity that was hemming me in on every side. This sort of determination had nothing to do with a robust personality or steely determination but more out of faith in God who promised that He would never allow us to be tempted beyond that which we are able to manage [1 Corinthians 10:13]. In my trial I confronted the truth that God had not brought me that far in life to abandon me and that it was His intention for me to wear out adversity rather than the other way round. This imbued me with strength.

The Bible says that if we faint in the day of adversity our strength is small [Proverbs 24:10]. This scripture makes clear that for a child of God, fainting under duress is not an option. God never meant for us to wear out adversity in our own strength but rather by reliance on His grace lest anyone boast. When we come to the end of ourselves in the middle of a crisis or strong challenge, the evidence that we are leaning on God is that regardless of the level of intensity we do not faint. What does it mean to faint?

Fainting means to weaken, quit, give up, expire, droop etc. Slumped shoulders are a classic example of one who has fainted in the biblical sense. An air of discouragement in one's mannerisms or countenance is evidence that one has quit the race and waved the white flag at the adversary. As the word implies, adversity comes from our adversary and every Christian knows this refers to the devil or Satan. In his quest to steal, kill, and destroy he unleashes all manner of challenges designed to undermine us and hammer our confidence in God and His word. Apostle Paul speaks about a season when he and his companions were afflicted to the point where they were pressed out of measure, above their strength and even got to the point of despairing of life; he says that they felt as if they were under a death sentence, but they trusted in the God who delivers from death and not in themselves [2 Corinthians 1:8-10].

Anyone who knows the life of Paul from the Biblical accounts, knows that he was a man well acquainted with sorrows throughout his time in Christian ministry. But we are grateful to Paul who taught us the secret of wearing out adversity. He refers to a moment when he was buffeted by a demonic agent who afflicted him with a thorn in the flesh – we are never told what this was and despite much speculation we will probably never know. All we do know was that it was painful, most likely agonisingly so, and uncomfortable. He begged God on three separate occasions to remove it, but God did not. However, according to Paul, God said 'My Grace is sufficient for thee: for my strength is made perfect in weakness' [2 Corinthians 12:7-10]. From this, Paul eventually learnt that when he was weak physically and emotionally, he was in fact strong because God was propping him up and enabling him to carry on regardless. Despite all that Satan threw at Paul, he failed to derail this fiery Apostle from fulfilling his divine mandate [2 Timothy 4: 6-8].

So how do we to wear out adversity? Simple, we follow Paul's example and turn to the Lord and seek His grace; we do not, however, try to do it on our own to show God how resilient we are. The starting point for building strength is God's word which contains all the nutrients we need to remain spiritually resilient in the face of the adversary's attacks. The battle always takes place in the mind, and it is here that the adversary amplifies situations and circumstances and makes them appear more overwhelming than they really are. The Bible is a book of wisdom and in the battle of the mind wisdom is strength [Proverbs 24:5].

No matter how hemmed in we feel, we should remember that God promises us that even the captives of the mighty shall be taken away and the prey of the terrible shall be delivered [Isaiah 49: 24-25]. No weapon fashioned by our adversary against us shall prosper [Isaiah 54:17] and if we are confident that God is for us then who can be against us? [Romans 8:31]. This is why we need to fill our minds with the truth which can only be found in God's word and trumps every lie and deception of our adversary. The Bible is clear that those who wait on the Lord will renew their strength, they shall mount up with wings as eagles; they shall run and not be weary; and they shall walk and not faint [Isaiah 40:31.] Finally, I want to remind us of what Apostle Paul says to those of us who are wondering whether to throw in the towel or carry on. He urges us not to grow weary in doing well for in due time we will reap the reward of our efforts if we faint not [Galatians 6:9].

9

A confidence that seems misplaced

When we are walking by faith, to the casual observer we may appear to have misplaced confidence, particularly where our circumstances indicate that all is not well or that we are heading for a crisis. A confidence that seems misplaced is the only way to describe some of our attitudes when facing the seemingly impossible. The evidence of this misplaced confidence lies in our words, our countenance, and our actions. This sort of attitude often rears its head when a Christian who is walking by faith receives bad news. There is a confidence that regardless of how bad everything is it will ultimately be all right. It is not uncommon to hear people say things like, 'We know that all things work together for good to them that love God, to them who are called according to His purpose' [Romans 8:28].

A person who senses that all things will work together for his/her good is apt to walk with a confidence that appears misplaced to those who perceive the situation with their five senses. Such a man was King David who as a young shepherd had carried out amazing feats because of the presence of God with him. Before famously slaying the Philistine giant called Goliath, David had killed a lion and a bear – both ferocious beasts far larger and physically powerful than human beings. When David appeared at the battlefield to face Goliath, he walked with a misplaced confidence that caught the attention of the King of Israel – Saul (who incidentally was the tallest man in Israel.) David was neither the tallest nor bulkiest of the men gathered at one end of the valley that day, in fact he had, had no military training and so was the least qualified on paper to face Goliath.

Saul tried to convince David that he was going to die because factually Goliath had a head start in terms of experience in warfare and size. However, David's confidence as misplaced as it may have seemed to all the army of Israel, was not rooted in his own experience or prowess but in the presence of God. David's self-assuredness disarmed Goliath who struggled to understand why the army of Israel had sent over a boy to fight him. However, the battle started before the main bout when Goliath cursed David by his gods and David made clear that God did not rescue His people with manmade weapons. David informed Goliath defiantly that he was going to kill him and feed his carcass to the birds and wild beasts [1 Samuel 17]. How could David exude such confidence when in the eyes of all watching on both sides of the battlefield, he was a dead man walking? It was because of where he had placed his trust.

He informed Saul that the Lord who had delivered him from the lion and the bear would deliver him out of the hand of the Philistine. When David eventually confronted Goliath, He informed him that he was coming to him in the name of the God of the armies of Israel whom Goliath had defied. Notice, he did not say he was coming against Goliath in his own name. Because of David's relationship with God, he knew the source of his inexplicable prowess. This confidence as misplaced as it seemed unnerved Goliath and may explain why he was powerless as David raced towards him twirling his sling. The whole battle was over in seconds.

A righteous person who has cultivated a close relationship with God is never perturbed by bad news [Psalm 112:7] because his heart is fixed trusting in the

Lord. Blessed is the man who trusts in the Lord whose hope (or confidence) is in Him [Jeremiah 17:7]. There is a blessing to the person who has made the Lord their refuge. I believe that the fearlessness that those who trust the Lord unwaveringly experience comes from their proximity to Him. The Bible is clear that there is no fear in love, but perfect love casts out all fear because fear carries torment; and the one who fears is not made perfect in love [1 John 4:18]. Again, the Bible teaches that God shall keep him in perfect peace whose mind is stayed on Him [Isaiah 26:3]. All these scriptures seem to capture the personality of David.

We have previously spoken about the three Hebrew administrators in Babylon – Shadrach, Meshach, and Abednego who defied King Nebuchadnezzar. Here again we have three men who had built up such a close relationship with God despite their circumstances to the extent that they were bold enough to defy the most tyrannical leader in the world at that time. To all the observers, they appeared to have misplaced confidence for having the effrontery to stand their ground before the king and refuse to obey his bidding. In the face of a fiery death, they refused to cave-in to his demands and effectively diminished his authority.

Without a doubt, the best example of a person who appeared to have misplaced confidence was Jesus Christ. Despite His well-publicised miraculous works, He was constantly exposed to the danger of losing His life at the hands of the priests and religious leaders in the region known as Palestine. Unlike the multitude of the Jewish population Jesus was never in awe of the prestige and status of the religious leaders or the Roman authority. When they eventually succeeded in arresting Him on trumped-up charges, they were unable to intimidate

Him. On one occasion he stood before Pontius Pilate who became so frustrated by Jesus' refusal to answer his questions that he said, 'Knowest thou not that I have power to crucify thee and have power to release thee? [John 19:10]. Jesus' response provides us with great insight Jesus said, *'you would have no authority over me if it were not given to you from above.'* Jesus understood that as a child of God, no one on earth no matter how powerful or influential had any authority or power over Him except God permitted it. Likewise, we need to learn to walk with the same confidence knowing that, as children of God, we would never have experienced any of the situations we face or challenges in our lives unless God permitted them.

10

Being prepared for loneliness in one's position

Being prepared for loneliness in one's position is one of the great hallmarks of faith. What does this mean? It means that you probably say "yes" when the majority say "no" and say "no" when the majority say "yes". It means you are not led by the crowd in terms of your perspective and opinion and are not seeking popularity. Loneliness is always a risk once a person decides to take an unpopular stance which aligns with God's will. There is a tendency for most people to toe the popular line for whatever reason. Some people want to be liked and resist unpopularity, others want the security of the generality – there is safety in numbers after all. Others may want to play it safe; and yet there are others who are insecure and will back the majority opinion even if they are not entirely convinced that it is the right one.

It takes a brave person to stand their ground on a position that is not popular. We live in a society today where many Christians, in trying to identify with the trends in society, choose to remain silent on issues that they should be outspoken about. These issues are sensitive socially and politically and many Christians navigate their way through them by taking a middle of the road position that is not offensive to those they are trying to identify with. In an age when the church is facing even greater persecution than at any other time in history because of perceptions about its politically incorrect perspective on mainstream issues, this is a time for Christians to be prepared for loneliness in their position. Sadly, many of us would rather cower in the shadows than stand in the light we claim to represent.

The Prophets Elijah, Jeremiah, and Isaiah were extremely unpopular during their day because of their 'controversial' views on righteousness and holiness in the face of societal decay. Israel had turned its back on God and embraced the heathen practices of the nations around them – nations that God had conquered to give them access. The people started serving other gods, sacrificing their children to them, and observing their festivals and rituals. They intermarried and committed all manner of evil which provoked God. In line with His long-suffering nature, God sent prophets to them to urge them to turn back to Him and to caution them about the sanctions for disobedience, but they remained obstinate.

One day the Prophet Elijah confronted King Ahab and informed him and the nation that there would be no rainfall for the next three and a half years [1 Kings 17:1]. What followed was forty-two months of drought across the nation. Yet the King, and his occultist spouse Queen Jezebel who had introduced the worship of Baal and created temples for this false god, refused to repent. For most of these three and a half years, Elijah moved from place to place with a consciousness that he was the only priest or prophet serving God in the land. The knowledge that he was in religious minority meant that he had to carry on his shoulders the weight of responsibility. The whole nation had turned to idolatry except a few and Elijah saw the survival of God's temple as falling to him. In this regard he was prepared to be unpopular.

When God eventually sent Elijah to present himself before King Ahab so that He could restore rainfall to the land, Elijah proposed a contest between himself and the four hundred and fifty prophets of Baal and the four hundred prophets of Asherah who ate at Jezebel's table.

When the prophets convened at the place for the contest along with the crowds of onlookers, Elijah stated that he was the only one of the Lord's prophets left but was willing to take on the four hundred and fifty prophets of Baal. The contest was for the souls of the people who had been misled by Jezebel and it was about determining which God was the real deal – the Lord or Baal.

At the end of the contest which Elijah won, because only the Lord showed up to endorse his prophet as opposed to Baal who was a no-show (no surprise there), he commanded the people to seize all the prophets of Baal and kill them. He subsequently discovered during an encounter with God that the Lord had preserved seven thousand people in Israel who had not bowed to Baal. I believe that this was not revealed to him earlier because he may not have accomplished as much as he did for God's kingdom if he knew that he was not alone in his position. This is what makes it all the more remarkable. Elijah stood his ground when the majority of the nation had turned their back on God, and he did so in the face of tyranny.

Similarly, the Prophets Isaiah and Jeremiah were of the minority opinion regarding the worship of the true God, but many had adulterated their relationship with Him and invited other diabolical symbols and practices into God's temple. God was furious with the nation and decreed that it would go into exile for seventy years. However, in Jeremiah's day many prophets were still preaching good news and lulling the people into a false sense of security. Jeremiah was isolated because of his views, warning them about the exile, and opposed by other so-called prophets. Even after the invasion by Babylon and the imposition of tribute, false prophets were still trying to prophesy in a way that reassured the people they would not be going into exile. During the reign of King Zedekiah of Judah, a false prophet named Hananiah prophesied that God was going to break the yoke of King Nebuchadnezzar and restore the articles taken from the Lord's temple as well as all those taken into exile. Jeremiah sought to correct the false prophecy even being so bold as to tell Hananiah that the Lord had not sent him and that he was persuading the nation to trust in lies. Jeremiah then prophesied the prophet's death and shortly after that he died. Hananiah's prophecy was the more attractive because it gave hope, but it was not a prophecy from God.

God is looking for those who will say "yes" when the majority are saying "no" and who will say "no" when the majority are saying "yes" even if it results in one being in a place of loneliness.

11

Having a story that nobody desires to experience

Faith is having a story that nobody desires to experience. Everyone marvels at God's miraculous works – His healing, deliverance and provision are the stuff of legend but as spine tingling as these testimonies are, who really wants to live out the story that precedes them? Many of us may either know or have heard people share testimonies of a wilderness trek where they had to put their faith in God because the circumstance was anything but encouraging. It might have been financial, health-related, family-related, or career-related, but the backstory is never pleasant. In fact, we often find ourselves marvelling at how the protagonist survived the events preceding their miracle. In the heat of adversity, I used to say that "I am a walking breathing miracle", simply because I had not lost my mind in the process.

Sometimes, the person sharing their story might still be in the chokehold of the challenging circumstance and still waiting on God for His intervention. This is often the most difficult time because from the facts it might look impossible – like a person facing terminal cancer who has been given weeks or months to live by the medical experts but is still holding on to a word they received from God. In the face of the sheer impossibility on paper of a healing, these people testify about how God has been good to them and has kept them strong regardless of the pain and discomfort. You may marvel at their spiritual fortitude but I daresay you will never desire their experience. This is not unusual; nobody wants a life riddled with problems or trouble. The preferred position is to walk continuously under the umbrella of God's grace in all areas of our lives. Sadly, this is not the case for the majority of us.

I knew a lady who was facing terminal cancer which impacted her and her family severely. Her husband had to give up regular work to become a fulltime carer and her children had to adjust to the possibility that despite their mother's faith she might not be with them for much longer. As with most cancer-sufferers she lost a lot of weight, shrinking almost to half her normal weight. She needed care for almost everything and was unable to eat or digest food. Yet, she was strong. My happiest moments were sitting with her and discussing God's word and His grace. She absolutely believed she was going to be healed and in a very short time her faith had become mountain-like in dimension. This lady had so much insight into the word of God that she was a source of encouragement to others who were going through far less than she was. Sadly for us she passed away after a brave fight and left many a sorrowful heart behind. But everyone who spoke about her only recalled her immense faith in God. She left a legacy through her testimony and even though I am sure no one wants to live out her experience, yet it will live on as the standard of faith that God expects.

The Bible is awash with stories of those who endured all kinds of contradictions in their walk of faith and left stories that we can still relate to in our present day and age. Hebrews Chapter 11 is often referred to as the heroes of faith hall of fame, because it describes a diversity of unlikely heroes who endured great adversity but retained their faith in God. Many of those mentioned were not exemplary characters in terms of their conduct – they were not perfect, but their hearts were devoted to serving God. They had many weaknesses, but their commitment to God's will was their strength. So, we read about Abel the third man whose faith in God cost him his life at the hands of his brother Cain, simply because he was accepted as righteous by God. We also read about Abraham the father of faith whose story I am sure no Christian desires. Here was a man whose wife was barren and who had been asked to leave his family and move into the unknown where he would receive his inheritance. Abraham responded by faith to this commission seeking a nation not created by the dictate of man but the will of God. Abraham died before he could see the fullness of God's promise – he only glimpsed the beginning of it in the person of his son Isaac.

We read about his wife Sarah (formerly Sarai) who by faith received the strength to conceive a pregnancy even though she was well past childbearing age. Sarah simply considered the faithfulness of God who had promised her that against the odds she was going to give birth to a child and become a mother. Her faith was all the more remarkable because she also had to believe that her husband who was almost a hundred years old was capable of impregnating her. When this child was past puberty, God asked Abraham to offer up the child as a sacrifice and Abraham obeyed even though it would have been gut wrenching for him. But he did so without hesitation because he believed that God was able to raise the child from the dead if it came to that. In a manner of speaking Abraham did receive Isaac back from the dead thanks to God's intervention.

What this chapter of scripture does not mention is Abraham's moments of doubt or his arrangement with his wife to procure a child through her handmaid. What is also not mentioned is the fact that they both laughed when God informed them that they would be parents in old age. None of this is mentioned in that chapter because their faith in God trumped their weaknesses. Nobody wants their story. Who wants to wait till they are aged and wrinkled before becoming parents of a child? Yet, we all marvel at their story and use it to encourage ourselves in down moments. Who wants to be Moses the temperamental stammerer who murdered a man in his zeal and became an exile for forty years before being called into ministry at the grand old age of eighty? The chapter does not highlight Moses' weaknesses but focuses on his testimony in that he forsook the pleasures and treasures of Egypt where he was a prince preferring instead to identify with his people who were in slavery. Who wants to be Samson the distracted womaniser with an awesome anointing who lost his eyesight because of his indiscipline, yet in his darkest hour was used by God to destroy the hierarchy of the Philistine nation? What about King David the man after God's heart who committed adultery and then killed the woman's husband. Anyone who has read about the suffering and torment that David suffered as a result of those actions would not wish to live his backstory. We all want to slay Goliath, but do we want to become exiles from King Saul hiding in caves for fear of losing our lives?

Do you have a story which you have either lived or are still living? Are you clinging on to a word from God? Then let me encourage you to stay the course because your story will empower many who hear it as they battle with their own challenges.

12

Singing a song when you really want to cry

Have you ever found yourself worshipping God on the verge of tears or oftentimes through the mist of tears? This is a powerful statement of faith. You feel like rolling up into a ball and crying your eyes out but instead your spirit motivates you to start worshiping in song. The bible is clear that weeping may endure for a night, but joy comes in the morning [Psalm 30:5]. Albeit this refers in context to a situation where a person is being subjected to the Almighty's discipline and assurance that it will not last forever, yet it is also relevant where we are battling with challenges that have reduced us to a tearful state.

There is a part of us that responds emotionally to trials and adversity, and we feel inclined to give in to it because it is our default mode, humanly speaking. When we face protracted trials, we may start off well but as time lapses, fatigue sets in and our emotions take over. These are the times when the adversary and his agents start nudging us towards the mindset of abandonment and rejection. I recall taking long drives in my car during challenging times so my family could not see my tears or hear my agonizing prayers.

The Bible records an episode where the Children of Israel were making the exodus from Egypt and encountered a dead end in the form of the Red Sea. They were hemmed in between a rock and a hard place with the wilderness and a pursuing Egyptian army behind and an expanse of water ahead [Exodus 14:8-10]. If they retreated it was to face death at the hand of their enemies and if they pressed forward, it was to drown in the water.

In despair they cried out to Moses blaming him for bringing them out of their comfort zone in slavery to die in the wilderness. Realising the need to urgently turn the tide of opinion and reassure the crowd, Moses told them not to fear but standstill and see the Lord's salvation [Exodus 14:11-15]. He assured the people that the Egyptians would be wiped out because God was going to fight their battle and cause them to retain their peace.

At this point, however, the Bible records something peculiar. The Lord spoke to Moses and asked why he was crying out to Him. Now why would the Lord say this? I believe that it was in response to something Moses had said which was not recorded. I am confident that having spoken those brave motivational words, Moses went to God and cried out for a strategy. He had no idea what to do and was clueless. He probably also repeated the people's complaints in God's hearing to emphasise the urgency. It was a desperate time, but God intervened and made a way for them through the Red Sea. Having been miraculously delivered the people rejoiced and gave God glory and sang a song of praise [Exodus 15], their hearts were full of joy until they came to Marah and could not drink the water because it was bitter. Then they grumbled again and cried out in despair. One would have thought that their faith in God's capacity to deliver them would have sustained the song on their lips but sadly as is so often the case they promptly forgot and behaved as if they had never seen His deliverance.

The perfect example of the kind of song that reveals our faith in God was the one sung by Paul and Silas after they had been thrown into prison for having the effrontery to cast out a demon from a young maiden who earned a living as a fortune teller or soothsayer [Acts 16]. The young lady who was possessed with a spirit of divination, had been following Paul and Silas around town loudly proclaiming that they were servants of the Most High God who had come to show people the way of salvation. After many days of this vexatious conduct, Paul turned around and commanded the spirit to come out of her in the name of Jesus Christ, and instantly the girl was delivered from its control. The girl's masters seeing that their hope of making profit was gone turned on Paul and Silas. They brought the apostles before the city's magistrates on false charges of sedition, resulting in them being stripped bare and thrashed severely after which they were thrown in prison. The prison warden placed them in the most secure part of the prison and locked their feet in stocks (a device for securing the feet and ankles so that the legs were held in a straightforward position).

If anyone had the right to give in to their emotions, it was Paul and Silas. In fact, they could be excused for having a pity party and bemoaning their fate with tears of anguish. Here they were, doing the Lord's work and yet their reward was a severe thrashing and imprisonment. They were obviously bruised and in pain and each man's confidence had taken its fair share of pummelling. If they gave in to their emotional side and bawled their eyes out, it would be deemed a normal reaction. However, rather than give in to the dictates of their flesh, at midnight, Paul and Silas started praying and sang praises unto God so loudly that other prisoners heard them. Suddenly there was a great earthquake that shook the foundations of the prison and caused all the doors to spring open and for the prisoners' manacles to fall off. The episode resulted in the prison warden along with his whole family receiving salvation and being baptised. This is what can happen when we yield to the right impulse. Paul and Silas looked past their pain and anguish and found the grace to worship God.

The Psalmist says, *"what time I am afraid, I will trust in thee. In God I will praise his word, in God I have put my trust; I will not fear what flesh can do unto me"* [Psalm 56:3-4]. Again he says, *"In God will I praise his word: in the Lord will I praise his word. In God have I put my trust: I will not be afraid what man can do unto me. Thy vows are upon me, O God: I will render praises unto thee."* [Psalm 56:10-11]. When our focus is on praising God regardless of the challenges, and not giving in to our emotions, we receive the grace to triumph.

13

Talking to yourself more regularly than is considered healthy

Faith is often about talking to ourselves more regularly than is considered healthy by people around us. Have you ever been overwhelmed by the heat of the moment and suddenly began to speak to yourself, reminding yourself of God's word in an effort to quell the lying voice in your head? This is an act of faith. People often caution that speaking to oneself is the first sign of insanity, but I believe it depends on what you are saying and its source.

Part of the adversary's strategy is to derail Christians by bombarding their minds with lies in the moments of weakness. He picks his moments when we are tired or worn out and then strikes with lies designed to get us to question the goodness of God or undermine our value to Him. Our way of counteracting this is by speaking the truth. Apostle Paul says that whatever is true, honest, just, pure, lovely, admirable, praiseworthy, or of good report we should allow such things to occupy our minds [Philippians 4:8]. All these things comprise the content of the word of God. When we allow such things to fill our minds, we will find ourselves speaking to them, because out of the abundance of the heart the mouth speaks. A good person speaks about good things and an evil person speaks evil [Matthew 12:34 and Luke 6:45].

Again, the Bible cautions us to keep our hearts with all diligence for out of it flow the issues of life [Proverbs 4:23]. The heart in the biblical context is the mind rather than the organ that pumps oxygenated blood to our brains. God commanded Joshua to ensure that the book of law (the law of Moses) did not depart from his mouth, but he was to meditate on it day and night so that he may observe to do according to all that is written within it [Joshua 1:8]. The Lord clarified that by so doing he would make his way prosperous and have good success. Provided we are speaking God's word to counteract the lies of the adversary, regardless of what observers may think or say we will be operating by faith.

However, speaking to ourselves about our problems or challenges will not empower us but undermine us. The evidence of a brain disorder is often said to be the sight of people speaking to themselves oblivious to what is happening around them. It is said when people start speaking to themselves in the third person this is potentially the evidence of schizophrenia. This phenomenon usually occurs when a person is mentally overwhelmed and starts to speak out loud what is taking place in their thoughts. If you are thinking faith thoughts, you will speak faith-based words but if you are thinking delusional thoughts these will escape your lips as delusional words.

Most of the Psalms are a soliloquy where the author speaks out his thoughts to no one in particular but everyone in general. They are very personal and so one gets the idea that they were spoken in private but the fact that they are recorded means that he intended them to be shared ultimately. So, when the Psalmist asks, *"Why art thou cast down, O my soul? And why art thou disquieted within me? Hope thou in God, for I shall yet praise Him for the help of His countenance"* [Psalm 42:5], he is not speaking to anyone but himself. He is obviously grappling with something personal and troubling. However, it starts off as a declaration to God for at the beginning of the passage [Psalm 42:1], he says, *"As the hart panteth for the water brooks, so panteth my soul for thee O God."* But as he progresses, he starts to address himself as if trying to shake off some prevailing mindset that has been weighing him down. By speaking to himself, he is trying to realign himself with God's will.

The Apostle Paul urges us to speak to ourselves in psalms and hymns and spiritual songs, singing melody in our hearts to the Lord, giving thanks always for all things …. [Ephesians 5:19-20]. This is a prevailing attitude that we are called to exhibit which as Paul says is evidence of being filled with the Spirit rather than being drunk with wine [Ephesians 5:18]. Therefore, God clearly expects us to speak to ourselves but rather than bemoaning our fate and reeling out our problems, He desires us to speak in psalms and sing hymns and spiritual songs. So, reciting psalms out loud to ourselves and decreeing God's word is the evidence of our faith in Him.

Some Christians speak out loud to God as part of a monologue but to anyone eavesdropping, it may sound very much like they are holding a conversation with themselves. You may recall Elijah who had just triumphed over the prophets of Baal whom he had arranged to have slain by the people. After being used by God to restore rainfall over the land, Elijah heard that Queen Jezebel (the custodian of the Prophets of Baal) had issued a death warrant for him [1 Kings 19:1-4]. Fearing for his life Elijah fled into the wilderness and kept running a whole day's journey until he collapsed under a juniper tree and began to cry out for death, pleading with God to take his life as he was no better than his fathers (forebears). He was clearly speaking from the place of discouragement and exhaustion, but his ultimate audience was God. This was not a man speaking by faith but one who had come to the end of himself and was ready to quit. Although he encountered God's mercy, it is a reminder of why none of us can serve God in our own strength. By strength shall no man prevail [1 Samuel 2:9].

When Jesus Christ was on the cross laying down His life for all of mankind, He spoke out from a place of agony and intense emotional burden. To casual observers He may have been reacting deliriously to his suffering but to those with insight He was both fulfilling prophecy and prophesying. When He said, "I thirst" [John 19:28], I believe it was firstly a fulfilment of Psalm 69:21 where David prophesied of the events that would take place and how Christ would be given vinegar to assuage His thirst. However, I also believe it was Christ's way of emphasising His willingness to drain the contents of the cup the Lord had handed Him to drink. That cup represented the price of redemption. When He says, "It is finished" after drinking the vinegar that was offered to Him, He was confirming that the cup was now empty and there was nothing left to do for the salvation of mankind.

By all means let's speak to ourselves in the hour of need but ensure that we are focussed on God's promises and avoid the temptation to focus on the facts.

14

Knowing the bible through experience rather than meditation

Knowing the bible through experience rather than meditation is a hallmark of faith. Most of us are familiar with the scripture that says faith comes by hearing and hearing by the word of God [Romans 10:17]. This has often been presented as the premise for faith, and it is absolutely correct. It is the starting point, but it is by no means the finishing point for the Christian. Four times in the Bible we are taught that the just shall live by faith [Habakkuk 2:3-4; Romans 1:17; Galatians 3:11; Hebrews 10:38], but Apostle Paul makes clear that we live from *faith to faith* [Romans 1:17], meaning that we start with faith and end with faith. Apostle James speaks about the need to show our faith through our works [James 2:17-18] because faith without works is as good as dead. He gives us an example of faith without works when he says that if a person is naked and destitute of food and all we do is pray for them to be in peace, and to be warmed and filled rather than giving them what they need, we have not fulfilled the requirements [James 2:15].

Whilst it is commendable for Christians to dwell on God's word and mull over it till their minds are flooded with light from the scriptures, it is more important to live the word. What do I mean? The word of God expressed through a person's lifestyle is the most vivid presentation of scripture and possibly the only encounter those outside the church will have with it.

Jesus said that a person is known by their fruits [Matthew 7:15-20]. He clarifies His statement by saying that a good tree cannot bear bad fruit, nor can a bad tree bear good fruit. This is effectively saying that a person is known by their works (or activities). So, Apostle John says that whoever hates his brother is a murderer and does not have the gift of eternal life [1 John 3:15]. He also says that if a man claims to love God and hates his brother, he is a liar, because he that does not love his brother whom he has seen cannot love God whom he has not seen [1 John 4:20]. John makes the critical point that whoever has worldly possessions and sees a brother in need but shuts his heart to him, how does the love of God abide in him? [1 John3:17].

It is possible to know what the Bible teaches and be able to recite it chapter and verse, but if the person does not live in accordance with the word of God, he or she has hidden in their heart they are hypocrites.

Apostle James makes a similar observation to John when he says that we should be doers of the word and not hearers only, deceiving ourselves [James 1:22-25]. James goes on to say that if any of us is a hearer of the word only and not a doer, we are like a person staring at their reflection in a mirror but forgets what they look like after they have turned away from it. He clarifies that anyone who looks into the perfect law of liberty and follows its instructions, will be blessed in their deeds.

Jesus cautions us against being like the Pharisees who loved to receive the adulation of men for their piety but were in fact hypocrites who put on a public display [Matthew 6:5]. He also described the Pharisees and scribes (teachers of the law) as being whitewashed tombs looking beautiful on the outside but dark and full of dead bones on the inside. They appeared to people as righteous but were full of hypocrisy and wickedness [Matthew 23:27-28].

Jesus described the greatest commandments in the Bible as being to love the Lord with all our heart, soul and mind and strength, and then to love our neighbour as ourselves [Matthew 22:35-40; Mark 12:28-34; and Luke 10:27]. In Matthew's gospel He is recorded as saying that all the law and the prophets hung on these. The Laws of Moses and all the writings of the Old Testament prophets were built on these two laws for life. These two laws comprise the fruit Christ refers to. In other words, anyone who knows scripture back to front but does not walk in love is not a Child of God. We may profess to love Him but unless we walk in love, we have no hope of ever pleasing Him. Jesus makes clear that whoever meditates on and keeps His commandments is the one who loves Him; and whoever loves Him shall be loved by the Father and Jesus promises that He will love him and manifest Himself to such a person [John 14:21]. In response to a query by one of His disciples, Jesus clarified that if a man loved Him, such a man would keep His words and if he does then the Father would love him and both Jesus and the father would make their abode with him [John 14:23]. This paints a picture of intimacy between God the Father, the Lord Jesus Christ and one who obeys God's word.

Jesus says that if we abide in Him and His words abide in us, we shall ask what we will and it shall be done unto us. He also promises that if we keep His commandments we shall abide in His love [John 15:7 & 10].

So, it is clearly not enough just to know the word. We need to live it out through our experience.

15

Life book not textbook

Faith is all about a life book not a textbook. I guess you could call it practical versus theory and authentic versus synthetic. In other words, faith is what we do not what we know. One of the practices commonly found amongst us Christians is discussing faith as a subject matter and getting really theological about it. We can quote all the relevant scriptures that discuss the subject, but our knowledge comes from a textbook rather than a life book.

There are two ways of viewing the Bible. Firstly, we can view it as a textbook littered with the documented thoughts of observers or witnesses, prophets, commentators, scribes, and the divinely inspired. The Bible viewed in this way becomes an academic text to be studied with a unique set of tools not readily available to the uninitiated. There are those that will analyse chapter and verse; Greek, Hebrew, and Aramaic; utilise exegesis (critical analysis of a text to draw out the hidden or less obvious meaning); delve into the discipline of hermeneutics as a means of interpreting the text where comprehension fails to provide globally acceptable clarity. These academicians deconstruct the bible using these theories and methodologies to arrive at definitions and interpretations that are taught to theological scholars.

The second way we can view the Bible is as a life book littered with accounts and principles that must be applied in everyday life. As a life book, the Bible does not lend itself easily to exegesis or hermeneutics but rather to revelation. Revelation is the fruit of the Holy Spirit, and it cuts across biblical interpretation and analysis to reveal what was on the mind of God when He commissioned the particular author to write. As a life book, the Bible is focussed on practice rather than theory, and rather than being confined to the pages of a book, it wants to be inscribed on the hearts of men.

Faith does not lend itself well to the bible as a textbook as there are far too many discrepancies for the scholar to navigate on their way to a satisfactory conclusion. Faith is relegated with textbook but emphasised with life book. Faith is not concerned with the Greek, Hebrew, or Aramaic interpretation or the findings of exegesis and hermeneutics. Rather it is concerned with everyday real application of the word. Faith seeks a promise that may seem flawed in presentation and then latch on to it with a healthy expectation. There is a clear dichotomy between life book and textbook which is amplified by the discrepancy in their content, the same words, but different context and appreciation.

Textbook has to be ratified by other textbooks and subjected to ruthless scrutiny before it can be justified. In other words, with textbook just because a passage of scripture in that book makes a proclamation does not mean that it is deemed authentic. It is never self-evident but must be analysed and scrutinised to determine its authenticity and relevance. Many passages of scripture interpreted or analysed from the perspective of a textbook have been questioned and ultimately described as allegories, prose, musings, and fiction. The idea being that the reader doesn't place too much confidence in the text but hangs on it loosely.

So, for instance, you may hear a commentator of the theoretical school of thought describe the books of Job and Jonah as allegory. The idea of a person being subjected to such intense suffering by Satan, or another being swallowed up by a large fish are deemed too farfetched to be authentic. They seek to pry aside the literary veil to discover what the writer's intent was when he or she scripted the text and believe that the motive was inspirational or insightful. With them, faith is never unconditional trust but a rational assessment of the facts.

Faith never latches on to anything that challenges the authenticity of God's word. To the academic, the written word is not the embodiment of truth but of a person's impressions which are inherently flawed. The word of God is not a safety net for the academician but a net with holes that need to be sewn-up before they are fit for purpose. Just like Peter's nets that needed to be washed and mended after a fruitless night toiling on the Sea of Galilee for an elusive catch, the word is processed before it is released [Matthew 4:201, Luke 5:1-2]. The word 'inspired' is never accorded any relevance by the academician when considering the written word because there is no independent corroborative evidence to substantiate it. So when Apostle Paul tells his protégé Timothy [2 Timothy 3:16-17] that all scripture is given by inspiration of God or when Apostle Peter [2 Peter 1:20-21] says that no prophecy of the scripture is of any private interpretation but was documented by holy men of God as they were moved by the Holy Spirit, they are not accorded the reverence reserved for historians.

Faith operates by a person reading or hearing the Bible in its life book context and then believing what they have seen or heard regardless of doctrinal discrepancies or controversies. So, a person is less bothered about whether it was Apostle Paul or his protégé that wrote the Book of Hebrews than about believing its content. The

Christian is not hung-up about the apparent differences between the presentations of the four Gospels and instead seeks what complements them. Those who receive the Bible as a life book and not a textbook discover its secrets and enjoy its blessings.

16

Hoping against hope

Faith is hoping against hope for the performance of something that looks impossible in the natural. Hoping against hope is daring to hope when hoping is deemed hopeless. When hoping is perceived as pointless the person of faith rises up in hope.

When the Bible teaches that faith is the substance of things hoped for the evidence of things not seen [Hebrews 11:1] it effectively places faith at the centre of hope. In other words, this is not just hope as many define it, but hope built on faith. But if the heartbeat of this brand of hope is faith, then what is at the core of that faith? It is a promise – a promise of God derived from the word of God whether Rhema or Logos. So, if you can, picture a circle within a circle within a circle. The innermost circle is a promise; the central circle is faith, and the outermost circle is hope. Promise within faith within hope = hope against hope.

This statement is accorded by Apostle Paul to Abraham known as the Father of Faith [Romans 4:18]. The passage reads, *"Who against hope believed in hope, that he might become the father of many nations, according to that which was spoken 'So shall thy seed be'."* So, as we can see Abraham had a promise which formed the heart of his hope but as we shall see this also drove his faith. The scripture goes on to say [Romans 4:19-20], *"And being not weak in faith, he considered not his own body now dead, when he was about an hundred years old, neither yet the deadness of Sara's womb: He staggered not at the promise of God through unbelief; but was strong in faith, giving glory to God."*

These passages encapsulate all the ingredients of the unique brand of hope that showcases a person's faith. The more we read and meditate on them the clearer it becomes that mere hope is insufficient. Many of us hope for good things to happen but often have to contend with contradictions. Many lose heart and their hope wanes in the face of a protracted gestation period. How long are we to wait on the Lord to answer us, and how long are we to hold on to our hope? These questions are in the hearts of many Christians who desire a degree of certainty.

To hope against hope, we need to visualise something beyond the periphery of our five senses. What does this mean? We need to perceive a reality that cannot be articulated by our senses of sight, smell, taste, hearing, or touch. Now I don't believe hallucinations count, but there is a reality we encounter through our spiritual perspective that persuades us beyond a shadow of doubt that we are on the verge of receiving what we perceive. To hope against hope our focus must be on the unseen.

Apostle Paul urges us not to focus our senses on the things which are seen but rather at the things which are unseen because the things which are seen are temporary but the things which are not seen are eternal [2 Corinthians 4:18]. Apostle Paul was effectively asking us not to get distracted by external stuff – the challenges and afflictions of day-to-day life which he describes as being momentary by comparison with the longer-term work that God is working out on the inside of us. There is a character-building exercise going on in our lives through the contradictions we face, but if we lose sight of this we will give in to discouragement and struggle [2 Corinthians 4:16-17]. Apostle Paul is asking us to focus on the big picture. What is really happening here? It is much more about what we shall become than what we currently are or what we are passing through. God is more concerned about our souls and their eternal destination than He is about this temporary mortality. Our short-term comfort is not His priority.

Abraham had a revelation that he was going to become the father of many nations. He was shown the constellation of stars in the sky on a clear night and informed that his descendants would be as numerous as them [Genesis 15:5-6]. This was what Abraham believed and as a result gained favour with God who counted that belief as the standard of righteousness that would apply not only to him but all his descendants [Romans 4:23-24]. Apostle Paul confirms that if we believe God in the same way as our father Abraham did, He will also count our belief as righteousness. This should fill us with great expectation and boost our hope.

So, our objective is to receive a promise from God, and this will only come as we spend time with Him and endeavour to obey His word. God has a promise for each of us and He will reveal it to us in the place of intimacy. If we draw near to Him, He has promised to draw near to us [James 4:8]. The Bible makes clear that the secrets of the Lord are revealed to those who fear Him [Psalm 25:14], so it is not everyone who will discover God's promises for them. It requires intimacy. Abraham was intimate with God and discovered the long-term plan for his life. Even though he agonised over parenthood and his wife's barrenness, he had a sense of the relevance of his child in relation to God's covenant. Even when he got to the stage where in the natural scheme of things God's plan looked impossible, Abraham believed in a God who had the power to raise dead things back to life. How did he get this perspective? Because he saw God restore his lifeless body as well as the deadness of Sarah's womb, he had a revelation of the God of resurrection. This was the God Abraham believed in. He also believed in the truth that God cannot lie [Hebrews 6:17-18] and this was his place of strong consolation.

To hope against hope, we must develop intimacy with God, receive a revelation of His plan for us, believe His plan as revealed through His Holy Spirit and focus on His greatness in the face of our earthly challenges. We must also learn to invoke the name of the Lord that is most relevant to our crisis (just like Abraham did). I don't know what we are facing right now but I am convinced that the moment we both see and believe God's purpose for our lives we will discover the grace to hope against hope.

17

Saying "yes" when the world says "no" and saying "no" when the world says "yes"

More often than not, faith is about saying "yes" when the world around us says "no" and saying "no" when the world says "yes"; it is about perspectives. If we hold a worldly perspective, we will show solidarity for the majority opinion on issues.

Life is about choices. Sometimes it comes down to a simple choice of whether to stick with your convictions and follow the unpopular path of greatest resistance or play it safe and stick with the crowd trampling along the populist boulevard.

For many of us sticking with the majority is the safe option as it guarantees sufficient company and the least resistance. "There's safety in numbers" as they say. For those who consider themselves the shy retiring type this is a place of refuge and great comfort. Mob psychology exerts an influential collective will which is extremely persuasive. Nobody wants to get trampled on and so they either stay out of the way or unashamedly join the tide of popular opinion. The construction of the Tower of Babel [Genesis 11:1-9] was the fruit of a collective will, driven by the fuel of mob psychology. As a result of the unity of language and culture, people pulled together to oppose God and elevate humanity through the building of a monument. God acknowledged that where there was a collective will anything was achievable.

Today we have many Towers of Babel, most of them being erected through the potency and influence of the media. People are targeted through marketing campaigns which subtly gun for certain age groups or cultures or professions or sexes programming them so as to regulate their choices. There are Towers of Babel in education, politics, arts, professions, relationships, the economy, and just about every sector we can identify. These towers are erected in opposition to God's way and seek to elevate humanity to a godlike status. Why do we worship at the altar of innovation and technology? Why are we so fascinated by works of art that we impose an almost celestial-like status on their creators and worship the ground beneath them? Why are we so much in awe of the works of men? How can we discover heaven on earth through our carnality? How can we see virtue in darkness but disdain the light?

In an age where politically correct opinion rules the media and people have adopted a liberal stance, God has been relegated. Where the Bible recommends a conservative path, the world advocates a liberal one which sways the majority.

In an effort not to be seen we try to blend in and become invisible. When Christ describes us like salt and light we prefer to be seen as sand and darkness. Those who blend in never change the crowd instead as is often the case they end up being influenced and eventually sympathising with the plight of the majority. We forget God's caution about friendship with the world or the warning not to be unequally yoked because light and darkness have nothing in common.

Jesus calls the popular route the wide road and the least popular God-ordained route the narrow way. According to Him, the wide way leads to destruction while the narrow leads to life. We are urged to stay on the narrow road rather than the wide road even though it is the more precarious of the two. Who can forget Joshua and Caleb's stance in the face of the report by the ten other spies who had been sent to spy the Promised Land? When the ten unbelieving spies delivered a negative report that discouraged the whole community, Joshua and Caleb maintained a report that relied on their faith in God [Numbers 13:25-33; and 14:5-9]. The ten spies died as a result of their faithlessness and none of those who believed them survived to see the Promised Land. Only Joshua and Caleb lived to step into God's promise.

David and Daniel are two characters in the Bible who eschewed the popular way in favour of the narrow route that leads to life. Daniel and his friends refused to eat food sacrificed to Babylonian gods unlike the majority of other young exiles. We can also recall Shadrach Meshach and Abednego who took the narrow path in their dealing with Nebuchadnezzar by refusing to bow down to the golden image. Because he feared God, David refused to give in to the pressure of his men to kill King Saul even though he had the opportunity to do so on two separate occasions.

We can contrast this with King Saul who sought popularity with the people and so disobeyed God. He was given the task of completely wiping out an enemy nation leaving nothing alive [1 Samuel 15]. God had commanded this to ensure that there was no residue left to corrupt the Children of Israel, but King Saul had the temerity to vary God's instructions. He not only preserved the best of the livestock, but also spared the life of the king Agag with a view to entering into an alliance with him. When confronted by the Prophet Samuel he admitted that he was afraid of the people. By his own admission he was afraid of losing their support and so made choices that ultimately culminated in his loss of status and subsequent death. At the root of this affinity with the majority is a fearful mind and a person who either does not know who they are or even if they do know are unwilling to embrace that difference.

Ruth is another example of a person who opted for the narrow route. Whilst gleaning for grain in the harvest fields she refused to mess around with the young men like the other women did in their desperation for more grain. Her virtuous ways brought her to the attention of Boaz, one of the wealthiest and most influential men in the town [Ruth 2:8-23].

God is looking for people who are not afraid of offending the crowd with politically incorrect perspectives that mirror God's. He is looking for people like Jesus Christ who are not afraid to stand out from the crowd by adopting a God-aligned view. Men and women who will say "no" when the world says "yes" and "yes" when the world says "no". This is faith.

18

Counting your chickens before they are hatched

Counting your chickens before they're hatched is one of the strongest symbols of faith. It is a mark of the certainty and confidence that a person has in God that provokes such action. Circumstantially all you have are eggs, yet you are sure of the size of the poultry awaiting you at the other side because you have received a promise from God.

There are many ways of counting your chickens before their hatched which have nothing to do with faith. You could count your chickens by speculation like most investors do, hoping that your seed will yield a healthy reward or harvest. You could also count your chickens based on your use of technological aids such as artificial incubators to replicate the conditions of an egg beneath its mother. However, these are not fool-proof routes to receiving a poultry laden with healthy chicks. When God promises, He brings them to pass in accordance with our faith. Faith always gives thanks in advance not in arrears.

In response to Thomas' belated worship, Jesus said, "*Thomas because thou hast seen me, thou hast believed; blessed are they that have not seen, and yet have believed*" [John 20:29].

Thomas had heard from the other disciples about Jesus' resurrection but because he had not seen the risen Christ for himself, he doubted. When Christ eventually showed up and presented Himself to Thomas, He invited the doubting disciple to touch His wounds to satisfy himself, but Thomas declined and instead worshipped Him. He was not commended for his reaction – believing after the event. Jesus made clear that it was important to believe in advance of seeing with the five senses. To expect anyone to believe in something they have not seen with their eyes is effectively inviting them to perceive another type of reality. A person cannot just switch from relying on their five senses to perceiving life through their spiritual senses. It is a process of faith that is cultivated through intimacy and proximity.

You cannot perceive the poultry when all you have before your eyes is a tray of eggs. To perceive it you must first surrender reliance on your five senses for dependency on your spiritual senses. The biggest obstacle to seeing the poultry is doubt. If we doubt that God has given us a poultry all we will perceive is a tray of eggs. Receiving the poultry becomes impossible without a firm belief that it has been given. Once we are able to believe that the poultry has been given to us, we are able to receive it by faith, and once we have received it, we have the capacity to perceive it regardless of what the facts are. It sounds more complex than it is in reality.

There is a childlike trust that accompanies anyone seeking to receive something from God. We simply believe that God has given and gradually start to perceive the poultry even though all we have factually speaking is a tray of eggs. When we perceive the poultry, our spontaneous reaction is thanksgiving. It makes no sense to anyone but us and we run the risk of being called deluded, because we are gazing into the unseen realm through the eyes of faith. Every Christian has to learn to perceive outside the limitations of their five senses. This is what sets us apart from those we call *unbelievers* or *potential believers*, as I like to call them. The uncanny sense of realism is what makes faith in God such a personal and unique experience.

No one can count their chickens before they're hatched without building trust in God. That trust is built through regular encounter with His word. The more we dwell upon His word the more we learn about His nature and find the capacity to trust Him. There are no hard and fast rules about how long this takes, suffice to say that it is a process in which the Holy Spirit plays an active role. The conviction we feel when we start perceiving as real, things we cannot connect to with our five senses, is powerful and attracts a blessing. Prophet Jeremiah says that "*Blessed is the man who trusts in the Lord, And whose hope the Lord is*" [Jeremiah 17:7].

Believing God attracts a blessing, and this is confirmed by Elizabeth the mother of John the Baptist when the baby in her womb (John) leapt for joy at the presence of the foetus in Mary's womb (Jesus). Elizabeth, speaking under the leading of the Holy Spirit said, "*.... blessed is she that believed; for there shall be a performance of those things which were told her from the Lord*" [Luke 1:45]. At this stage, Jesus was still in the first trimester of development and John was at the six-month point, but both Mary and her cousin Elizabeth were counting their chickens because of what they perceived by faith. Factually, all they had was a tray of eggs but by faith they were counting the chickens in their poultry.

The capacity to count our chickens in advance of hatching is grace-provided. We must hear from God, see the promise, and receive the promise. When God makes a promise, He wants to be believed because that is the standard of the righteousness that comes through faith. Abraham set that standard for all his descendants (us) when he believed God that he would be a father of many nations. Likewise, we too must believe to receive what our natural eyes cannot see and then act like we have received it in the natural – this is faith.

19

Seeing something no one else can see

Faith is often about seeing something no one else can see. It is about charting a course to a location that you've never been before. All you have is a destination and a conviction. There is a limit to what we can perceive with the five senses. When God created humans, He gave us five senses to enable us to interact with our environment. It was never His intention that we should become limited by our sight, hearing, smell, taste, or touch. We were originally designed to interact with God through our spirit, because God is a spirit [John 4:24]. This was how Adam engaged God – he did so via his spirit. This was also how he exercised authority in the earth before the fall.

Imagine having the capacity to see stuff that no one else in your community sees and making accurate forecasts of events that have not yet happened. Faith has eyes that perceive the future. If we spend long enough time in His presence, He will reveal things to us that cannot be perceived with the five senses. The Bible is clear that the secrets of the Lord reside with those who fear Him [Psalm 25:14]. Those that fear God spend time in His presence and obey His commands. We cannot claim to be in faith if we don't spend time with Him. How can you have faith in the words of one you barely know? A person who spent a lot of time in the Lord's presence was Moses and the Bible says that God revealed His ways to Moses, but the Children of Israel only saw his acts (the outward manifestation of His works) [Psalm 103:7].

Thanks to redemption and salvation through Jesus Christ, we receive the gift of the Holy Spirit by faith. The indwelling of the Spirit provides a dependable source of insight, revealing things that natural senses cannot perceive. Before the birth of Jesus Christ, the Holy Spirit did not indwell those who had a relationship with God by faith, but His presence abided with them, and His power rested upon them. If you recall, Samson was anointed and carried the presence of God, but the power of God resided in the seven locks of hair on his head which he could not shave off. The Prophets in the Old Testament likewise carried God's anointing for various purposes, and this was evidenced in the mighty feats they performed.

The story of Elijah comes to mind. Elijah was described as having a normal personality. Outside the presence of God in his life, there was nothing remarkable about him [James 5:17-18]. Yet he prayed that it would not rain in the nation and there was no rainfall for three and a half years. During the famine that followed Elijah's pronouncement, God sent him to a widow's home in a town called Zarephath. God said that He had commanded the woman to feed him but when Elijah arrived there and asked her for a meal, she explained that she only had enough ingredients to prepare a last meal for herself and her son. However, Elijah knowing that God could not lie commanded her not to fear but to first make a meal for him and thereafter for herself and her son because her ingredients would not deplete until the day rainfall was restored [1 Kings 17:9-16]. Elijah saw something the widow could not see – he perceived that she was his meal ticket for the rest of the famine, and this led him to issue forth the command, which was effectively a command from God.

In another account, Elijah had successfully triumphed over the prophets of the idol god Baal and thereafter he began to pray for rain to fall. Before praying, however, Elijah asked the king to go and have a meal because he heard the sound of the abundance of rain [1 Kings 18:41-46]. Now at this point in time, there were no clouds in the sky to signify that rain was about to fall. But whilst the king went to have a meal, Elijah sent his servant to look out to sea and inform him if he noticed rain. Elijah kept praying and each time his servant returned he would enquire of him whether there was any sign of rain and be informed that there was nothing. This happened seven times, but on the seventh occasion the servant reported that there was arising a little cloud no larger than the size of a man's hand. At the mention of this, Elijah urged the king to prepare his chariot for departure so that the coming rain did not frustrate his journey. Shortly afterwards there was a downpour, but Elijah had already perceived it when there was no physical evidence to suggest rain.

When Joshua and Caleb perceived victory, ten others saw failure and caused the whole camp of Israel to sin against God [Numbers 13 and 14]. In the natural, they had seen the same things but their interpretation of what they had seen differed. When Goliath rose up to intimidate Israel, and all of Saul's army was quaking in its shoes, only David perceived an uncircumcised Philistine who was marked for death [1 Samuel 17]. When all the ship's crew were predicting good weather and a pleasant voyage, only Paul perceived that they were going to encounter inclement weather (in the form of Euroclydon – a North Easterly cyclone) and suffer loss of their cargo [Acts 27:9-44].

A story that best captures the phenomenon of seeing something no one else can see is the biblical account of Jairus' daughter as recorded in the Gospels of Mark (5:21-43); Matthew (9:18-26); and Luke (8:40-56). Jairus' daughter was very ill, at the point of death, and her father came to fetch Jesus to heal her. On their way to the house some people from the household came to meet them and inform them that the little girl had died. However, Jesus told Jairus not to be afraid but believe. When Jesus arrived at Jairus' home, He informed the mourners that the little girl was not dead but sleeping and they laughed at him scornfully. However, when Jesus had removed them from the home, He took the girl by the hand and asked her to arise. Immediately the girl arose to the astonishment of all present – except Jesus Christ that is.

Has anything died in your circumstance? Are you seeing what the crowd wants you to see? The Bible urges us not to be conformed to this world (and the mindset of the world) but to be transformed by the renewing of our minds [Romans 12:2]. To see something no one else can see, we need to be tuned in to God's wireless and receiving the signal He transmits to those that have faith in Him.

20

Touching something intangible

Faith is touching something intangible. In other words, faith enables the tangible to make contact with the intangible. Imagine if you can, a bridge between one realm and the next; that bridge is faith. Faith effectively links two realms enabling the material to make contact with the spiritual. Why is this important? Well, because the material, natural realm which we perceive with our five senses cannot exist without the spiritual realm which is inaccessible to those same senses. If this is the case, then faith is about us accessing the spiritual realm to obtain the substance we need to enhance our experience in the natural realm.

In the first place, the visible natural realm was created from the invisible supernatural realm we call the *spirit realm*. The Bible makes clear that God who made the heavens and the earth created the things which are seen from things which cannot be seen [Hebrews 11:3]. We see that in the beginning of creation, God made the heavens and the earth and started calling forth things into existence over a six-day period, culminating in the creation of human beings [Genesis 1:1-27]. To understand how this works, we need to explore scripture to see what it says about the two realms and how we are called to live.

In the first case, God is a spirit [John 4:24]. Please digest that. God is not a man [Numbers 23:19]. If we try to relate to God as if He were a man, we will encounter frustration. The arrival of Jesus Christ in the earth and His death and resurrection were all about giving us access to God the father. Between the fall of Adam and the resurrection of Christ, only a select few (mainly Prophets and Priests) had direct access to God. Many had to go through rites of purification to gain access to the creator and sustainer of the universe, and even then, they did not possess the hope of eternal life because all had sinned and fallen short of the glory of God [Romans 3:23]. Just as sin entered the world through one man's disobedience so also did righteousness and grace access the world through one man's obedience [Romans 5:12-19]. Whereas Adam had free access to the spiritual realm before his fall, he lost it because he died – spiritually.

Death comes in two forms, physical (the first death) and spiritual (the second death). Adam died spiritually the moment he disobeyed God, but physical death was a longer process which lasted over nine hundred years. The spiritual death meant that the bridge between the natural and spiritual realms was shut to human access. From now on, the only form of access was through the bridge of faith. Because humanity was limited to the use of its five senses, it led to the creation of gods in the shape of idols. People were desperate to see their god and created idols to address this desire. Idolatry is still prevalent in many parts of the world and is practised by those who don't understand the futility of the practice. They pray to these idols, sacrifice to them, and seek to appease them in the hope of gaining their favour but the Bible makes clear that idols are fashioned from earthly materials (not spiritual). These idols cannot see, hear, speak, or move and those who create them are just like them [Psalm 115:4-8].

God was very clear that the Children of Israel were not to have or create idols – graven images [Exodus 20:4] but in a moment of treachery, the people created a golden calf and declared it to be their god simply because

Moses had spent longer in God's presence and away from them than expected [Exodus 32:1-4]. The challenge for humanity is serving a God that cannot be perceived with the five senses and it is why most religions are fashioned around idols. The fallen nature of man lacks the capacity to perceive the existence of a spiritual God.

However, those who have submitted to the lordship of the unseen God through His son Jesus Christ have the privilege of being spiritually alive. Their dormant spirits are resurrected to life at the moment they submit to God through Christ and these spirits begin a relationship with God's Holy Spirit – the third man of the Holy Trinity. The resurrection of the dormant, fallen spirit in man enables him to become a child of God [Romans 810-11]. All God's children are spiritually reborn – this is what it means to be born again [John 3:3-8]. Those who are not spiritually reborn are not the children of God [Romans 8:9] Those who are born again in spirit are called to pursue the things that are spiritual [Romans 8:12-16] rather than things which are material. The evidence of a child of God is one who prioritises the spiritual over the material [Romans 8:5]. We are therefore urged by Apostle Paul to fix our focus on the unseen realm which is eternal rather than the seen realm which is temporary [2 Corinthians 4:18] because this is the only way we can rise above earthly challenges.

Why is this preamble important to know? It is because we need to know what faith is given for and why it is demanded. Faith is not about enhancing material possessions as has been wrongly taught in many quarters of the church but rather it is a medium for a child of God accessing the supernatural provision of God to establish His kingdom on earth. Adam walked in the spirit through his submission to God's authority and obedience to His commands and we are called to do likewise. This is why faith is about touching the intangible from the material realm through the gateway of faith. Any material benefits that are received through the exercise of faith are incidental and in addition to the spiritual enhancements [Matthew 6:33].

So, for the avoidance of doubt, the primary purpose of faith is to enable the child of God access the unseen spiritual realm to obtain the materially intangible substance required to enhance his or her experience in the earth. That experience is primarily a spiritual one because each of us is a spirit who lives in a body and has a soul, and it is in our spiritual capacity that we establish God's kingdom here on earth.

21

Aiming at a bullseye that cannot be seen with the naked eye

Aiming at a bullseye that cannot be seen with the naked eye is the aim of faith. The objective is never physical but rather the spiritual that cannot be perceived with the naked eye. The unseen objective or target (bullseye) is a spiritual one which can only be aimed at and successfully hit by faith. This means that we submit to the leading of the Holy Spirit in how we execute, and we consult regularly.

When Abram was called by God out of Ur of the Chaldees, [Genesis 12] there was a lot of uncertainty in his life. He was married to a beautiful, virtuous woman, who was unfortunately, barren and because of his love for her he made no effort to marry another woman or have a concubine. Therefore, his prospects of becoming a father were nil. He was in his seventies and nearing retirement. To compound matters, he was still living at home under his father's headship. There is nothing to suggest that he was independently wealthy and capable of managing on his own. From his circumstances, we can deduce that he lacked a personal vision for his life and by nature appeared to be a man who avoided taking risks.

God called this man to step out of the shadows of his father's influence and chart his own course in life. This must have been extremely daunting for Abraham. We know this, because even though he had been called to step out alone, he took his father and his nephew along for company. He clearly lacked the confidence to make his own way in life. Even after his father died along the way, he carried on with his nephew. He also appears to have been a timid man. We can tell from how he conducted himself, when forced to go to Egypt during a famine, that he was more concerned about self-preservation and was often guided by his fearful imagination. Abram asked Sarai, his wife, not to disclose their marital relationship so that he would not be killed by the Egyptians who might desire to have her. We can also detect a selfish streak in him. Like most fearful people, he was only preoccupied with his own safety.

The challenge for Abram was that God had asked him to take aim at a bullseye that could not be seen with the naked eye. Having spent most of his life aiming at easy, reliable targets, Abram was being dragged out of his comfort zone. It takes conviction to look beyond one's five senses. That conviction is not based on information acquired in the natural but the rather the supernatural. How many of us live 24/7 in the spirit? It is impossible. Not even the most determined Christian can live that way, because we have an impediment in the form of our flesh. Like many of us, Abram heard the voice of God but was divided in his heart between what he perceived with his five senses and what he was being asked to do.

God promised Abram, that if he went to the land (bullseye) that God would lead him to, that He would produce a great nation through his lineage. In Abram's mind, this nation was going to be a physical one. For a man whose wife was barren and who had no intention of remarrying, this was an impossible feat, but still he obeyed. Why? I believe it's because he was desperate to become a father and God's promise provided a glimmer of hope that this might come to pass. How do we know this? Because, after God had promised him that his descendants would be as numerous as the stars, Abram bemoaned his lack of a male heir. This tells us that

Abram's focus was on a physical lineage that would become large through biological reproduction. However, God's focus was on a spiritual lineage – the Body of Christ. This was the bullseye.

The gateway to Abram's bullseye would start with a child – Isaac, morph into a family under Jacob, become a nation called Israel – birthed in captivity and delivered through a man named Moses, and ultimately become the Church of our Lord and Saviour Jesus Christ. This was the bullseye that Abram could not see. All he had at the outset was faith the size of a mustard seed. That faith was built around a kernel known as hope. When aiming at a bullseye you cannot see, we often start out with hope, and as we take the next steps like Abram we grow until we achieve strong conviction.

Jesus taught a parable about the kingdom of heaven which He likened to a mustard seed [Matthew 13:31-32]. Jesus said the kingdom of heaven is like a mustard seed that a man planted in a field. Although it is the smallest of all seeds, yet it grows into the largest of all garden plants and becomes like a tree, large enough for birds to come and nest in its branches. If we judge our mustard seed faith by size, like Abram we will be daunted and paralysed with fear. But what we don't realise is that this level of faith has capacity to achieve great things [Matthew 17:20]. For Abram, the promise that he would become a great nation started with the first step. That first step was built on hope, but the bible defines it as faith [Hebrews 11:8-10]. The scripture informs us that by faith Abraham, when called to go to a place he would later receive as his inheritance, obeyed, and went without knowing where he was going. He was aiming at a bullseye that could not be seen with the naked eye. What was the end of that process? Although he died in the natural without receiving what had been promised, that wasn't the end. Before he died, he saw something. The bible teaches that Abraham was looking forward to a city with foundations, whose architect and builder is God. That was his bullseye – the final resting place of the church which no eye has seen, nor ear heard, nor any mind perceived. But God has revealed this to us by His spirit [1 Corinthians 2:9-10].

22

Ignoring time and distance

Faith is all about ignoring time and distance. The desire to receive God's promises means that we are not restricted by the length of time it should ordinarily take or the distance between us and that promise. Sometimes a promise can take longer than expected to be received even though in the natural it seems close at hand. A case in point is the Promised Land which took the children of Israel a whole generation to access because of their spiritual misalignment.

The one who walks by faith is able to transcend both time and distance to receive what has been promised. Yes, there will be occasions where we are required to wait on God and exercise patience because in His sovereignty, He is doing a greater work than we can perceive. However, there are a number of instances in the Bible where the metrics of time and distance were transcended for the purpose of God performing the miraculous in people's lives. So, Joseph had to go through a twenty-two-year journey between his dream and its manifestation, incorporating thirteen years as a slave and a prisoner. When his brothers eventually bowed down to him, it was the confirmation of everything God had shown him. Likewise, David went through over thirteen years between his anointing to be King and his becoming sovereign over firstly a part of Israel and then subsequently king over all of Israel. Sometimes time is necessary for the fulfilment of God's will.

However, faith can in certain instances bypass the distance and duration to perform a miracle. When it aligns with the will of God, faith can shrink time and distance. To believe this we have to look beyond the natural and focus on the spiritual because it is only from this realm that such phenomenon can come. We are required to suspend our five senses and just believe.

The Roman Centurion is an example of how distance was overcome because of his faith [Matthew 8:5-13; Luke 7:1-10]. The Roman Centurion was commended for his exemplary faith. He approached Jesus with a request to heal his servant who was seriously ill and confined to his home. Jesus offered to accompany him to his house but immediately the centurion resisted this, informing Christ that he was not worthy for Him to come under his roof. All he required was that Jesus pronounced a word of healing and he was confident that his servant would be healed. The Centurion explained that he was man both under authority and in authority who issued commands to his men which had to be obeyed. Jesus marvelled at this and asked him to go and that it would be done for him as he believed it would. At that moment, the Centurion's servant was healed. The word of God was not restricted by distance.

Then again, we have the evidence of the first miracle Jesus performed in public which was at a wedding in a place called Cana in Galilee [John 2:1-11]. Jesus attended the event with His disciples and His mother Mary was also present. At some point during the ceremony the wine ran out and His mother informed Him of the situation. Jesus protested that it was not yet His time, but His mother, oblivious to His position, informed the servants that whatever He asked of them they were to do. Jesus then asked them to fill six stone water pots used for purifying of the Jews with water. Each water pot had capacity for about twenty to thirty gallons and the servants were asked to fill them to the brim. Once the pots were full, Jesus asked the servants to draw some of the water and serve it to the master of the ceremony. The man tasted the water that had been turned into wine without realising its source and began to tell off the bridegroom for preserving the best wine till last rather than bringing it out first as was the custom. What this miracle demonstrated was how faith can transcend time. Firstly, there was the faith of Mary and the servants, which facilitated the miracle. Then there was the miracle that bypassed the process for producing wine from grapes, processing them, and then distilling the alcohol and leaving the wine to settle for a period of time because as everyone knows, the best wine is the one that has been left to settle for a period of time.

On another occasion, Jesus was leaving a town called Bethany when He saw a fig tree in bloom and went to find out if it had any fruit [Mark 11:12-22]. However, when He arrived at the tree, He discovered that it had no fruit because it was not the season for figs. In other words, the tree was an aberration. So, He cursed the tree saying that no one would ever eat from it again. He subsequently travelled to Jerusalem and the following morning as he was heading back, Peter, His disciple, saw the tree withered from the roots and remarked at the phenomenon which had been orchestrated by Jesus' curse. In response, Jesus told him to have faith in God. For a tree to wither from its roots overnight was miraculous because it takes many years for withering tree to die. Again, Jesus had bypassed time by exercising His faith.

I guess the lesson here is that faith can bypass time and distance to produce miracles where and when they are needed.

23

Investing in something regardless of the returns

When we say that faith is investing in something regardless of the returns, it is slightly misleading. This is because very few of us would sink something of value into something that will not guarantee a healthy return. Those who walk by faith are often not bothered about the material gain associated with their investment. Whilst nobody actively invests with an expectation of not making some sort of returns or profit on that investment, those who walk by faith are more concerned about the spiritual returns on their investment.

As Christians, we invest with expectation. This expectation or hope is the envelope within which our faith resides. Giving with no thought of receiving anything in return is at the heart of the Gospel of Jesus Christ [Luke 6:35]. Jesus asks an insightful question. He asks rhetorically, if we lend to those from whom we expect to receive what credit is it to us? He clarifies that even sinners (unbelievers) lend to each other in order to receive something back in return [Luke 6:34]. It is a radical concept which contradicts the earthly wisdom at the root of capital investment.

Charitable giving under the umbrella of philanthropy is at the top of most corporate bodies' objectives as part of their "giving back" to society or being seen to embrace social values. For some, it is a heart-led thing but for others the decision is a head-led decision. Incentives like taxation benefits for charitable giving are attractive stimulants but behind the giving is a desire to boost one's profile and brand image. Likewise, for individuals who are given to philanthropy, they have a desire to be seen doing something to tackle poverty and social inequality. Individuals and corporations do their bit as part of their corporate social responsibility but in some cases, this is all about the kudos of being seen to be involved in tackling social issues.

As Christians, our motivation for continuing to give to God has to be the love of Christ in us which leads us down paths of generosity. We are driven to give as an act of love and when we do so we do not expect anything in return. When we look at the example of the early church [Acts 4:32-35], we see a church that majored in giving generously just like Jesus. The people in the church shared all things in common and did not lay claim to personal possessions. They sold real estate and brought the proceeds to the Apostles who then distributed the funds unto those who had needs. As a result, the Bible records that there was no lack within the community. Everyone had their needs met through the love and generosity of others.

Jesus taught that when we invite guests to dinner, we ought to invite those who are unable to reciprocate [Luke 14:12] rather than those who are able to. In the natural realm it is hard to see what benefits or returns one is able to receive when they give with love with no thought of return. However, this is the very embodiment of giving by faith because it is focussed on the unseen spiritual realm and the rewards that accrue from there. The Bible assures us that those who give to the poor lend to God and He will reward them for what they have done [Proverbs 19:17].

Again, the Bible promises that those who give to the poor shall not lack [Proverbs 28:27]. This is a challenge for many because they cannot see how giving to the poor who are unable to repay their generosity could ever result in a reward. However, God who cannot lie tells us that those who invest regardless of returns shall never lack. The unbelieving heart might sneer at this and scorn those whom it perceives as gullible and simple-minded. Even those who have some form of religiosity and believe in God struggle to embrace this philosophy.

There is the story in the gospels of the rich ruler who approached Jesus Christ seeking eternal life [Luke 18:18-23]. When Jesus asked him to ensure that he kept the commandments, the man mentioned that he had kept all of them since he was a boy. So here was a man who understood the importance of obeying God's commands and in many respects, he was more disciplined than some of Jesus' disciples. When Jesus heard the man's testimony, He pointed out that there was one thing still lacking. He asked the ruler to sell everything he had and give the proceeds to the poor, so that he could have treasure in heaven and thereafter become His disciple. However, the ruler became very sad when he heard this because he was very wealthy.

Jesus was testing the man's heart but at the same time revealing the distinction between religion and relationship. The rich ruler wanted to obtain eternal life without obeying the most important commandments – to love the Lord God with all his heart, soul and might and to love his neighbour as himself [Luke 10:27]. Apostle John points out that those who do not love their neighbour whom they can see cannot love God whom they have not seen [1 John 4:20]. The evidence that we love God is that we are able to give to the poor without thought of return. The failure to do this is a sin. The story of Lazarus and the rich man is hinged on this teaching. We all know the story told by Jesus of a rich man who had a poor man at his gate named Lazarus but refused to show him any kindness or generosity. The rich man ultimately went to hell because he had not loved his neighbour as he loved himself [Luke 16:19-31].

Why did Jesus take time to teach on this issue? Because He understands the implications for those who refuse to invest in the lives of the less fortunate or less well-off in society. Those who are only concerned about personal gain will end up like the rich fool (as the bible calls him) who did not care about anyone but himself and was accused of not being generous to God [Luke 12:16-21]. By not giving to those unable to repay him, he was not being generous to God.

24

Having no plan B

Faith is about having no plan B. It is about sticking with God's plan without succumbing to the temptation to devise a back-up plan in case things don't work out. If God tells us to jump out of a plane, we have to trust Him to catch us without the need to strap on a parachute.

The challenge with having no plan B is that we leave ourselves vulnerable and exposed. Our natural instinct is to plan for failure, and there is nothing wrong with this. Even Jesus asks us to count the cost of any action or activity we embark on to ensure that we have enough resources to complete it. Planning is a kingdom thing. Kingdom people plan but they also trust that God's plans and purposes could usurp them if they are out of alignment with His.

What a plan B says is that we either trust plan A but accept that we are not in control of all the external factors, or that we don't have confidence in our plan A and need the security and safety of a back-up plan. This is a logical position to adopt especially when we are not sure what God's will is. It is not that we lack faith, but we are being pragmatic and prudent by keeping something in reserve to mitigate potential failure. No human is infallible, and a plan B is an acknowledgement of this.

We serve a God who does not operate with plan B's. God is omniscient – all knowing, which means nothing is hidden from His awareness. He knows all things that have ever occurred or will ever occur. However, added to this formidable and incomparable capacity is His omnipresence – universal presence. His presence transcends time which means He dwells in the past, the present and the future all at the same time. Ponder over this for a moment. Look beyond where you are right now and your limitations and consider that God is unlimited. His capacity for knowing every scenario that will ever play out in the earth realm means that He is uniquely positioned to stick to one plan. When God makes a plan, He does not repent of it because before the plan was initiated in the depth of His omniscience, He has computed every possible outcome and He is never wrong.

When God created Adam and Eve, He knew that they would fall and made provision for such an occurrence. It did not take Him by surprise that Eve was deceived or that Adam rebelled against His authority. However, the coming of Jesus Christ was not an afterthought or a plan B because plan A had failed. The Bible says that Jesus was a lamb slain from the foundation of the world [Revelation 13:8; 1 Peter 1:20] meaning that even before the creation of humans God had already provided a solution for man's frailties. Jesus was all part of the original plan. God knew Adam would fall and factored Jesus into His plan. He informed Adam, Eve, and Satan that the woman would bring forth a seed that would trample the serpent's head, destroying its capacity for poisoning mankind [Genesis 3:15], and despite the long interval of time, things happened exactly as He said they would.

To walk by faith is to function like God and when He gives us a promise which seems to take an inordinately long time to come to pass, we do not devise a back-up plan. Sometimes a plan B is constructed at the outset because doubt kicks in. At other times, the plan B is hatched in a moment of panic when things don't seem to be tracking well and failure is imminent. The evidence of a plan B is that it arises as a result of human reasoning rather than conferring with God. When it comes to trusting God, a plan B is evidence of doubt. Doubt weakens our resolve and causes us to attempt to salvage the situation. When we doubt, our perspective is impaired, and our vision becomes blurry. Having a plan B is also an act of disobedience because when it is triggered, we deviate from God's plan.

Examples abound in the Bible of people who resorted to a plan B because they wanted in their limited understanding to salvage the situation. How can any person salvage the plan of God? Sarai, Abram's wife learnt that her husband had received a promise that he would be a father of a child and decided to bring it to pass with an idea concocted from her own imagination. She urged her husband to have a child with her maid who was young and fertile [Genesis 16]. This was not God's plan; this was a human strategy aimed at facilitating His plan but in fact was a deviation and by default a plan B. Just because she had incomplete information and had no confidence that she could ever be a mother she decided to assist God and created a problem which still exists in the Middle East in the Twenty First Century.

When King Saul was at war with the Philistines and felt the battle turning against him, he sent for the Prophet Samuel who was the spiritual medium between Israel and God [1 Samuel 13:6-11]. However, when Saul saw his men deserting the battlefield, and there was no sign of Samuel, he committed a travesty by stepping into the Priest's office to burn incense to God (an abomination which shortened the reign of his family in Israel).

To understand how God expects us to function, we need to study the principles instituted by Jesus in relation to Christian ministry. When Jesus sent out His disciples to preach [Matthew 10:5-10], He instructed them not to carry any money in their purses, no bag for the journey, or an extra cloak or sandals or a staff because the labourer was worthy of his keep. This was a valuable lesson because it taught the disciples how to trust Him rather than themselves and to trust in His unseen provision. In other words, they were being sent out by faith. Faith means having no back-up or plan B but sticking with God's plan regardless of what happens or how long it takes to materialise because He is faithful.

Crying with expectation

Faith can often be about crying with expectation. We feel the pain and react with tears, but our focus is not skewed. For those Christians who have experienced the pain of affliction and torment, they will attest to their physical and emotional agony. However, for many of us the pain no matter how intense is not sufficient to distract our focus or diminish our expectation. For the suffering Christian, the promise of God is the source of their resilience in the face of the devil's torment.

The Bible reminds us that tears endure for a night, but that joy comes in the morning [Psalm 30:5]. The unbeliever in a similar situation will likewise feel the pain and react with tears of anguish but the difference is that they do not have the gift of expectation. One of the characters in the Bible who suffered most in his Christian service was Apostle Paul. Recounting his challenges, Paul says that just as we share abundantly in the sufferings of Christ so also our comfort abounds through Christ [2 Corinthians 1:5]. Paul goes on to narrate a catalogue of sufferings. He speaks about the pressure he and his companions experienced which was far beyond their ability to cope or endure to the extent that they despaired of life itself [2 Corinthians 8-9]. His suffering was immense, and one can almost imagine him with tears of agony as he was subjected to yet another beating, yet he did not lose his focus.

Crying with expectation is what one would call tears of faith because they do not deny the suffering but don't let it obstruct them or dictate their perspective. One who comes to mind is Job, a man who lost his children,

wealth, and health, along with his status [Book of Job].
In pain and torment both emotionally and physically he
nevertheless refused to speak out against God even
though urged to do so by his wife. Job's suffering was
excessive, and he became a man well acquainted with
sorrow. His tears did not however blur his focus.

The Bible clarifies that the expectation of the
righteous shall not be cut short for there is a future and
their hope will not be cut off [Proverbs 10:24 and 23:18].
The assurance that God's promises never fail enables a
Christian to remain steadfast despite their tear-inducing
affliction. There is an attitude that God expects of us in
the midst of challenges which delights Him because
without faith it is impossible to please Him. The Prophet
Jeremiah was a man whom many identify with sorrow
especially as there is a whole book in the Bible labelled
the *Lamentations*.

God sent Jeremiah to warn the Children of Israel
about their sinfulness and His forthcoming judgment.
The people however largely ignored him, as did the
ruling elite resulting in their being held captive for
seventy years in Babylon. Whilst the people were
enduring the pain, shame, and humiliation of their
conditions in exile, Jeremiah wrote them a letter which
has become for us the text of God's expectation for His
children when they are enduring His correction
[Jeremiah 29].

Jeremiah advised the people in exile to adjust to the
situation and carry on with their lives as normal, building
houses, settling down, farming, marrying, and giving
their children in marriage; refusing to diminish but rather
increasing. He advised them to seek the welfare of the
country where they were held captive, doing all to ensure
its peace and prosperity by praying for it. He made it

clear that their prosperity was tied to the prosperity of that nation. There was a set time of seventy years for them to dwell there and the prophet cautioned them about listening to false prophets who were prophesying contrary to God's will (probably assuring them that they would not have to dwell in captivity for the full seventy years). If Jeremiah left off his advice at this stage, one could forgive the people for becoming despondent. However, God gave them a word of encouragement to fuel their wait.

In the climax of the letter, God, speaking through Jeremiah, informed the people that He knew the plans He had for them, plans for their prosperity and not to harm them, plans designed to give them hope and bring them to an expected end [Jeremiah 29:11]. For a browbeaten people with nothing to smile about this was a lifeline. God was informing them that there was light at the end of the tunnel and giving them fuel through His word of assurance that they would be preserved through the circumstance to come into a glorious future. Those who had witnessed Jeremiah's earlier prophecies come to pass with unerring accuracy, were assured that God did not mean for them to die in the situation they found themselves in.

Hope from God cancels tears and lifts shoulders. Today, many quote this scripture in isolation and even then, draw strong confidence from it. But, in context it is an assurance to us that when we pass through God's correction (as most of our suffering inevitably is), we need to adopt the right attitude. It doesn't mean that we don't harbour expectation of getting out, but we also understand that the situation is for a set time and even if we don't know how long that is we are confident that it will not be forever. Life does not and should not come to an end just because we are passing through a challenge that has reduced us to tears. This may seem easier said than done particularly for those facing terminal illness or the death of a loved one. However, when we remember that this world is a temporary experience compared to the eternal experience awaiting the faithful, we can draw strength from that and remain expectant.

26

Travelling on a journey where only you know the destination

Faith is travelling on a journey where only you know the destination. This sounds reclusive but is actually about perspective. The embodiment of vision is confidentiality. A vision has a confidential quality that lends itself to discretion. The information possessed by the bearer or carrier is usually for their eyes and ears only. Even though the general outline might eventually become public knowledge it is still a private affair, and its core features will be shrouded until the day of manifestation.

When God reveals His plans to us, it is normal for Him to share the destination with us but not the route. He shows us where we are going but then takes us there by a route known only to Him. When God called Abram out of Mesopotamia to go to a land that God had prepared for him, he chose to travel with his father and nephew. The Bible records however that God had called Abram alone [Isaiah 51:2; Acts 7:2-4] and as God led him step by step to the destination the family followed. Although the Promised Land was a place where Abram had never been before, God gave him the directions and led him there. God did not however share the directions with Terah his father or Lot his nephew because He had not called them. When Abram eventually arrived there, he knew it and built an altar there to honour God.

When God calls us, others may follow and seek to know the destination. However, God will only reveal that destination to us because His calling is very specific. In Abram's case, his father had to die, and his nephew separated from him before Abram could clearly see

God's plan. What was Abram's destination? It was not Canaan but rather it was the nation of Israel and ultimately the Church, something that he did not live to see but received by faith.

Knowing our proclivity for sharing our visions, God may often choose not to show us the fullness of the destination but give us types and shadows, symbolical reference that reveal His plans. If like Joseph, the son of Jacob, we choose to share the destination with our brothers it will never be the specific location. Once we embark on the journey, however, those who are not called by God to join us will drop off along the way, leaving us to trudge on alone. The reason for this is that the hangers-on lack the capacity to make the trip because of the absence of God's grace. Lot, who had no appreciation of the relevance of Abram's journey, was soon caught up in strife with him which resulted in them going their separate ways.

When Angel Gabriel visited Zechariah the priest to inform him that he and his wife Elizabeth were about to become parents to a child named John in their old age, the angel appeared to him alone [Luke 1]. Because Zechariah doubted the angel, he was struck dumb and unable to discuss his experience until the child was born. Doubt and unbelief block our access to God's grace, so maybe Zechariah's dumbness was God's mercy. No one else knew why Zechariah was unable to speak but it ensured that the destination of his vision was known only to him and his wife.

Six months later when Mary became pregnant with Jesus by virtue of her encounter with the Holy Spirit, Joseph believed that it was an act of infidelity on her part. However, God appeared to Joseph alone and reassured him. From that point onwards Mary and Joseph shared a common vision which no one within their family or circle of acquaintances knew about. That journey led them to a manger in Bethlehem where the saviour of the world was born, but no one knew that destination except for those God chose to reveal it to. Even King Herod who was looking to kill the child could not figure out where He was and so ended up killing a host of children.

When sending His disciples out to preach, teach, and heal, Jesus instructed them to greet no man along the way [Luke 10:4]. The reason for this may have been to avoid them getting distracted from their objective by others who might try to dissuade them. Imagine the disciples walking along on their assignment and then coming across friends and family who are eager to know where they are going. Ordinarily they might have mentioned it in passing but in line with Christ's instructions they could not. This reveals that in the eyes of God the journey and how we conduct ourselves along the way is as important as the destination.

The Bible tells us about a man of God from Judah whom God had sent on a specific errand to bring a word of prophecy to the king regarding his idolatry [1 Kings 13]. The king was upset with the man of God and tried to seize him, but his hand withered. After the man of God had prayed for the king's hand to be restored, the king asked him to come home with him to have a meal and receive a reward. But the man of God refused on the grounds that the word of God forbade him from eating or drinking or deviating from the route he had taken. However, as the man of God was heading back the way he came, an old prophet deceived him into believing that an angel of God had asked him to bring the man of God to his home and feed him. Falling for the deception, the man of God deviated from his route and went home with the old prophet. As the man ate, the old prophet received a word of prophecy pronouncing the man of God's death due to his disobedience. Shortly afterwards, on his way home, the man of God was sadly killed by a lion.

Faith is heading somewhere God has shown you but which you can't often discuss with others to avoid being distracted. The journey may seem lonely because others do not have the grace to accompany you all the way, but your discretion and confidentiality will ensure that you arrive at your destination.

27

Taking a risk when the odds are against you

Faith is taking a risk when the odds are against you. This needs to be understood in context. With faith there is always an element of risk. What we are considering here are scenarios where, on paper, defeat or failure is inevitable. These are situations where not even our closest friends or family would bet on us.

The Bible records the account of a man named Gideon who had no feelings of grandeur or sense of greatness [Judges 6 to 8]. He had never accomplished anything noteworthy and had no intention of ever doing so. He was, like many of us, content to stay in his corner and tackle the issues of life in relative obscurity. In other words, Gideon was an unlikely hero. However, God always approaches us not according to how we are perceived but how He perceives us. When he was summoned out of his comfort zone, Gideon was in hiding within a winepress, carrying out the mundane task of threshing wheat. Why was he in hiding? He was in hiding because he had the unenviable situation of having been born in an era where his nation – Israel – was under the dominion of the nation of Midian, as a result of its disobedience.

The Midianites were a fearsome nation, and they were in league with other nations in the region that were hostile to Israel. For seven years this oppressive coalition forced the Children of Israel to hide in dens, caves, and strongholds from where they carried out their affairs. However, every harvest time the Midianites and their coalition partners invaded Israel with the sole aim of destroying the harvest and livestock deeply impoverishing the nation. The invading forces were like grasshoppers in number and voracity, and totally dominated the land. It is within the context of this climate that Gideon was summoned forth to display valour in the face of impossible odds. When an angel appeared to him and called him a mighty man of valour and assured him that the Lord was with him, Gideon must have done a double take. He felt anything but brave. When he started reeling out complaints about the situation facing the nation, as some of us do, he was told to go out and deliver the nation. In reaction to this gauntlet, Gideon laid down the reasons why he was not qualified for the task – his family was the poorest in his community, and he was the least in his family. However, the Lord assured him that He would be with him. How often do we disqualify ourselves from the assignments that God commissions us to fulfil because of our sense of inadequacy?

The first task God gave Gideon to do was to destroy the altar that had been erected in Israel for the service of the idol named Baal and then build an altar for God. Gideon obeyed but because he was afraid of the people's reaction, he opted to do it at night. How many of us obey God only if we feel safe enough? So, we obey discreetly and stay in the shadows where we can't be easily identified. However, as is always the case, the people found out about what Gideon had done and wanted to kill him but for the timely intervention of his father. When God's Spirit provoked Gideon to gather an army from the various tribes, he obeyed but remained sceptical. Despite God's assurance he still felt inadequate.

To further reassure himself, Gideon put God to the test. On one occasion he placed a fleece of wool on the floor and said that if the wool was soaking wet, but the ground remained dry then he would be convinced that God would use him to deliver the nation. On another occasion he asked God to cause the wool to remain dry but for there to be dew on the ground beneath it. On both occasions, God produced the desired outcomes and with nowhere left to hide Gideon gathered an army of people and prepared for battle.

But when God took stock of the army, He observed that the people were too many for Him to use against the Midianites. One could imagine Gideon's pulse rate and blood pressure when God explained that if He used an army of that size (thirty-two thousand), the people would boast that it was their own prowess that had secured them victory. Instead, God told Gideon to discharge everyone who was fearful or apprehensive and twenty-two thousand departed. God again took stock and noted that ten thousand was still too large an army to be used by Him and so He asked Gideon to get them to drink water from a stream and separate them into two groups. Those who lapped the water with their tongues like dogs were to be separated from those who stooped down to drink. Three hundred men lapped water like dogs and God selected these as the army He would use to deliver the Midianites into Gideon's hand. Now we need to put this into context. The army of the Midianites and their coalition partners numbered over one hundred and thirty-five thousand men. Even with an army of thirty-two thousand men the odds were stacked against Gideon, talk less of three hundred. Are you in a place where the odds are against you and the challenge confronting you seems overwhelming? This is the moment to seek the Lord and listen to what He says.

To further reassure Gideon, because God knows the heart of every man, God caused a person within the camp of the Midianites to have a dream and gave the interpretation of that dream to another, then caused Gideon to overhear them talking. The interpretation of the dream was that God had given victory over the army of Midian to Gideon. On hearing this, the residue of doubt was expunged from Gideon's mind. With three hundred men and facing impossible odds, Gideon overcame a vastly superior army. God intervened in the battle causing confusion in the camp of Midian so that the men turned on each other and killed themselves. If we believe Him, we can experience the same overwhelming victory regardless of the odds against us.

28

Appearing to plant in the wrong season in the wrong soil

Faith is about appearing to plant in the wrong season in the wrong soil. Think about that. Faith does not follow convention. The natural path for any farmer is to sow in the right season in the right soil. The Bible instructs that there is a season for everything and a time for every purpose or activity under the heavens [Ecclesiastes 3:1-2]. Therefore, there is a time to sow and a time to reap or harvest what was sown. This flows from the law of Cause and Effect. This law is the basis upon which everything reproduces. For every action there is a reaction, and so it is with farming. You cannot get a harvest without first sowing a seed. When we sow seeds, depending on the conditions of the soil, we should in the normal scheme of things receive a harvest.

So Jesus teaches about the parable of the sower who went out to sow seeds, and sowed some along the wayside where it was devoured by birds; he sowed some in stony ground where the seeds were unable to tap into the nutrients within the soil and therefore withered; he sowed some amongst the thorns and thistles which suffocated it and stunted its growth eventually killing the plant; and then he sowed in good soil of varying grades of quality where the seed produced a harvest thirty, sixty and a hundredfold [Matthew 13:1-23; Mark 4:2-20; and Luke 8:4-15]. Although this parable focuses on the growth of the word of God in the heart of a Christian, it also confirms what many of us know to be the pattern of growth for ordinary plants.

Farmers know the difference between the time to sow and the harvest time. They understand the different seasons and the impact of the climate on the soil and the potential for growth. Farmers know what weather conditions suit which type of crop and they plan accordingly. No farmer starts to plant without a proper understanding of these factors and although they may occasionally suffer the ill effects of unforeseeable freak weather patterns this is the exception rather than the norm.

However, faith can provoke a person to plant in the wrong season and in the wrong type of soil because it is not governed by the natural but the supernatural. Therefore, against all earthly wisdom, faith opts to move in tandem with the word of God rather than expert opinion. This is because faith understands that the spiritual rules over the natural and that the word of God is the most reliable source of instruction. So, for instance, expert opinion would caution against making an investment in a particular climate because of how the sector is performing or what is happening in the stock market or economy. Faith defies such knowledge because it receives its guidance from a higher source which transcends earthly limitations. Faith swims against the tide and those who are able to disengage their common sense form their spiritual sense reap the rewards.

When I think about this, I recall the Biblical account of Isaac. Isaac famously sowed seed in the wrong season and in the wrong soil but suffered no loss. Isaac did not follow the conventional wisdom of farmers but submitted to the instruction of God. As a result, he obtained something miraculous [Genesis 26: 1-6 and 12-13].

The background to this story starts with the conception and birth of Isaac. In summary, Isaac was a child born out of season. He was conceived in the wrong season of his parents' lives from questionable seed sown into questionable soil. His mother was well past the age of childbearing at eighty-nine years old when she conceived him, and his father was well past the age of potency and fertility at ninety-nine years old when he impregnated his mother. Isaac's genesis and orientation was of the faith that produced a bountiful harvest from seed sown into wrong soil in the wrong season of life. He was therefore well-positioned to understand and exploit the spiritual principle that defied human understanding. If his parents were stuck in conventional thought, he would never have been born.

In the Biblical account that forms the spine of this principle of faith, we are told that there was a famine in the land where Isaac dwelt. Following his natural instincts, he went to a place called Gerar enroute to Egypt [Genesis 26:1-6]. But God appeared to Isaac and told him not to go down to Egypt, instructing him to dwell in Gerar, and promising that He would be with him and bless him because of the covenant He had made with Abraham his father. Isaac therefore chose to remain in Gerar and sowed in that land ignoring the fact of the famine. Against all odds, that year he received a hundredfold harvest [Genesis 26:12].

Farmers typically never sow all their seed in a famine, as they expect to make a loss. Whilst wisdom may suggest that sowing more seed means chances of a larger harvest factoring in potential losses, the reality is that without sufficient water to irrigate the land there may be a total wipe-out of all seed planted. Some farmers end up with nothing, so reserving some seed to plant in a good year is wisdom. We do not know whether Isaac sowed all the seed at his disposal. All we know is that he sowed in a famine in soil that was not fit for purpose. I suspect that he sowed all the seed he had, as he normally would have done, because he was not operating by sight but by faith. While the Philistine farmers bemoaned their paltry yield, Isaac celebrated a full harvest with no loss. Even in a good farming year, few farmers receive a hundredfold harvest because of pests like insects and birds. However, Isaac did good business in a famine because he operated by faith. This tells us that our prosperity as Christians is not linked to the economy of our respective nations but to our faith in the word of God.

29

Making a fool of yourself

Faith is making a fool of yourself. Faith in God and His word can provoke certain behaviours that many will deem foolish. However, it is a matter of perception because foolishness in the eyes of the world is not the same thing as foolishness in the eyes of God. After all He said that His thoughts are not our thoughts neither are His ways our ways; He made clear that as the heavens are higher than the earth, so much higher are His ways than our ways and His thoughts than our thoughts [Isaiah 55:8-9]. Because of this gulf between God's perspective and the human perspective, some things that we deride He endorses and some behaviour we disdain He delights in.

Therefore, God's definition of *foolish* is different from the world's. What the world calls wise, God calls foolish and what God calls wise the world calls foolish. For instance, Apostle Paul clarifies that the preaching of the cross is foolishness to those who are perishing but to Christians it is the power of God [1 Corinthians 1:18]. However, God has promised to destroy the wisdom of the so-called wise and frustrate the understanding of those who deem themselves prudent [1 Corinthians 1:19]. Explaining the gulf between God's perspective and the world's, Paul says that God has made foolish the wisdom of this world for even as the world in its supposed wisdom refused to acknowledge God, it pleased Him through the foolishness of preaching to save them that believe [1 Corinthians 1: 20-21]. This preaching, according to Paul, was a stumbling block to the Jews who were seeking a sign to convince them and foolishness to the Greeks who were seeking earthly wisdom.

Today in many communities the practice of bible-based Christianity attracts hostility and derision from those who advocate and promote tolerance through lip-service. The name of Jesus is used in profanity and those holding fast to Christian values are targeted by those operating under the protection of an intolerant legislative agenda. This is nothing new, for those who worship the true God have historically been the subject of ridicule. One can only imagine the sort of mockery and scorn that Noah was subjected to when he began to construct a large ocean-going vessel on dry land. Despite his attempts to save many within his community, they rejected his caution until the floods washed them away [Genesis 6:8-22; and 7; Hebrews 11:7]. In their eyes Noah was a foolish man and sadly they perished in their so-called wisdom. This is the same scenario being played out in our world as we approach the end of the age.

What many don't realise is that the perceived foolishness of God is wiser than men and He has chosen the things that appear foolish to the world to confound the things deemed by the world to be wise [1 Corinthians 1:25-27]. When we look at the people used by God to carry out mighty feats, He appeared to have a preference for those who were not highly regarded within their communities. David was such a person. When the Prophet Samuel turned up at his family home and requested to see all the sons, David was left out in the fields to tend sheep. He did not make the grade in his father's eyes and was treated accordingly. Yet, David was God's choice.

Confronting Goliath in combat was foolhardy because on paper they were not evenly matched, and no one was taking bets on the outcome. From both sides of the arena, it was a settled outcome. In the eyes of all observers David was a dead man. The wise soldiers and their commanders stayed within the safety of their camp and sent the shepherd boy to die.

Many years later, when David became king over all Israel, he decided to bring the Ark of Covenant into Jerusalem. Having failed at his previous attempt, resulting in the death of one of his men, this time he was determined to get it right. He arranged a procession in line with the instructions given by Moses and brought the ark to the city. Along the way David danced before the Lord like a madman, out of a heart overflowing with joy. In fact, so vigorous and wild was his merriment that his loin cloth barely preserved his dignity before the people who were celebrating around him. This was not some mild wardrobe malfunction but a wholesale exposure of himself before his subjects as he leapt and pranced about in celebration. Yet he did not lose dignity in their sight in fact I wager that he earned their admiration [2 Samuel 6:12-17]. Yet his wife Michal, the daughter of King Saul – David's predecessor, observed him dancing before the Lord and despised him in her heart.

Later that day, she confronted David and berated him for his conduct which she deemed unbecoming of the King of Israel. She tongue-lashed him for uncovering himself and dancing half naked before the young female slaves like a vulgar person. But David displayed no remorse for his perceived foolishness. Instead, he defended his actions, by pointing out that he was dancing before the Lord who had chosen him to be King over Israel rather than her father's descendants. He then hurled fuel into the furnace by claiming that he was prepared to be even more undignified than he had been that day and be humiliated in his own eyes. But he made clear that he would be held in honour by the female slaves she spoke of [2 Samuel 6:20-22]. For David, worship was a lifestyle and an act of thanksgiving. It was also an act of faith because he truly believed that God desired a sacrifice of praise from his people [Psalm 22:3]. Therefore, David's exuberant obedience in this area was reflective of his faith in God.

30

Doing and saying crazy stuff

Faith is doing and saying crazy stuff. This might sound awkward at first but if you dwell on it, you will eventually grasp the context. Crazy stuff is mad and extreme or just plain weird and inappropriate. Crazy stuff makes no sense because it does not follow a conventional path. The Bible is littered with examples of people who had a close relationship with God either doing or saying crazy stuff. But in each case, they were acting strictly by faith.

We all know the story of David and Goliath, and how David's oldest brother and King Saul disdained the young shepherd when he offered to fight and kill the giant [1 Samuel 17]. That was crazy! Goliath was twice his size and better experienced in the art of war. He was also better equipped for combat and supported by a vastly superior army. King Saul's observations are noteworthy here. He said, "You are not able to go out against this Philistine and fight him; you are only a young man, and he has been a warrior from his youth." Saul was being polite. What he probably wanted to say, is "you're going get squashed. You do not stand a chance." I can only imagine what must have been going through Saul's mind when David narrated how he killed a bear and a lion. He was probably thinking that he was either in the presence of a mad man or a fantasist. Who risks their life confronting wild beasts to rescue a sheep?

At age eighty-five, Caleb declared that he was going to possess Hebron one of the most dangerous territories within the Promised Land – Canaan [Joshua 14:9-12]. To younger observers, he must've looked insane. Here was this grandfather stepping forward with gusto and declaring that he was ready to fight and felt as fit as he was forty years ago. Yes, if I had been there, I would have struggled to keep a straight face. But there was substance to Caleb's demands. He was basing his stance on a promise from God, made through Moses forty years earlier. Moses told him that the land on which he had set his feet would be an inheritance for him and his children forever, because he had faithfully followed the Lord. Caleb believed God had spared his life so he could possess Hebron the land of the giants.

Faith reveals itself in all sorts of crazy ways such as when Jesus observed some men breaking through the roof of a house He was in just so that they could beat the crowds and get to the front of the queue. The account which is documented in the Gospels [Mark 2:1-12 and Luke 5:18-26] reveals the crazy lengths faith will go to in search of a miracle. On this particular day, Jesus was in a house teaching and as one version recounts, He was surrounded by Pharisees, doctors of the law who had come from every town in Judea and Galilee. Now even though Jesus was teaching, the power of the Holy Spirit was present for the purpose of healing those in need of it [Luke 5:17].

Some men arrived at the house carrying a bed on which lay a paralyzed man. Seeing the crowds surrounding the house and having no way of gaining access through the door, they instead climbed up on the roof and began to dismantle a section. Having broken through the roof, they lowered the man on the bed into the house through the hole they had created and laid him at Jesus feet. All the while they were breaking through the roof, Jesus was observing them whilst the house owner was probably beside himself and incandescent with rage. It is very likely that the Pharisees and Doctor of Law were also indignant at the rude disruption to the teaching session by the insanity of those carrying the paralyzed man. Yet, the Bible records that Jesus saw their faith [Mark 2:5; Luke 5:20] and pronounced the forgiveness of the man's sins before eventually healing the man in the presence of the sceptical dignitaries. The example of these men proves that crazy faith does get results.

What about saying crazy stuff? Well, the Bible proves that that also gets results. Making crazy statements, giving crazy commands, and making crazy pronouncements could also be the evidence of faith at work. The Bible records the account of a king of Judah named Jehoshaphat who commanded his people to head into battle with the choir ahead of the army singing songs of praise to God; now how crazy is that? [2 Chronicles 20:21]. Jehoshaphat had a situation he could not dislodge in his own strength. He was under siege from a coalition of three powerful nations namely Moab, Ammon, and Mount Seir. Having prayed about the situation and received assurance from a prophet of God that the battle was the Lord's, the following morning he informed the people that they were going out to the battleground and arranged them with the choir leading the way. Now which commanding officer does that? To the casual onlooker that is crazy. Even though they had assurance from God's prophet, telling the choir to march in front ahead of the army is crazy. Obeying such a command was even crazier. This was crazy faith in motion.

Yet even though they looked ridiculous to onlookers, on Jehoshaphat's command they sang songs of praise to the Lord. Who does that? Faced with annihilation, rather than facing their adversaries with weapons they relegated the army and elevated worship. The Bible records that as they extolled God's praise and sang of his mercy that endured forever, God caused confusion in the camp of their enemies who turned on each other and wiped themselves out. Jehoshaphat's instruction was crazy, and the people were even crazier for obeying it, yet it obtained for them victory.

Like Elisha asking Naaman the Syrian commander to bathe seven times in the impure River Jordan as a cure for his leprosy or Joshua asking the children of Israel to march around the walls of Jericho as a means of overthrowing the city, saying crazy things can be the hallmark of faith if the origin of that stuff is God.

31

Believing in something you cannot prove

Faith is essentially about believing in something you cannot prove. This is both the most intriguing quality of faith as well as its most challenging. Many of the debates between Christians and non-Christians centre on substance of conviction. The non-Christian believes because they can perceive the evidence of what they believe in with their five senses. They can see, hear, smell, taste, and touch what they believe in, and their reality is established through this medium. The Christian believes in what is not tangible from a natural, material perspective and therefore often lacks credibility in the heat of debate.

By way of counterargument, some Christians often ask their doubting audience, "Have you ever seen your brain?" They then follow-up by pointing out that "the fact you haven't seen your brain yet believe you possess one is faith." I have heard other Christians use the analogy of sitting on a chair but trusting that it will hold your weight, as the evidence of faith. Whilst I appreciate the analogies, I believe that they diminish the essence of faith. I may not have seen *my* brain but if I really have a red-hot burning desire to see it, a scan can be taken of my brain and shown to me. And, of course, I can see the chair before I lower myself onto it. Faith is not merely about believing, but about believing in something you can't prove through your five senses.

When Thomas, one of Jesus' disciples doubted the resurrection of Christ [John 20:24-29], despite the report given by other disciples on the truth of the matter, Jesus showed up again just for him. But He did not commend him. After inviting Thomas to touch His wounds to prove that He was alive, Jesus informed him that he only believed because he had seen but said that those who have not seen and yet believe are blessed. The most quoted definition of faith says that it is the substance of things hoped for and the evidence of things not seen [Hebrews 11:1]. We cannot see what we are hoping for but believe in its substance, we have no visual evidence of what we are expectant for yet do not doubt. The natural mind does not put its trust in what it cannot prove, and this is why the Biblically derived Intelligent Creation theory is derided and ridiculed by some intellectuals.

However, the Bible points out that by faith we (Christians) believe that the worlds (Universe) were created by the word of God [Hebrews 11:3] so that the things which are seen were not made of things which can be seen. We cannot prove scientifically that the world was created by God, but we believe it was. We were not there when God created it, but we believe He did. But our scientists believe they have a fairly clear idea how it all came together. The prevailing theory at the time of writing this book still favours the Big Bang as the source of the Universe. Apparently at some point in the distant past, space and time emerged. Emerged from where? Well, this is still being debated but by the use of diverse complex calculations astronomers have mapped out a theory which describes a process by which space and time expanded. According to them, as this expansion continued it resulted in the energy and matter present within those elements (space and time) decreasing in density and ultimately leading to the creation of hydrogen atoms, subatomic particles and dense dark matter which contributed to the creation of planets, stars, galaxies etc. This is a simplification of what is an impressively complex theory constructed by very intelligent people who have performed experiments and conducted tests to gather empirical evidence capable of being codified into a field of study.

However, the impressive theory does not address the elephant in the room – what is the origin of time and space? As Christians, we believe by faith that it is God. I am not qualified to disprove the scientists as I have conducted no experiments or tests. I simply believe what is written in the Bible because faith comes by (consistently) hearing the truth that is embedded in the word of God [Romans 10:17]. The more I meditate on the word of God the stronger my conviction becomes until God's truth becomes my truth. Therefore, when the Bible teaches that God created the Universe, I believe it because it is the truth. Jesus confirmed that God's word was the embodiment of truth [John 17:17] and He prayed that we should be sanctified [set-apart from everything else] by that truth. Let God be true and every man a liar [Romans 3:4]. God cannot lie [Numbers 23:19; Hebrews 6: 18]. It does not matter how convincing and clever manmade theories are, neither does it matter whether the whole world believes in them; if their source is not God then they are lies.

During a trip to Rome, Apostle Paul advised a ship's crew and a Roman Centurion, in charge of Paul and some other prisoners, not to embark on the next leg of the journey [Acts 27:10-14]. Paul cautioned that the voyage was going to be disastrous with great loss. But rather than listen to Paul, the Centurion chose instead to follow the advice of the ship's crew who were bent on making the journey. The ship's crew were governed by their knowledge and experience of weather patterns.

They had probably sailed those waters dozens of times and knew the weather pattern for that time of year. The Centurion chose to put his confidence in their skill and expertise rather than Paul's spiritual insight. But for God's intervention on Paul's behalf, the journey would have resulted in loss of lives [Acts 27:14-44]. The ship and its cargo were lost but the lives were preserved.

Standing on a conviction which you cannot prove with any tangible evidence will expose you to ridicule and scorn. You will be dismissed by intellectuals and written off by your peers as being mediocre or a charlatan. However, not having any physical evidence to prove what you know in your spirit to be true is the hallmark of faith.

32

Seeing an impossible outcome

Seeing an impossible outcome is the evidence of faith. What do I mean? When you are confronting a problem for which you have no solution or facing a challenge which defies all your efforts it is easy to become despondent. That is the time that the devil projects a discouraging outcome to your senses. You struggle to see how things can get better or how escape from it is possible. At times, you may be confronting a multitude of issues, each in need of resolution, and despite your efforts at triaging them, your structured approach disintegrates. As the stronghold in your mind consolidates an array of bad outcomes, a cloud of impossibility smothers your reasoning, neutralising your capacity for seeing light at the end of the tunnel. This is where many of us often find ourselves and this is Satan's stomping ground. He strikes when we are tired, frustrated, angry, and discouraged, loading our thoughts with negativity. This is the time that impossibility becomes our reality.

If, however, we are able to see a positive but impossible outcome in the midst of the impossibility, then we will find the strength to walk towards the light at the end of the tunnel. Jesus promised that in this world (or life) we will have trouble or tribulation [John 16:33]. However, He also informed us that we should fear not because He has overcome the world. Therefore, the key to seeing an impossible outcome in an impossible situation is to remember that Jesus has already obtained for us victory. How did He obtain victory? He obtained victory when in the flesh He died on the cross for our sakes and through that death He destroyed the one who had the power of death – the devil and by so doing released us from bondage to the fear of death [Hebrews 2:14-15]. The Bible informs us that whoever is born of God overcomes the world through faith [1 John 5:4-5]. It clarifies that those who believe that Jesus is the Son of God are the ones who overcome the world. These are the ones who have the capacity to see God's deliverance because regardless of how challenging the challenge is, they have already experienced greater deliverance from darkness to light and from bondage to salvation.

The most discouraging event for Jesus' disciples and followers was the cross. Seeing the hope of the world brutalised, humiliated, and executed in such a cruel manner was harrowing for them. Even before Jesus was executed, His disciples were in hiding and the one who had the courage to follow part of the way ultimately denied Him. Like most devious schemes, it was an inside job executed by a disciple named Judas who, like the serpent in the Garden of Eden, was a willing vessel for the inhabitation of evil. After the crucifixion and resurrection, Jesus appeared to His disciples and followers to confirm that His earthly assignment had been successfully accomplished and that salvation and redemption were freely available to all who put their trust in Him and received Him as Lord. In one account of a post-crucifixion revelation, Jesus appeared to two of his disciples as they journeyed to a town called Emmaus but prevented them from recognising Him [Luke 24:13-35].

Jesus listened as they spoke about Him in dismal tones, describing Him as a prophet powerful in word and deed who had been crucified. They had hoped that he was the Messiah (the one who was going to redeem Israel) but it was the third day (when Jesus had promised

He would arise from the grave) and, despite the fact that His tomb was empty, no one had seen Him. Jesus then rebuked them for being foolish and slow to believe all that the prophets in Scripture had written about. Jesus asked them rhetorically whether Christ should not have suffered this manner of death and thereafter entered His glory. As they were pondering over His words, He took them through the Scriptures explaining all that the prophets starting from Moses had written about Him. What did the prophets write about Him? They wrote about God's promise of redemption for mankind through the sacrifice of a lamb without spot or blemish. Jesus was explaining to His disciples that Christ was that lamb and without His death mankind would never be delivered from its eternal sin. In other words, though the situation was gruesome the outcome was glorious.

The Prophet Isaiah says that *surely, He took up our pain and bore our suffering, yet we considered Him punished by God, stricken by him, and afflicted. But He was pierced for our transgressions, he was crushed for our iniquities; the punishment that brought us peace was on Him, and by His wounds we are healed….He was oppressed and afflicted, yet He did not open His mouth; He was led like a lamb to the slaughter, and He was as a sheep before its shearers is silent, so He did not open His mouth…..for the transgression of my people He was punished…….Yet it was the Lord's will to crush Him and cause Him to suffer….*[Isaiah 53 paraphrased NIV©].

Apostle Paul reminds us (Christians) that all things work together for good to them that love God and are called according to His purpose [Romans 8:28]. He did not say *some* things but *all* things. That means there is a solution to every problem and a way of overcoming every challenge. We might pass through fire and water along the way and acquire scrapes and bruises like badges of honour, but God promises that He will be with us and that the outcome will be good [Psalm 66:12; Isaiah 43:2]. In other words, there must be a testimony at the end of the trial and God must receive the glory. It may be difficult to see the possibility of an impossible outcome in your situation because of the doctor's prognosis or the expert's opinion or the judge's ruling. But if you are able to see Christ victorious and the devil defeated then you will access the grace necessary for seeing a glorious end.

33

Parking your five senses

Parking your five senses is an essential element of faith. The challenge of faith is that it demands you shut down reliance on your five senses and step out over the edge of the cliff ignoring the two hundred metre drop beneath you. You shut-down the facts and step out in obedience with no parachute or safety net.

When Queen Esther set out to see her husband the King Ahasuerus during a season when a decree was in force forbidding anyone even his own wife from approaching him, she faced the risk of losing her life [Esther 5:1-7]. Even though she probably believed that the heart of a king was in the hand of the Lord who directs it as He pleases [Proverbs 21-1] yet she was full of trepidation. Before embarking on a three day fast, ahead of her act of faith, she had exclaimed that if she perished as a result of her faith in approaching the king then she perished [Esther 4:16]. It was almost as if she had resigned herself to a certain fate. Her defiant remark was probably her way of controlling her apprehension. She had no idea how the king would react but by confronting the worst-case scenario it weakened her fear.

Because of Esther's faith however the king was favourably disposed towards her when she appeared before him and rather than putting her to death as per the decree instead, he offered her anything she wanted even up to half of his kingdom [Esther 5:2-3]. By parking her five senses and just trusting God, Esther did not lose her life but was granted an open door to present her petition.

One way of overcoming the control of our five senses is to be in the spirit. I know this may appear ominous to some of us, but it is not as scary as it sounds. To be in the spirit requires keeping our focus fixed squarely on God. Why do we need to do this? Because what is impossible with man is possible with God [Luke 18:27]. Another way of phrasing this is whatever man finds impossible to do, shall become possible for him when he turns to God. An example of this is when the angel told Sarah that at eighty-nine years, she was about to become a mother and when she sniggered within her at the thought, God asked whether she believed there was anything too hard for the Lord [Genesis 18:14]. God was not going to carry the pregnancy for her but by discarding her confidence in her five senses and focussing on Him she would receive the power to conceive even though she was way past the age of childbearing.

When Mary was approached by Angel Gabriel and informed that she was going to become pregnant with a baby even though she had not yet had sexual relations she sought clarity. From her perspective this was a new dimension because to her knowledge she had only ever seen women become pregnant after sexual relations with a man. When the angel explained that she would be impregnated supernaturally by the power of the Holy Spirit, she accepted it [Luke 1:26-38]. Because Mary responded by faith, she conceived the child who was to become the saviour of the world. She had to bypass her five senses in order to believe the angel and because she did, she became one of the most famous women in history.

For Sarah and Mary, it was a state of mind that had to be overcome. Both women had to look past what their five senses had conditioned them to believe and reach into a supernatural dimension where impossibility becomes possibility. By focussing on God and His ability they were able to access the grace needed to receive what was promised. To focus on God is to divert our minds from the world. When Adam and Eve fell from grace, they lost the capacity to relate with God in the spirit and became limited to the function of their five senses becoming no better than superior primates.

Focussing on what is revealed via the five senses is what the Bible calls being in the flesh and is used to distinguish a lifestyle lived according to sensual pleasure from one lived in the spirit [Romans 8:5]. Being in the flesh prevents one from accessing things in the spiritual realm. It can also be referred to as carnality. The carnal mind lacks the capacity to form a relationship with God talk less of accessing the spiritual realm [Romans 8:7-9]. The Bible makes clear that those who live out their lives through a carnal mind (living in the flesh) cannot please God. The Bible also states that without faith it is impossible to please God [Hebrews 11:6] and that those who come to Him must believe that He is and that He rewards those who diligently seek after Him. This means that those who are carnally minded cannot have faith in God because they are limited by their five senses to things in the world.

Apostle Paul tells us not to be conformed to this world but to be transformed by the renewing of our minds [Romans 12:2]. Conforming to this world is living life like the people of the world and sharing the same lifestyle. Apostle John says that everything in the world including the lust of the flesh and of the eyes, and the pride of life does not come from God but from the world [1 John 2:16]. Apostle James says that friendship with the world is enmity with God [James 4:4] and that anyone who chooses to befriend the world becomes an enemy of God. It is therefore clear that anyone who chooses to live like the people of the world, the ones whom Paul calls the "children of disobedience" who are governed by the prince of the power of the air (Satan) [Ephesians 2:1-3] cannot focus on God. Because they have been blinded by Satan, their five senses limit them to the earth realm.

However, those who possess the Holy Spirit are children of God and co-heirs with Christ and are therefore capable of accessing the spiritual realm through various mediums including prayer, confession, fasting and meditation on God's word. Once we access this realm, we are able to park our five senses and connect to truth.

34

Trusting in one you have never seen

Trusting in one you have never seen is faith. No one has ever seen God except Jesus Christ who came from God to reveal Him to us [John 1:18; John 6:46; 1 John 4:12]. Since the fall of Adam only Jesus has seen God the father face to face. Even the most faithful Christian cannot claim to have seen God face to face in their humanity. They may have had a revelation of Him or seen an angel or some presentation of Him but never in the fullness of His glory. God said no man could see Him and live [Exodus 33:20]. When Moses was on the mountain with God receiving the commandments, He beheld God's likeness but even that was far more exposure than any other prophet ever saw before or after. As a result of the intimacy between God and Moses, God revealed His ways to him, but the Children of Israel only saw His deeds [Psalm 103:7].

We are told that the Lord used to speak with Moses face to face as one does with a friend [Exodus 33:11] but we know that it was not face to face with God in His full glory because subsequently he asked God to show him His glory [Exodus 33:20]. God however said that Moses could not see His face for no man could see Him and live. Instead, He passed before Moses and only revealed His back to him [Exodus 33:20-23]. Therefore, when the Bible says that those who come to God must believe that He is and that He rewards those who diligently seek Him, [Hebrews 11:6] it is not referring to His actual appearance but rather His presence. Those who seek Him are seeking His presence. His presence is manifested in our dispensation through the Holy Spirit.

In the Old Testament God revealed Himself in various ways through angels and the elements; in the gospels He reveals Himself through Jesus Christ and in our time, it is through the Holy Spirit [John 14: 16-17 and 15:26].

Even when God reveals Himself through angels as He did throughout scripture, those who saw them feared for their lives and believed they would die [Judges 6:22-23; Daniel 8:15-18, 10:5-9; Revelation 1:10-17]. The mere sight of an angel in all its splendour was enough to strike terror into the hearts of even the most faithful prophet or apostle. Because our physical domain (our body) is contaminated with sin and marked for death we are unable to see God face to face the way Adam did before he fell.

Although God does not reveal Himself to us in all His glory, we are aware of His presence through the works of His hands [Romans 1:19-22]. Apostle Paul makes clear that what may be known about God has been made plain to humanity and that God's invisible qualities including His eternal power and divine nature are revealed through His works of creation so that people have no excuse and cannot feign ignorance. Instead, people chose to worship God's creation rather than Him, exchanging the truth about Him for a lie – swapping the glory of the immortal God for images of mortal creatures. As a result, God gave them over to their sinful and lustful desires. Their senses were eventually blinded to the existence of an eternal God who created the earth and everything in it as well as the sun, moon, stars, and planets. The fallen nature of man gravitates towards idolatry and rituals and therefore he cannot walk by faith.

So how does one believe in a God, one has not seen in person? I believe we do this by imbibing His Holy Word until our minds are saturated with the truth of it.

Meditating on God's word is the pathway to knowing Him and experiencing His reality. The Bible teaches that blessed is the man who does not walk in the counsel of the wicked or sit in the domain of the scornful or stand in the congregation of sinners, but such a person finds delight in meditating on God's word day and night so that he becomes like a tree planted by rivers which yields its fruit in season, and whose leaves are green and do not wither and whatever he does prospers [Psalm 1:1-3]. The person, who meditates on God's word, gets to know the God of the Bible, and become intimate with him. Such a person prays in a more effective word-based manner, quoting God's word accurately and in context. Such a person hears from God on a variety of matters concerning his life and makes plans based on God's counsel. Such a person realises that man does not live by bread alone but by every word that proceeds from God's mouth [Deuteronomy 8:3].

Outside of God's word it is impossible to build up faith in Him because He rarely reveals Himself outside His word. It is deliberate to ensure that we understand His principles and precepts and apply them to our lives. The one who does not know God's word cannot obey it and such a person will at best be reduced to a religious person who loves to hang around church and even serve within it but lacks intimacy with God. The challenge with trying to have faith in God outside His word is because of our carnal nature (our flesh) which causes us to cleave to the things of the world.

Jesus says we cannot serve two masters because we will ultimately love one of them more than the other to the point where the unloved one will be despised [Matthew 6:24]. By way of analogy, He says that we cannot love God and Mammon (the god of this world system). Trying to serve two gods is akin to schizophrenia. A person becomes double-minded because of their split allegiance, and this creates instability. A double-minded person is indecisive and prone to doubt. Apostle James says such a person will never receive anything from God [James 1:6—8]. Those who come to God must believe that He is even though they have never seen Him and through dwelling on His word, they learn that He is not partial but will reward everyone who diligently seeks Him [Hebrews 11:6].

35

Believing that water can come out of a rock

Faith believes that water can come out of a rock. In the natural scheme of things, water does not come out of a rock. Rocks contain minerals but because of their solid construction they are not known for containing or concealing water within their structure. A rock is a stronghold; so, believing that water can gush forth from a rock is stretching the imagination a bit. Yet the Bible records two episodes where God caused water to gush forth from rocks in the wilderness.

Whilst leading the Children of Israel out of Egypt, they became thirsty in a place where there was no oasis or well and as was their nature began to mob Moses and put God to the test. This happened on two occasions. The first was at a place called Rephidim where there was no water and the crowds accused Moses of bringing them and their livestock out of Egypt to die of thirst. Moses turned to God for a solution and was told to use his staff to strike a rock at Horeb and water would come out for the people to drink. Moses obeyed this and he called the place Massah and Meribah because the people quarrelled and tested God there, asking whether the Lord was among them or not.

Now this was a miracle because they were in a situation that had no natural solution. The wilderness is a place where no one tends to dwell, and no one tends to pass through especially if they have an alternative route [Jeremiah 2:6]. God was revealing to them His power as their provider, Jehovah Jireh [Genesis 22:14]. God was determined to cultivate intimacy with the Children of Israel by getting them to recognise Him as their provider.

Even after they provoked Him and ended up wandering for forty years around the wilderness, He was still determined to cultivate a relationship with them individually and corporately. He was also testing them to see whether they would respond to Him in the right way and submit to His laws [Deuteronomy 8:2]. God wanted them to ultimately know that man does not live by bread alone but by every word that proceeded forth from His mouth [Deuteronomy 8:3]. However, their fixation with self-preservation prevented them from seeking a relationship with God.

The second incident where God produced water from a rock occurred in the Desert of Zin in a place called Kadesh. Again, a quarrel broke out because of the lack of water and Moses and Aaron were under siege. Many began to wish they had died when their brothers who had rebelled died before the Lord. Again, they moaned that Moses had brought them into the wilderness to die along with their livestock. The people whinged about the lack of grapevines, fig trees, grain, or pomegranates and, above all, the lack of drinking water. Moses and Aaron presented themselves before God and Moses was told to speak to a particular rock in the presence of the people and it would pour out water before their eyes. However, in a fit of anger at the people's rebelliousness Moses struck the rock twice with his staff and although water gushed out as before, he had offended God through disobedience.

Again, God had shown them his nature as Jehovah Jireh, but it was clear that the people were more preoccupied with their needs than in forming intimacy with God. God had brought them out of Egypt by displaying His might against the Egyptians; He had parted the Red Sea for them to escape from the pursuing

Egyptian army; He had fed them with manna and quail on a daily basis for six days giving them enough to eat for seven days; He had fought their battles for them; provided them safety from the hostile nations within the region; kept wild beasts at bay; and brought water forth from a rock to satiate their thirst, yet they doubted His nature. There was no better place for them to know God as provider than in a wilderness, but they missed the opportunity because they would not walk in faith.

Moses was prevented from leading the people into the Promised Land because he had failed to revere and honour God through obedience when asked to speak to the rock. In short, he had not acted by faith. For God, it was important that Moses obeyed His instructions to the letter because that was how He had ordained to receive glory. The people needed to know that God could provide through actions or words. The first time Moses struck the rock at Rephidim that was an act of obedience and a mark of faith. On the second occasion God wanted to reveal that he also provides through confessions made by faith. However, that opportunity was lost through disobedience.

We can translate this experience into our current situations and consider whether we are between a rock and hard place where we need a solution that cannot be provided through natural means. Believing that water can come out of a rock involves a level of faith that has been cultivated through association; the reason being that it is so extreme in concept that the five senses have to be completely discarded and banned from any form of involvement. The natural tendency is to try to consider how water would flow out of solid matter which is not porous. The engagement of intellect has a way of frustrating these sorts of miracles from occurring. Moses had walked with God long enough to have developed the level of faith required for a miracle such as this and that is why God was upset with Him. His anger focussed him on the people's rebellion, and he disobeyed God. If his eyes were on God rather than the people, he would never have struck the rock with his staff.

It reminds one of the father of the child possessed by a demon [Matthew Mark 9:17-29]. Jesus' disciples had been unable to cast out the demon and the father turned to Jesus and asked if He could do anything to assist. After asking the father about the history of the child's condition, Jesus informed him that if he could believe, all things were possible to them who believed. The father said he believed but asked for help to overcome his unbelief. It is easy to see why the father struggled. He had lived with the child and was distracted by the overwhelming nature of the condition. He was operating with his five senses despite his desperation for a miraculous intervention. Jesus cast out the demon and later on informed His curious disciples that this type of spirit only came out with praying and fasting. There is a level of faith for every situation, and we often have to dig a bit deeper to get results. To bring water from a rock requires strong faith because a rock represents a stronghold, but as Jesus says, all things are possible to them who believe.

36

Seeing riches when everyone else sees poverty

Faith is all about seeing riches when everyone else sees poverty. It is about seeing harvest when others see famine and seeing provision when all around see lack. As you will have gathered, it is all about perception. It is not about denying the facts. It is about not letting the facts cloud your vision or smother God's promises. Am I advocating adopting the prosperity teaching model? Absolutely not! This is not some illusory Eldorado-type mindset where God is a slot machine and all you need to do is slot in the coins long enough and keep tugging on the handle to get a breakthrough. I am merely suggesting that we learn to see our lives from God's perspective and say what His word says about us and our situation.

To put this in perspective, you might be on minimum wage or worse still out of work with no savings to fall back on. You may be struggling to keep up with your bills and falling behind on your mortgage or car note, however, faith does not declare the facts; it declares the truth. The facts say you are broke and facing a financial crisis, but your faith says that you serve a God who shall supply all your needs even in a famine (Psalm 37:19 and 37:25; Philippians 4:19). Your capacity to see yourself better off than the facts of your situation, is tied to your faith in the promises of God. What has He promised you? I am not saying you should dive into the Bible and start repeating Scriptures to yourself in the hope that that will change your situation. That may not provide the outcome you are looking for at least not in the short term. I want us to think about the promises God made to us during our time of devotion or quiet time with Him.

What did He share with us in that place of intimacy and what are we expecting Him to fulfil in our lives? [Psalm 25:14]. This is not an exercise for daydreamers but for those who spend time with God.

Faith relies on promises. Chew on that for a moment. If you don't have a promise you will struggle to exercise the brand of faith that attracts God's intervention. Faith does not latch on to daydreams or wishful thinking. You may be living in a shack and dreaming of a mansion but unless you win the lottery, get an inheritance or cash in on some investment it is very unlikely to happen. You first of all need a promise from God. The promise may be either collective or corporate, aimed at a certain community or group, or it may be personal to the person who received it. The promise of the Promised Land was to Abraham and his descendants, so it was in a sense a collective one. However, the promise to Mary regarding the conception and birth of Jesus was for her consumption alone. So, in the former, every descendant of Abraham (tribes of Israel) had the right to be expectant for an inheritance in the Promised Land whilst in the latter Mary had every right to expect to become the mother of Jesus.

The comfort of a promise is that because we know God cannot lie [Numbers 23:19] all we need to do is remain expectant and regularly dwell on and confess the promise. Isaac was not moved by the fact that he was residing in a land afflicted by famine. Because of God's promise [Genesis 26:2-5 and 12-14], Isaac could ignore the facts and maintain a prosperity mindset which was entirely legitimate. As a result of that mindset, he reaped a hundredfold harvest with no loss of crop during a severe famine.

God's promises to us are conditional but trustworthy. God can never change His mind regarding any promise He has made to us because each promise cannot return to Him void or unaccomplished [Isaiah 55:10-11]. To further reassure us about His commitment, He seals each promise with an oath as He did for our father Abraham [Hebrews 6:13-19]. God's promises to us are effectively covenants and He assures us that He will never break His covenants nor alter what promises He has spoken [Psalm 89:34]. God's promises often contain His purpose for our lives. The whole idea behind revealing His purpose through promises is to give us something to aim at, like the Promised Land. However, if we reside in doubt and unbelief then we may miss our Promised Land because access and possession depend on our faith.

It is therefore not wishful thinking to speak about God's promises, as this reinforces in us a conviction, as well as in the hearing of our audience, that we know who we are and where we are going. Your shack no longer defines you, neither does your low-income job label you. You may endure the challenges associated with those affairs now, but you do not dwell on them because anything you meditate on will possess your mind. Whatever possesses your thoughts owns your life [Proverbs 4:23; 23:7]. This is why meditation on the Word of God is highly recommended.

When God first approaches a person, He does not call them according to where they are but rather according to where He is taking them. A case in point is Gideon who was called a mighty man of valour whilst he was still hiding to thresh wheat [Judges 6:12]. Another is Jeremiah the prophet [Jeremiah 1:4-8] whom God called a prophet whilst he deemed himself too young to bear that mantle. Because God does not change [Malachi 3:6] we can rest assured that as we meditate on His word, we will receive promises from Him which will define who we are and where He is taking us. Joseph had a dream of greatness which he shared with his brothers [Genesis 37:5-9]. His brothers hated him because they believed the dream. Joseph went into slavery and prison but did not lose sight of who he was. We should likewise focus on who He says we are and possess in our spirits what He has promised to give us because this is pleasing to God. Remember those who come to Him must believe that He is and that He rewards those who diligently search for Him [Hebrews 11:6].

37

Being pitied or avoided

Faith is often about being pitied or avoided. Yes, really! Depending on the surrounding circumstance many who are walking by faith have been the subject of pity for their weird belief or stance on some issues and in other cases have been avoided as if they were carrying some contagious disease. When we walk by faith we are submitted to God's will and may be convicted to exhibit our faith in ways some may deem unorthodox.

When God engages us, He never addresses us in relation to where we are or what we are passing through but instead speaks into our future. The future He paints will always be more glorious than our current situation. If we have difficulty adjusting to seeing ourselves the way He sees us, imagine how difficult it must be for those who know us. Because our God-given potential is often not on display, people tend to label us according to what they perceive. The common reaction is to either question our judgment or side-track us.

For instance, if you are poor and don't have enough money to pay your rent, wandering around declaring yourself to be rich will guarantee that you are either pitied or avoided. A common one is the reaction you receive when you choose not to accept an expert opinion because it clashes with what you believe God told you. How many of us have been subjected to the professional pitying smile, usually thin-lipped with a faux benevolence in their eyes?

When David informed King Saul that he was willing and ready to fight Goliath, he was most probably treated to a pitying stare as the monarch tried to explain to him why he didn't stand any chance of defeating the defiant man-mountain. In the king's eyes, he was a young man whose greatest skill lay in his ability to play exquisite rhythms on a harp which seemed to drive away evil spirits. Every soldier in the army of Israel had a template of what a warrior looked like, and David didn't fit the mould.

When Moses showed up at Pharaoh's court in Egypt after a forty-year sojourn in the wilderness of Midian, his clothes and appearance much altered, it is more than likely that he was subjected to a pitying look. The once great prince of Egypt was now an outcast who was babbling some nonsense about Pharaoh letting the Hebrew slaves, who were fuelling the Egyptian economy, leave the country [Exodus 5:1-21]. For having the effrontery, Moses' actions increased the burden on his people who now had to search for straw to make bricks rather than being given the straw. Apart from an initial attempt to mob him, most people pretty much avoided Moses. If they had been waiting for God's deliverance, they struggled to see Moses as His agent.

Jeremiah was a man well acquainted with the challenges of being accepted as he tried to establish himself in the office of a Prophet. God had forewarned him about the hostile reception awaiting him and made clear that he was not to give in to an inferiority complex. Jeremiah considered himself too young, but God clarified that he had been ordained a prophet whilst he was still in his mother's womb [Jeremiah 1:4-8]. When Jeremiah started ministering in the office of prophet he was disdained and side-tracked by those who were more established in the role. Jeremiah was a minority prophet in their midst whose prophecies always contradicted theirs. Despite their efforts to shove him into the corner of obscurity and silence him, God confirmed Jeremiah's prophecies through performance.

The reason why many who walk by faith are either pitied or avoided is because they are walking in a domain that is not easily accessible. It is weird for a naturally minded person governed solely by their five senses to understand the defiance that possesses those who claim to walk by faith. Why would anyone refuse medical treatment or reject surgical intervention when their prognosis demands it?

When Jesus paid a visit to His hometown of Nazareth, He was disdained by the people who only remembered Him as the carpenter's son. This led to Jesus remarking that a prophet is not without honour except amongst his people and community [Matthew 13:54-57; Mark 6:1-6; Luke 4:16-30; John 4:44]. As a result of their perspective, the majority were not able to benefit from His presence. Here was the carpenter's son claiming to be the son of God and inviting them to come and be miraculously healed. It was all a bit too much for them to take in.

When we are walking by faith, confessing God's promises, and seeing ourselves the way He sees us, we inevitably come up against opposition in the form of detractors or mockers who scornfully side-track us or try to get us to see ourselves the way they see us. Some legitimately believe that we are overreaching ourselves and sensitively try to manage our expectation. When we are walking in line with our kingdom expectation, we will experience this. This is why we need to be resolute in our conviction regardless of the opposition.

38

Investing without due diligence

Faith can involve investing without due diligence. This is usually the default reaction by a Christian who is walking by faith in response to an instruction from God. Such Christians adopt a "hear and do" approach to God's word. If God commands them to do something, provided they are convinced that it is God, they obey. There is no due diligence to weigh the risk or count the cost. This is often because such Christians are disciples and have already counted the cost of following Christ.

In discussing discipleship and the cost of following Him, Jesus spoke about the need to count the cost before embarking on any project or activity [Luke 14:25-34]. He said if anyone came to Him and did not prioritise Him over their own families and even their own life, they could not be His disciples and whoever did not carry their cross and follow Him could not be His disciple. He then added that anyone who did not give up everything they had could not be His disciple. The position therefore is that as disciples of Christ we have already counted the cost of following Him. We have already conducted a general due diligence when we dedicated the rest of our lives to Him and so we do not carry out due diligence whenever we are called by Him to invest of ourselves in some particular service or project.

Faith responds to God's word. Where God's word proclaims a promise, faith just believes and then acts on it without pausing to weigh the cost. Faith acts on the insurance policy of God's faithfulness [Hebrews 11:11]. When God's word provides an instruction, faith just obeys it because it knows that obedience is the evidence of love [John 14:23]. Real faith does not count the cost. It does not analyse the facts and consider the options. There is only one option – obey.

When one considers investing without first conducting due diligence, the name of Apostle Paul easily comes to mind as one who suffered substantially for the sake of the Gospel. He embarked on many journeys or missions to places where he was beaten, stoned, imprisoned, and tortured for his faith but he never let the memories of past experiences dissuade him. For example, in one account, Paul had a vision in which a Macedonian man requested for his help. He immediately headed to Macedonia, believing that it was God calling him to go there and preach [Acts 16:9-12]. The only due diligence conducted by Paul was whether it was the will of God.

The Bible is awash with examples of characters who did not count the cost or conduct due diligence before embarking on the journey of faith and one of the most prominent of these is Ruth. For those who know the story, Ruth was married to Naomi's son Mahlon. Naomi and her family had fled to Moab from Bethlehem because of a serious famine in that land. Whilst in exile, Naomi's husband Elimelech, and her two sons Mahlon and Chilion died leaving Naomi with two daughters-in-law and no reason to go on living. Naomi asked her daughters-in-law to return to their families but whilst Orpah – Chilion's widow went back to her parents, Ruth staunchly refused. In a passionate speech, Ruth informing her mother-in-law that wherever she went, Ruth would go, wherever she stayed, Ruth would stay; she said Naomi's people would be her people and Naomi's God would be her God; she added that where

Naomi died, she would die, and be buried there [Ruth 1:16-17].

Ruth's speech reveals that she had decided within herself from the outset that Naomi's family was her family and that she would never be returning to her parents. It was not a spur of the moment thing because her declaration was not something she had hastily cobbled together, but a carefully constructed piece that revealed reflection. It is possible that she had counted the cost before marrying Mahlon because it was a well-known fact that the Hebrews did not marry the Moabites because of their controversial history. The Moabites are descendants of Lot's incest with one of his daughters after the fall of Sodom and Gomorrah. Lot was the nephew of Abraham the father of the Hebrews. But the bad blood between the nations stems from the refusal by the Moabites to assist the Children of Israel when they fled Egypt and dwelt in the wilderness. Also, the Moabite king – hired a prophet-for-hire named Balaam to curse Israel [Numbers 22:1-6]. Even though God turned the curse to a blessing [Numbers 23:19] still the incident created a rift between the nations. Moses who was leading the nation at the time pronounced God's command that the Moabite could not enter into the congregation of the Lord for ever [Deuteronomy 23:3-6] and Israel was not to seek their peace.

Ruth – a Moabitess was forbidden by the Law of Moses from entering the congregation of Israel, yet God permitted her to not only enter it but also to be married into it to one who would form the lineage of Jesus Christ. Unlike Elimelech, Ruth had entered into a covenant and acted purely by faith.

Ruth did not have to accompany her mother-in-law to Israel. The danger was well known, and her safety was not guaranteed but she did not even refer to the risks when she made her proclamation. She invested her life in Naomi without pausing to consider the immediate risk to life and limb because of her commitment to become a part of Elimelech's family. When Ruth left her parents, she clearly had no intention of returning and was determined to become a part of their lives. The death of her husband did not dislodge that commitment because she still had a connection to Israel through Naomi. In short, Ruth had made up her mind to become an Israelite, so she did not pause to consider the danger she was exposing herself to by going to Israel. In a sense she could be considered rather naïve, but isn't this just how children behave? Did Jesus not say that we had to become like children to enter the Kingdom of God? [Matthew 18:3]. Ruth had the innocent faith of a child and God accepted her into the congregation of Israel because of this. She had made God her God and He accepted her. She had not counted the immediate cost because of her covenant but God allowed a man named Boaz to become her covering. Real faith does not count the cost.

39

Not dwelling in the past

Faith is about not dwelling in the past; it is about looking to the future. Someone once said if we keep looking in the rear-view mirror of our life we will crash. I find this very graphic but accurate. Those who walk by faith are forward looking and live in the future rather than the past. They have learned that looking over one's shoulder with a sense of nostalgia is the easiest way to stagnate and even regress. The God we serve is a God of progress. He is a God of the living, not the dead.

The story of the Exodus patently illustrates God's perspective on the issue of faith and is our one-stop shop for the guidelines that we should comply with. It is an aide memoir for those who either stumble or stray off the straight and narrow path. What led to the deaths of a whole generation in the wilderness over a forty-year period so that the oldest men to enter the Promised Land were in their eighties? It was the people's proclivity for looking longingly at the captivity that God had rescued them from and the bondage that consigned them to the status of third-rate citizens.

With each physical step towards the Promised Land, these people longed in their hearts to return to Egypt simply because their recollection was warped. Rather than recalling the frequent whipping, hard labour, murdering of their male children, and violation of their womenfolk, all they remembered was the variety of food and wine that they had gorged themselves on as a panacea for their suffering. They forgot their toil and how they laboured to build successions of Pharaohs' cities and the torment inflicted on them for over four hundred years. On their way to the Promised Land as free men and women, a nation in their own right with the God of all creation leading them, they craved slavery. More than once they sought to return.

When hunger struck, they cried out in anguish wishing that God had left them alone in Egypt and killed them there rather than bringing them to the wilderness to die [Exodus 16:2-3]. They craved for the fleshpots, and bread of Egypt where in their shallow memories they ate their fill. They forgot how exhausted their men were at the end of a hard day's labour and how they could barely taste the food entering their mouths as they ate mechanically, wincing in agony. Even after God provided them with a nutritious meal called Manna [Exodus 16: 14-31], a substance resembling coriander seed that tasted like wafers laced with honey, they still craved meat. They remembered the fish, cucumbers, melons, leeks, onions, and garlic which they used to eat [Numbers 11:1-11; 18-20; 31-34] and began to despise the manna. All they remembered were the momentary highlights of a dismal past. Despite this, God fed the multitude with meat. When they were thirsty, God through Moses produced water out of a rock for them to drink [Exodus 17:3-6] but this did not pacify them and as soon as Moses' back was turned, they abandoned serving God in favour of worshipping a golden calf [Exodus 32]. The last straw that broke the camel's back was the negative report of ten of the twelve spies whom Moses had sent to spy the Promised Land which caused the congregation to mourn and regret why God hadn't seen fit to let them die in Egypt [Numbers 13 and 14].

Looking back with regret at the places God has delivered us from, is Satan's strategy to cause us to take our eyes off God and fix them instead on the facts.

Those who don't walk by faith are wedded to the idea of perpetual comfort even if the reality is far from it. They learn to adapt to changing tides and absorb the fluctuations of life because they are in survivalist mode. The spirit of self-preservation possesses them, and they function according to the psychology of survival of the fittest. The more protracted their season in the wilderness the more conditioned they become to the environment and never ever see God as their provider and sustainer. These are the sorts of people targeted by Satan because they are susceptible to his deception. He can remind an unhappily married man of all the fun he used to have with ex-girlfriends and make him wonder why he did not marry one of them instead. He sells the virtues of dishonesty to the one who used to thrive off fraudulent activities but is now less well-off living an honest life. He will try to convince such a person of why there was nothing wrong in what he used to do and assure him that many Christians are still living that way.

Walking by faith is not backsliding or moonwalking, but step by step progression towards a promise. The Bible makes it clear that God has no pleasure in anyone who puts their hands on the plough (embarks on the Christian journey by faith) but then withdraws that hand [Hebrews 10:38]. Jesus spoke about seed that fell among the stones (on stony ground) which represented those who receive the word joyfully but then fall away in the face of persecution on account of that word. They retreat to a safe position which is often the one they just came from. Many fall back into their old ways because that is where they are most comfortable.

When the facts are more overwhelming than the truth we start to malfunction. The lesson from the story of the Children of Israel is that those who look back long enough will ultimately die in the wilderness. Apostle Paul urges us to copy his example and forget the things behind us and press forward to the things ahead [Philippians 4:13-14]. Why was this important for Paul? Because before Christ enlisted him, Paul (then named Saul) had been persecuting the church and was complicit in the murder of Stephen – the first Christian martyr. Paul however pointed out that in his past life he had acted ignorantly in unbelief when he persecuted the church but obtained mercy [1 Timothy 1:12-13]. Paul pressed forward towards the mark for the high calling of God in Jesus Christ. This is why at the end of his life he could victoriously announce that he had fought a good fight, finished his course, and had kept the faith [2 Timothy 4:7]. Faith is forward looking, and it does so with energetic expectation.

40

Becoming pregnant with invisible seed

Faith is about becoming pregnant with invisible seed. It is about conceiving something which natural eyes cannot perceive and cultivating it until it becomes a manifestation that everyone can relate to. Apostle Paul puts it this way; he says no eye has seen, nor ear heard and neither has any heart perceived what The Lord has prepared for those whom He loves but by His Holy Spirit He reveals it to them as it is only the Holy Spirit that is able to search out the deep things of God [1 Corinthians 9-10]. The Apostle goes on to clarify that a natural man (someone who lives in the flesh and is restricted to their five senses) cannot receive the things of the Spirit of God because they are foolishness to him; neither can such a person know these things because they are spiritually discerned. What this means is that the invisible thing that God has prepared for His people is of spiritual origin. Only those who have access to the mind of the Holy Spirit are able to receive and conceive spiritual seed.

The seed referred to is the word of God as is discussed by Jesus in the Parable of the Sower and it is always delivered to us via the Holy Spirit. If we don't have a revelation of God's word, we will never become pregnant with it. Revelation produces enlightenment within us [Psalm 119:130]; this enables us to see things from God's perspective and know the things that are freely given to us by God [1 Corinthians 2:12]. Revelation gives us the opportunity to make the necessary adjustments to ensure that the pregnancy is sustained. If you do not know you are pregnant you will continue to live in a way that might harm that pregnancy. However, when you know that you are pregnant you make adjustments to your lifestyle. The seed sown into us in word form is for the expansion of the Kingdom of God and God entrusts it into our care so that we can partake of the Kingdom.

The analogy given by Christ is of seed that grows of its own accord once sown [Mark 4:26-29]. Jesus described the Kingdom of God as if a person should cast seed into the ground and sleep. The person goes about their business waking up every morning and going to bed at night, without knowing stages of growth the seed is passing through beneath the soil, because it is invisible to the naked eyes. As Jesus explains, the earth brings forth fruit of itself, first the blade, then the ear and after that the full corn in the ear. When the fruit is manifested, the person harvests it. The insightful thing about this teaching is that it describes the pathway of faith in relation to God's word. God gives a promise; the person receives the promise by faith and the word is cultivated in the soil of their heart. That seed grows in secret, invisible to the five senses and it may appear that nothing is happening. The person may act by faith on the promise by watering the word seed with prayers and declarations and may undertake acts of faith as prompted, but it may still look like nothing is happening. It is not until the ear appears that there is confirmation; and when they see the blade their expectation increases and when the ear is manifest it is clear that harvest is near. This is similar to the trimesters of pregnancy that a woman passes through. Some women experience no sensation of pregnancy until third trimester and can be going about their normal lives. However, the ideal situation is that they are aware so that they can make adjustments.

Mary, the virgin who conceived and gave birth to Jesus is a case in point. I believe every Christian knows the story. Mary was a virgin who was chosen by God to be the surrogate mother of Jesus Christ. She was informed by Angel Gabriel that she had been chosen and that she was to conceive and bring forth a son named Jesus [Luke 1:26-38]. Mary wanted to understand how she could conceive a child when she was still a virgin, but the angel clarified that the child would be implanted by the Holy Spirit. Mary accepted this explanation and granted permission for her womb to be used in the service of God. The moment she consented; she instantly became pregnant. How do we know? Because the pregnancy was supernatural and as there is no time in the spiritual realm, it had to be instant. Everything was predicated on her faith.

God's word spoken by the angel and her response to it produced the pregnancy. This was faith in motion. A fertilised egg was placed within Mary because the angel had said that the Holy thing born within her would be called the Son of God [Luke 1:35]. If one of Mary's ovaries had been fertilised, the child would not have qualified as holy because of the sinful blood of Adam. For Jesus to be the saviour of the world, He had to be holy in every spiritual sense of the word. Likewise, the seed of God's Word that is implanted in us is holy because its origin is the Holy Spirit not man.

Mary did not know she was pregnant until she started seeing the signs and it became obvious (manifested) so that it was clear to her husband-to-be, her family and community. The presumption from everyone including Joseph was that she had been wayward. No one knew that the pregnancy was supernatural or that she was carrying the Messiah. With the exception of Joseph, who had a revelation about the origin of the pregnancy, no eye had seen, nor ear heard and neither had it entered into the heart of onlookers what God had done within Mary. Like the analogy of the seed, all they saw was the ear and then the full corn in the ear. As a result, they probably castigated Joseph for violating the law by not waiting until the marital rites were concluded before enjoying intimacy with Mary. However, because of their faith, today hundreds of millions have become Christians.

41

Telling a story nobody believes

Faith is telling a story nobody believes. Why should they when it sounds so incredible and inexplicable? The story of faith is one that challenges even those who ought to believe because it usually exceeds anything they have experienced or witnessed before. They believe nothing is too hard for God and that with God all things are possible, yet even to these faithful ones it sounds far-fetched.

When David stood before King Saul and narrated how whilst out shepherding, he had killed a lion and a bear because the wild beasts posed a threat to his father's livestock, it was clear that the king did not believe him. David spoke passionately about how when a lion or bear came to carry off a sheep from the flock, he went after it and rescued the animal from its mouth. He described in intricate detail how he seized the animal by its hair, striking and killing it.

The difficulty for Saul was visual. The optics didn't stack up. How could this teenager have performed a feat that even the king's most valiant warriors could not? The animals referred to are some of the most powerful in the world. The lion is called the king of the jungle for a reason. It is a fearless beast that will hunt and attack animals larger than it and once its powerful jaws clamped around its prey that was effectively the end. Yet David was claiming to have killed such a beast and from his narrative it looked like he had done so with his bare hands. When David added insult to injury regarding his killing of the bear, the king must have been convinced of David's lunacy.

To emphasise his mindset, the King offered him the use of his own armour in the hope that it would delay the inevitable. David could not move with the armour on and so handed it back. In the king's mind all David wanted were the trappings of success but he did not stand a chance of emerging victorious. By the end of the encounter, however, David had killed Goliath and the Philistine army was in retreat. That was a totally unexpected outcome. Yet the king had doubted him. Even when David proclaimed that the Lord who rescued him from the paws of the lion and the bear would rescue him from the hand of Goliath, the king was not convinced [1 Samuel 17]. How could a shepherd boy overcome and kill the greatest warrior on the battlefield? King Saul was measuring David by the size of his physical stature rather than his spiritual stature.

One of the most memorable accounts in the Bible which vividly depicts this theme is the story of the four lepers at the gate of Samaria [2 Kings 7:3-20]. The background to the events was a siege by the Syrian army against the city of Samaria in Israel. As a result of the siege the people of the city were unable to go out to farm or trade and the economy collapsed under the duress of the resulting inflation [2 Kings 6]. Starvation gripped the people who turned to cannibalism in their desperation for self-preservation. The Prophet Elisha was summoned to see the king and prophesied that within twenty-four hours food prices would fall drastically but an administrator doubted this prophecy and said that even if God opened the windows in heaven it would not be possible in the current situation for such a rapid turn of events to occur. As far as that administrator was concerned, the Syrian Army was still laying siege to the city and that fact registered more vividly in his mind than the words of the prophet. Now the God who uses the ridiculous to confound the credible, chose to perform a miracle with the assistance of four lepers.

The lepers were seated at the city's gates because it was forbidden for them to mingle with the people as they were deemed unclean under Jewish law. They were starving and almost at the point of death and so they weighed their options. They had the option of risking going into the city but because of the famine there they knew it was certain death. They had the option of remaining where they were but that was also certain death. They however had the riskier option of going to the Syrian camp and throwing themselves on the invaders' mercy. They considered that going to the Syrians could result in one of two options – mercy or death. They went with this option because it was the only one that had a guarantee of food attached.

Their heading to the Syrian camp was an act of faith, but as the four lepers progressed, God amplified their footsteps so that the Syrian army heard the clamouring of approaching chariots and horses. Fearing that the king of Israel had gone to hire the Hittites and Egyptians to attack them, the Syrians arose and fled for their lives at twilight leaving behind their tents, horses, livestock, and everything in the camp as it was. The lepers arrived at the camp and on discovering it empty they went from tent to tent eating and drinking as well as carrying gold, silver, and clothing which they hid. After a while their consciences pricked them, and they decided to go and inform the King of Israel's household. They therefore returned and told one of the porters of the city (the city's gatekeeper) who in turn relayed the message to others.

When the king heard the news that the siege was over and that the Syrian camp was loaded with foodstuff and other necessities like horses and livestock, the king disbelieved it. His suspicious mind conjured up the possibility of the Syrians pretending to leave and then lying-in wait for the people of the city to come out so they could catch them and then invade the city. If not for one of his servants who persuaded him to send some people to investigate the story, the hunger in the city would have continued. However, when the messengers discovered that the lepers were telling the truth and that it was not some ruse the people went out and invaded the Syrian camp. The price of food dropped to the prices prophesied by Elisha but the administrator who had publicly challenged him was killed as he tried to control the crowd. The four lepers were disbelieved because they lacked credibility because of the stigma associated with their disability. Yet like David even though their testimony was doubted, they had more faith than all those "credible" folk who feared to venture out of their safe haven.

42

Wrestling with doubt and boxing with unbelief

Faith is wrestling with doubt and boxing with unbelief. As we walk by faith it is not uncommon for us to wrestle with doubt and box unbelief. As punches are traded in this most brutal of battles, the only thing that matters is that faith comes out on top. It doesn't matter how many rounds are fought and how many times faith gets knocked to the canvas, provided it emerges victorious at the end of the bout. The idea that somehow faith is impervious to knockdowns is unscriptural. The Bible is full of accounts of unlikely and reluctant heroes who wrestled with doubt and boxed unbelief. Many times, it looked like they were defeated and that the story was about to wrap but then they bounced back by faith and delivered a technical knockout to doubt and gave unbelief a pinfall.

How many times do we feel like we are on a losing streak where doubt seems to have the upper hand and unbelief is delivering all the uppercuts? For many of us this may be a regular occurrence as we stand on God's word. The aims of doubt and unbelief are to knock us off our perch and convince us that faith is a myth. The Apostle Paul says after we have done all we can, we should just keep standing firmly [Ephesians 6:13]. This combat takes place predominantly in the mind and each side vies for supremacy over our thought life. There are probably thousands of books on this subject which comb over the devil's strategies, however no matter how much knowledge you have of the enemy's wiles, without practice it is just theory.

When Moses passed away, Joshua, his protégé battled with doubt and unbelief; doubt about his abilities to lead, despite being anointed by Moses, and unbelief regarding the enormity of the task. How do we know this? We can deduce this from the conversation between God and Joshua [Joshua 1:1]. God must have noted the thoughts racing around Joshua's mind. How could he lead such a rebellious community into the Promised Land when Moses had failed to fulfil that task? Was he equipped for the task? Would he be accepted by them in the same way as Moses? Would God use him in the same way as He had used Moses? To assure him, God showed up and commanded him to be strong and of good courage, informing him that Moses was now dead and that He would be with Joshua in the same way He had been with Moses [Joshua 1:2-9]. Why was this necessary? It was because Joshua had some big shoes to fill in the natural. He had witnessed God using Moses and never dreamt that he would be selected to replace such a mighty prophet.

God then gave Joshua the strategy for defeating doubt and unbelief in the ring and there is a lot we can learn from this. The first thing God gave Joshua was an assignment – he was to lead the people across the Jordan into the Promised Land. This was divine independent confirmation to Joshua of his assignment and purpose. God mapped out the territory He had given the Children of Israel if only they would step foot in those territories. The second thing God did was give him a promise. He told Joshua that no man would be able to withstand him all the days of his life and that as He had been with Moses so He would also be with Joshua and would not fail him or forsake him [Joshua 1:5]. This promise was to encourage Joshua and empower him for the assignment he had been given.

Next God gave Joshua an instruction regarding his conduct; God told him three times at intervals to be strong and of good courage [Joshua 1:6, 7 and 9]. When God says something once it is important, when He repeats it, we should pay extra attention but when He mentions it three times it is mandatory and non-negotiable. If Joshua was going to achieve any sort of success in his assignment, then he would have to be strong and of good courage. Why was this important? God knew what manner of adversaries were awaiting Joshua in the Promised Land and if Joshua was not strong and of good courage, he would struggle to complete his assignment. There were mighty nations in the land which were well established, some of them living in fortified cities that could not be invaded. Moreover, many of the nations had advanced technology and greater armies which on paper could annihilate the Children of Israel. Possessing the promise was not going to be easy.

When God told Joshua to be strong and courageous, He was addressing Joshua's state of mind. The opposite of strength is weakness and of courage is cowardice. How was Joshua supposed to summon up the required level of strength and courage? The knowledge that God was present with him was supposed to generate faith in him. Faith was the strength and courage expected of him. As faith comes by hearing and hearing comes by repetitively hearing God's word, God was telling Joshua that the key to victory was in the Law of Moses. God instructed Joshua to meditate on the Word and not turn from it to the right hand or the left – he was not to add to it or subtract from it. In this way, God assured him that he would prosper in the fulfilment of his assignment. God also instructed him to keep confessing the Word openly in addition to meditating on it to ensure that he did everything in it. God was telling him effectively to be transformed by the renewing of his mind [Romans 12:2]. God rounded up the session by telling Joshua not to be afraid neither dismayed because He would be with him wherever he went. Judging by Joshua's success on the field of battle and in land distribution, we would all do well to adopt a similar strategy as we bid to defeat doubt and unbelief.

43

Reaching up with conviction

Faith is reaching up with conviction. We reach up with conviction to access what has been promised or what we believe has been promised. Reaching up is the act of extending one's reach or stretching towards someone or something in a higher position; it is about elevating one's access to the place of provision.

An example of this sort of activity is when David said that he would lift up his eyes to the hills from where his help came and then he clarified that his help came from the Lord [Psalm 121:1-2]. Reaching up entails stretching beyond the natural realm to the superior spiritual realm where God's Kingdom is located and from where all our blessings come. David had learnt the importance of reaching up with his gaze to perceive the truth when all around him was contradictory. Those who get into the habit of reaching up never put their confidence in anything located within the earth because God's kingdom is everlasting but the earth, at least in its current configuration, is not.

God, speaking through the Prophet Isaiah, confirmed that His thoughts are not the same as ours neither are His ways the same as ours and that as high as the heavens were above the earth so also were His ways higher than our ways and His thoughts than our thoughts {Isaiah 55:8-9]. This is why David symbolically looked to the hills – the term "hills" was representative of a higher level. David was saying that his focus was on God, not man, and that God was his source. We run into mortal danger when we substitute the help that God alone can give, for the help of a man, no matter how influential or highly placed he or she may be within society.

A pastor I know once said God asked him whether he could use one eye to look upwards whilst simultaneously keeping the other eye focussed on the ground. The pastor said he tried it and was unable to. God then told him that he should never claim to be looking at God when he was in fact looking at man or around him. Divided focus means that at times we will be reaching across and at other times we will be reaching upwards, but this is schizophrenic.

Reaching up with conviction is about having an uncanny certainty, as our hands reach up to God's kingdom. Apostle Paul urges us to seek things above and not beneath as we have been raised to new life with Christ and should be focussed on Him [Colossians 3:1]. Because Christ is seated at the right hand of God, we have access to the Father through Him. The Apostle then advises us to set our affection or desire on things above and not on things in the earth [Colossians 3:2]. This means that our choices must be governed by our spirits and not our flesh (or carnal nature). The Bible clarifies that every good and perfect gift is from above and comes down from the Father of the heavenly lights [James 1:17]. This explains why things that don't have a divine origin, no matter how desirable and alluring they are, will never enrich us. Their premise is earthly, and they are therefore limited to the earth.

When a lady named Hannah was unable to conceive and have children she reached up [1 Samuel 1:1-11]. She had grown weary of reaching across with no results and instead turned her attention upwards. She focussed on Him and received a revelation regarding His need. God clearly needed a new priesthood because the sons of the current priest – Eli - who served under their father in the temple were reprobates. Hannah tapped into that revelation and promised to give God something He desired if He gave her something of worth. After that vow, God paid her a visit, and she became the mother of Samuel one of the most faithful priests in Israel and the last priest to rule over Israel before the succession of kings. To compensate her for her faithfulness, God gave her five more children. There are many stories in the Bible of people reaching up to God, but Hannah's story is unique because she presented God with an opportunity to enter into a covenant with her and He accepted her terms.

Those who reach up to God do so in the knowledge that what is impossible with man is possible with God [Luke 18:27]. He asked a barren eighty-nine-year-old woman whose husband was an infertile and impotent ninety-nine-year-old whether there was anything too hard for Him and she became afraid because she realised that against all probability, she was about to become a mother [Genesis 18:14].

When King Hezekiah of Judah was besieged by the forces of King Sennacherib of Assyria, he reached up [2 Kings 18: 13-37, and 19; 2 Chronicles 32:1-22; Isaiah 36:1-22]. He knew that he was in an impossible situation because of the Assyrians' reputation as brutal warriors who had invaded and conquered many mightier countries whose armies were vastly superior on paper to Judah's. King Hezekiah had already tried diplomacy and entered into a political arrangement that allowed him to remain on the throne in Judah as a vassal king paying tribute to the Assyrians. However, this was not enough to appease the invaders who soon besieged Jerusalem the capital of Judah with voracious intent. Hezekiah had given them all the silver and most of the gold in Jerusalem most of which was extracted from the temple, but this was nowhere near enough to assuage their bloodlust. The Assyrians began a campaign of propaganda aimed at striking fear into the hearts of the people within the city so that they would capitulate but amidst the torment and apprehension, Hezekiah turned to God through the Prophet Isaiah. What he needed was an urgent miracle because in the natural he stood no chance. That miracle came in the form of an angel who in one single night slew the entire Assyrian army. Hezekiah's assurance came from the word of the prophet of God who had assured Hezekiah that the army would not set foot in the city and not even shoot an arrow over its walls. Hezekiah and Judah were delivered, but the story raises an important issue; who do we turn to in a crisis? Do we first negotiate with our adversary before reaching up?

44

Focusing on God's integrity

Faith is focusing on God's integrity. The dictionary definition of integrity is the quality of being honest and having strong moral principles that you refuse to change. At a human level this would certainly suffice, but in relation to God it is deficient. When He says that His ways and thoughts are distinct from ours [Isaiah 55:8-9] He is making clear that there is a gulf in relation to standards. His principles are so much higher than ours could ever be. This is why our focus on His integrity generates a heightened sense of expectation.

God's integrity is embedded in His holiness, righteousness, faithfulness, and unchanging nature. All these attributes of God are documented in His word. Faith gathers stamina from meditation on the word till the truth about His nature is unleashed from it. For all the promises of God are "yea" (meaning "sure") and "amen" (meaning a firm assurance] [2 Corinthians 1:20]. He says that He will not break His covenant nor alter what His lips have spoken [Psalm 89:34]. For we know that when God was about to bless Abraham, He chose to seal His promise to him with an oath so that by the unchangeable nature of His purpose (embedded within His promise) Abraham could have strong assurance [Hebrews 6:13-18]. God will never violate His word, and this is our assurance. He says through Prophet Malachi "For I am the Lord, I change not;" [Malachi 3:6].

God does not change and neither does His word. Jesus said that Heaven and earth will pass away, but His words will never pass away [Matthew 24:35]. Between the Prophet Malachi and the birth of Jesus was at least a four-hundred-year gap but the recorded word makes clear that God remains the same. Because His son, our Lord and Saviour, Jesus Christ bears the same genes as God the Father, the Bible confirms that He is the same, yesterday, today, and forever [Hebrews 13:8]. This tells us that we are called to aspire to this level of integrity which I will term spiritual integrity.

The challenge for us is relating with someone who does not change regardless of whatever is happening around us. Because humanity is prone to fail, we struggle to find reliable, dependable people who are constant in and out of season. Even our loved ones, in whom we have so much confidence, bend to the winds of change. Not so God. The Bible says that God, the Father of lights, does not experience any variation nor the shadows that are associated with turning [James 1:17]. This means that His light produces no shadows as it never turns, and nothing turns around it like the sun. Every light source produces shadows but not God's; it is that constant and fixed. Because He does not dwell in time everything around Him in eternity is still. That level of constancy should encourage us.

God never changes His mind. He never has a change of heart in the way that humans do. When the prophet for hire – Balaam was invited by the king of Moab to curse the Children of Israel as they trudged through the wilderness, he was unable to do so [Numbers 23:19 NKJV]. Thanks to this event, we are gifted one of the most vivid images of God's nature ever constructed with words. Balaam said:

"God is not a man, that He should lie, nor the son of man, that He should repent. Has He said, and will He not do? Or has He spoken, and will He not make it good?"

Balaam made clear that God cannot lie or change His mind and that whatever He promised to do will be done. Even though Balak, King of Moab, wanted Balaam to curse Israel, the prophet said he had received a command from God to bless them and could not reverse it [Numbers 23:20].

Confirming Balaam's insight, Prophet Isaiah said "*The Lord of hosts has sworn, saying, surely as I have thought, so shall it come to pass; and as I have purposed, so shall it stand.... for the Lord of hosts has purposed, and who will annul it? His hand is stretched out, and who will turn it back?*" [Isaiah 14:24, 27].

God's integrity is spiritually pure, and we know this as His holiness. There is none holy as the Lord and there is none beside Him [1 Samuel 2:2]. God is Holy and Christians are called to also aspire to this brand of holiness [1 Peter 1:15-16]. Even though we are called to holiness, God knows we are unable to achieve it in our own strength which is why Jesus sent us assistance in the form of the Holy Spirit [John 14:16-17, 26]. God's integrity is available to those who are filled with the Holy Spirit. It is the Holy Spirit that not only empowers the spirits of Christians to focus on God's integrity, but He also instructs our spirits on God's ways as we meditate on scripture.

When God promises never to leave us nor forsake us, because of His integrity we can rest easy and like Jesus fall asleep in a storm [Mark 4:35-41]. David says that he has never seen the righteous forsaken nor their seed begging bread [Psalm 37:25]. This speaks of a generational blessing. God remains faithful from generation to generation of those who obey His commands and walk in integrity [Proverbs 20:7]. Finally, we are reminded to fix our eyes on Jesus the author and finisher of our faith [Hebrews 12:2]. As Jesus was the express image of God on the earth, this scripture is applicable here. When we fix our eyes on the integrity of Jesus who endured the cross and despised the shame associated with it, we will grow in faith and find the grace to emulate his example.

45

Not keeping up with the Joneses

Faith is refusing to keep up with the Joneses. As a benchmark for assessing the level of one's social status within a community, the idiom finds its root in covetousness. The idea that one's social class is measured by how many material possessions they have in comparison to their neighbour, is at the root of societal dissatisfaction. Envy and rivalry propel a person to measure their success by the yardstick of their neighbour. They want to always outdo their neighbour regardless of whether or not the stuff they are accumulating brings them satisfaction. At the very least they do not want to fall behind and are plagued by FOMO (fear of missing out). This aspiration breeds anxiety and leads to idolatry.

At the core of this idiom is comparison. Comparison is always a dangerous thing because it produces wrong outcomes. Comparison will either tell you that you are inferior or superior. To assess inferiority or superiority you have to resort to comparison. Apostle Paul was no stranger to the tragedy of comparison because even in his day there were other preachers and teachers of the gospel who were comparing themselves with each other and in some cases were even comparing themselves with Paul. But Paul had this to say: *"For we dare not make ourselves of the number or compare ourselves with some that commend themselves; but by measuring themselves by themselves, and comparing themselves among themselves, are not wise"* [2 Corinthians 10:12].

Keeping up with the Joneses is the easiest way to lose yourself. When you make another person your reference point, you risk becoming a carbon copy. You never end up becoming what God intended you to be. This is why the tenth commandment warns us about covetousness [Exodus 20:17]. We are not to covet our neighbour's property or spouse or anything belonging to our neighbour. To flaunt this commandment is to fall out of God's grace. In fact, the surest way to live a long life is by despising covetousness [Proverbs 28:16].

The Bible teaches that our conversation is to be without covetousness and that we are to be content with such things as we possess because God has promised never to leave us nor forsake us [Hebrews 13:5]. This is a caution against our inordinate ambition and craving for worldly stuff – storing up treasure for ourselves. Our communication should not be dominated by discussion about the acquisition of material things as this is the evidence of faithlessness and a worldly view of life. Instead, we are urged to be content with our present condition or state of affairs. This does not mean we rejoice in poverty but that we appreciate that God is our provider and knows what we need even before we ask for it.

Apostle Paul assesses the baseline for gratitude when he teaches his protégé Timothy that if one has food and clothing, they should be content [1 Tim 6:8-10]. When we start grumbling about the type or quality of clothing, housing, vehicles, and career that we have in comparison to others, this is covetousness. When we speak like this we behave as if God is not aware of our situation and effectively label Him an irresponsible parent. Apostle Paul said that he had learnt to be content in whatever state he found himself whether with plenty or little, whether he was full or empty [Philippians 4:11-12].

No matter how we seek to justify it, there is no biblical basis for covetousness. Any teaching that compels us to crave for more material stuff is not of Christ. No matter how authentic it sounds or comforting it feels, it is of the world, and we are commanded not to love the world or the things of the world [1 John 2:15-17]. Apostle John reminds us that all that is in the world, namely the lust of the flesh, the lust of the eyes and the pride of life is not of the Father but is of the world.

Faith in God rejects the craving for material stuff because it knows that real faith trusts God for its needs and believes God to bless the works of their hands as they faithfully and diligently seek His will [Hebrews 11:6]. God does not reward covetousness, because He knows it promotes idolatry. Jesus warned against accumulating and storing treasure in the earth where it could be stolen, consumed by rust, or destroyed by moths [Matthew 6:19-21]. Instead, we are advised to store treasure in heaven where moths cannot destroy, rust consume, or thieves break in and steal. The thief referred to is Satan who comes to steal, kill, and destroy.

Christ makes clear that where our treasure is that is where our hearts will be also. He also teaches that we cannot serve two masters without having a favourite one. We are unable to serve God and the world [Matthew 6:24], as these are two parallels that can never meet. In the same sermon, Jesus teaches that we should not be concerned about what we shall eat or drink or how we should be clothed because this is an attitude reserved for those outside the family of Christ. Christ emphasises that God knows what we need even before we ask it, but we should seek God's Kingdom and righteousness and everything the unbeliever pursues will be added to us [Matthew 6:31-33]. Jesus also warned us to beware of covetousness because a person's life does not consist in the abundance of their possessions [Luke 12:15]. Many of us have heard this teaching a number of times but have not meditated on it sufficiently to let it marinate our hearts.

The evidence of spiritual growth is often seen in the state of our souls in the middle of challenges. A restless soul is clearly in infancy whilst a rested soul has learnt to trust in God. A restless soul enquires about its next meal and ponders over the bills whilst a rested soul looks to God. The latter state of being is often derided by those who mistake it for procrastination or indolence. The early church understood the need for dependency on God. Because its members had discovered contentment and realised that, for the Christian, this world is not the final resting place, they distributed their goods according to the needs around them, eliminating want [Acts 4:32]. Rather than competing amongst themselves, they began to support themselves. Rather than trying to keep up with the Joneses, they learnt moderation and made the necessary adjustments. This is real faith.

46

Not following the majority

Faith is not following the majority. When we are led by God's Holy Spirit, we never follow the crowd. In a fallen world, the majority are never right. Jesus describes following the majority as heading towards destruction.

Jesus cautioned about the wide gate and the narrow gate. According to Him, we are to access the narrow gate because wide is the gate, and broad is the way that leads to destruction, and many go through it. However, the narrow gate is serviced by a narrow pathway which leads to life, but only a few find it [Matthew 7:13-14]. This is a command for us not to follow the majority. Following the majority is effectively the same thing as identifying with the world and this will lead to destruction.

The narrow gate and wide gate are two separate, but parallel doorways to the eternal realm; one leads to everlasting life whilst the other leads to everlasting damnation. Likewise, the narrow and wide paths leading to these gates are separate but parallel and depict the exercise of choice. We have two ways of living, God's and the devil's. If we choose to serve God, we end up on the narrow path but if we choose to serve the devil then we end up on the wide path. Sadly, the narrow path is the one chosen by the minority whilst the wide path is the one chosen by the majority.

There are many who believe they are on the narrow path but are really on the wide path. They may even be in church, singing in the choir, serving as ushers, or helping out in Sunday school, worst still they may be preaching from the pulpit but wittingly or unwittingly, they are marching along the wide road. The wide road is easy and has lots of room for choice. Along the wide road you make up the rules as you go along and define your own standard of morality. Along the narrow road you are governed strictly by God's rules, and these regulate your character and personality. In the natural realm, the wide road is the one that appeals to the senses. The benefits accrued along this road are always material and status is a big thing. The narrow pathway may cause a person to lose their status and possessions as the cost for accessing eternal life, for others it may result in a loss of personality. The narrow gate does not admit material stuff which is why they have to be deposited along the way.

Someone once described the narrow path as being similar to walking on a tight rope where balance and focus are critical. If you lose your balance or focus on the tight rope, you better pray that there's a net beneath. This is why few find it; the way is too precarious and compared to the wide road it is not popular or fun. All the worldly trends reside on the wide path. There are fewer challenges along the wide road and fewer hurdles to scale. The rich young man was asked to sell all he had and give the proceeds to the poor and then to follow Christ and become His disciple. However, he wandered away sorrowful because it was too high a price for him to pay [Luke 18:8-23]. He had kept all the Ten Commandments but unknown to him he was still on the wide road that leads to destruction. Christ was testing his heart because as we know where a person's treasure is, there will their heart be also [Matthew 6:21].

Jesus described Himself as being the gate or the door by which His flock (Children) enter into the fold [John 10:9] and are saved. This door leads to life everlasting in God's kingdom. However, with so many religions in the world, many believe that Jesus was no better than a prophet and one of the many ways of attaining life. Viewed in this light, He is just another option along the wide path which is why many who believe they are Christians call out His name and profess to identify with Him. But He said it is not everyone who calls out "Lord, Lord" that will enter the Kingdom of Heaven [Matthew 7:21]; only those who obey the will of God will make it. Jesus said in the last days many will come saying that they had served Jesus and performed many miracles in His name, but He will tell them that He never knew them [Matthew 7:22-23]. The reason is that their fruit (works) reveal who they really are. Jesus said that by their fruits we shall know them [Matthew 7:20]. A person can pretend to be walking the narrow path, but their works will reveal who they really are.

When God brought the Children of Israel through the wilderness to the boundary of the Promised Land, Moses cautioned them about their choices. He said "… I have set before you, life and death, blessing and cursing; therefore, choose life" [Deuteronomy 30:19]. There was a way God wanted them to live in the Land because the majority of the inhabitants from other nations were living lives that God disapproved of. However, after the death of Joshua, Moses' successor, and all the elders of that generation, the Children of Israel succumbed to the allure of the lifestyle and culture of the surrounding nations and began to serve idols and indulge in abominations. As a result, God delivered them into the hands of their adversaries [Judges 2:7-15].

Faith does not toe the line of the majority no matter how influential it is. When God decided to destroy all of humanity with a flood because of its wickedness, He spared the lives of Noah and his family because Noah was a just man and perfect in his generation [Genesis 6:7-9]. In Sodom and Gomorrah, Lot and his family chose to maintain their righteousness despite all the wickedness around them [2 Peter 2:7]. Lot may have been wrongly located but his righteousness saved him from God's wrath when the whole country was burned with fire and brimstone. When the majority were bowing to an idol constructed by King Nebuchadnezzar of Babylon, Shadrach, Meshach, and Abednego refused to follow suit and were thrown bound hand and foot into a furnace [Daniel 3]. But because of their faith in God, they were delivered miraculously. Likewise, when all in the Nation were banned from praying to their gods for thirty days, Daniel maintained his routine of praying to God three times a day. Even though he was thrown in a lions' den, God rescued him because of his faith. These heroes all had one thing in common: they refused to follow the majority.

47

Not feeding your appetites

Faith is about not feeding your appetites. We have different types of appetites, spiritual and natural. The context here is the natural appetites. Faith is about self-restraint and not indiscriminately satisfying your appetites. It is not wrong to satisfy your hunger with food and drink, but this doesn't mean we have to be gluttonous. Apostle Paul reminds us that the kingdom of God is not about eating and drinking, but righteousness, peace, and joy in the Holy Ghost (Holy Spirit) Romans 14:17. This is all about moderation and for this we need to exercise the spirit of self-restraint [Galatians 5:22-23]. Without moderation we will abuse the grace of God which is given to us so that we can be a blessing.

In Jesus' parable, the rich fool said to himself that after many years of hard work he would extend his barns for the storage of his goods and would live the rest of his life in selfish luxury rewarding himself for his diligence [Luke 12:16-21]. He planned to eat, drink and be merry, living a life of ease and splendour. There was nothing in his early retirement plan for the less fortunate in his community. It was all about him. Unfortunately for him, on the first night of his retirement God recalled his soul and he died leaving all his acquired goods for others to possess. The Bible says that those who give to the poor lend to God and He will reward them for what they have given [Proverbs 19:17]. Jesus further teaches that we should sell our possessions (superfluous items) and give to those in need so that we can store treasure in heaven [Luke 12:33-34]. The rich fool was accused of being selfish towards God because he had no plan to share his excessive goods with anyone.

We should eat to live and not live to eat. There comes a stage where a Christian should take stock and sincerely analyse their motives and motivations. There is nothing wrong in living in a nice house or driving a nice car or wearing nice clothes. I use the word 'nice', but perhaps I should substitute that with 'opulent'. God has nothing against His children living in mansions, driving Rolls Royce cars, wearing Rolexes and designer clothing. What God frowns on is greed – a life that only invests in itself and seeks to acquire more than it genuinely requires. When Jesus says that a person's life does not consist in the abundance of their possessions, He is cautioning us against greed [Luke 12:15].

Unfortunately, many confuse greed with faith. They believe that large appetites equate to great faith in God's provision. Rather than asking for what they need, they function with a sense of entitlement and seek the most opulent believing that this is what God expects of them. No one stops to consider that in the wilderness God fed the Children of Israel with manna. It contained all the nutrients they needed but was light as a wafer. Because of this, the Children of Israel rebelled against this food and craved for meat which infuriated God. Rather than being grateful for being given a regular nutritious meal in a place where farming was impossible, they grumbled. They didn't just want a meal they wanted to feed their appetites.

Although we may say "Food for the belly, and the belly for food", however the Bible says God will destroy both; now the body is not for sexual immorality but for the Lord who cares about how we use our bodies [1 Corinthians 6:13]. Those who have no self-restraint will stray from their marriages into another person's arms without any sense of guilt. For these ones, all that matters is that their cravings are satisfied regardless of with whom. The fact that they are desecrating God's temple (our bodies) never occurs to them. They are pleasure-seekers who only desire to feed their appetites with complete disregard for the Lord's guidelines.

The scale of the problem runs deeper than many of us realise, because it is responsible for the current state of affairs in our society where we have totally abandoned God's definitions of marriage, family, and sex in preference for that which is abhorrent to Him [Romans 1:21-28]. Just because we have a craving for a particular experience does not mean that indulging in it carries no consequences. Feeding our appetites in a way that contradicts God's standard carries grievous penalties. Read verses 26 and 27 of the first chapter of the Book of Romans which is corroborated by the Law of Moses. We cannot live the way we want with disregard for God and expect to get off scot-free. The Christian who lives in this way cannot exhibit faith that gets results. No matter how long and hard they pray and fast, God will not respond to their requests.

The Psalmist learnt that if he harboured iniquity (sin) in his heart God would not hear him [Psalm 66:18]. There is a well-known story involving King David who committed adultery with a woman he observed bathing. The woman's name was Bathsheba, and she was the wife of one of David's officers. David did not think his deed would be discovered until the woman became pregnant with his child. David had flaunted God's tenth commandment regarding not coveting one's neighbour's spouse. However, in his bid to cover up his sin he ultimately arranged to kill Bathsheba's husband. God was very upset with David and pronounced judgment on him and his household which included the death of the child borne from the adultery. To appease God, David fasted and prayed earnestly as he had always done but could not sway God from His wrath [2 Samuel 11, 12:1-23]. The child ultimately died. If David, whom God called a man after His own heart was not able to dissuade God from carrying out His judgment on the grievous sin, what makes us think we can succeed where he failed? Feeding our appetites carries consequences and for a Christian it undermines our faith and ultimately prevents us from receiving any answers to our prayers. So, knowing what we know, why would we take the risk?

48

Being patient

Being patient is the evidence of faith. In fact, I would go so far as to state that patience is the core of faith. As we may know, patience is one of the fruits of the spirit [Galatians 5:22-23]. It is cultivated in us by the Holy Spirit so that we can be moulded into the image of Christ and reflect His glory.

Regarding Abraham, the Father of Faith, the Bible teaches that he had to exercise patience as he waited for the fulfilment of God's promise in his life [Hebrews 6:15]. Between the moment of God's promises to us and the moment of manifestation, there is often a period of waiting. That waiting becomes tedious if we have not learnt patience. Impatience robs us of peace and joy and introduces worry and anxiety. We struggle to see God as faithful and wonder whether what He has promised will ever come to pass. We believe it is taking too long and as we wonder whether we heard God correctly we experience a drift in our expectation. What was vivid becomes distant, and what was crystal clear becomes opaque. God's voice loses its resonance, and every other voice becomes amplified.

Being patient does not come naturally to most of us. When the delivery date becomes protracted and uncertain, we start to analyse the facts and ascribe all sorts of interpretations to this season of our lives. Waiting indefinitely can test our capacity for patience and God never shies away from propelling us through those hoops. Apostle James understands the process well and clarifies that the trying of our faith works out patience in our lives and that when patience is perfected in us, we will be mature and whole lacking in nothing [James 1:3-4]. Apostle Peter, speaking along similar lines, urges us to add virtue to our faith, and to virtue – knowledge, and to knowledge – temperance, and to temperance – patience, and to patience – godliness; and to godliness – brotherly kindness, and to brotherly kindness – charity [2 Peter 1:5-8]. Peter makes clear that without patience we cannot attain godliness, because patience is the foundation upon which godliness rests.

Apostle Paul agrees with his fellow apostles on the immeasurable value of patience when he invites us to glory in tribulations because tribulations produce patience and in turn patience produces experience [Romans 5:3]. Our patience in tribulations is the strongest evidence of our faith which is manifested through experience. This experience produces hope and those who hope in God will never be ashamed because through that hope the Holy Spirit reveals to us the love of God [Romans 5.4]. Love is manifested in so many different ways, but the greatest manifestation was by Christ's death on the cross for us whilst we were still deep in sin. Therefore, if God is for us who can be against us? [Romans 8:31]. If God did not spare Christ for our sakes, then why would He not together with Christ gives us all things in accordance with our faith in Him? [Romans 8:32].

Therefore, as the Bible teaches, we have need of patience so that after we have done the will of God, we might receive the promise [Hebrews 10:36]. We are similarly urged not to be slothful in our dealings, but to be followers of those who through faith and patience inherit the promises [Hebrews 6:12].

Patience is one of the chief attributes of God our father. He is called longsuffering [Numbers 14:18] which is indicative of the measure of His patience for humanity. God's longsuffering nature and patience are closely related because patience produces longsuffering and longsuffering is the evidence of faith, God is slow to anger [Psalm 103:8; Nehemiah 9:17] and quick to forgive those who genuinely repent of their sin. God's patience can often be misconstrued for slackness, but God is longsuffering toward us not willing that any of us should perish [2 Peter 3:9]. However, His longsuffering nature is not an eternal one because we know that one day, He will judge humanity for its sins.

Our patience is the evidence of our trust in Him. Like Abraham, we patiently wait for the manifestation of God's promise. From the time Joseph was given a promise to the date of its manifestation was at least thirteen years and a further nine years before his dream came to pass. From the moment Prophet Samuel anointed David to be the next King of Israel to the moment it was manifested after the death of Saul was about fifteen years. Both of them had to exercise patience as they waited for God to perform what He had promised. From of old, no one has heard or perceived God by ear, and no eye has seen a God besides Him, who acts for those who wait for Him [Isaiah 64:4]. And so, we have this incredible promise that those who wait on Him shall renew their strength [Isaiah 40:31]. To wait for Him or wait on Him connotes a level of patience but allied to this comes the assurance that our waiting shall not be in vain.

49

Seeing light in the midst of darkness

Seeing light in the midst of darkness is the evidence of faith. When all around is dim and visibility is poor the eyes that can see are the eyes of faith. For some of us, that darkness may come packaged as a negative outcome or a protracted state of affairs and with these scenarios are the expert opinions that quench any glimmer of light on the horizon. Sometimes the darkness arrives unexpectedly but oftentimes it follows swiftly on from a promise. The evidence of the light in these circumstances is the ability to still see the promise despite the natural darkness.

Apostle Paul teaches that no eye has seen, nor ear heard, neither, he says, has it entered into a person's heart what God has prepared for those who love Him, but He reveals it to them through His Holy Spirit [1 Corinthians 2:9-10]. The premise for this is Paul's teaching on the distinction between the wisdom of men (the wisdom of the world) and the wisdom of God which is hidden from natural senses and was instituted before the creation of the world [1 Corinthians 2:7]. In the gloom, those who have been blinded to the presence, authority, and power of Almighty God, see only darkness despite their brave narrative and stoic positions [2 Corinthians 4:4]. The one who has blinded them is the god of this world and his intention is that they never see the light of God's glory as captured in the gospels. The light of the gospel which is a lamp on to our feet and a light on to our paths [Psalm 119:105] is hidden from those who are limited to their five senses. However, this light shines out of darkness through the hearts of Christians empowered by the word of God – for the entrance of God's word into a person's heart brings light [Psalm 119:130].

In the midst of darkness God's word brings light. Those who habitually meditate on God's word, storing it in their sub-conscious have a resource in the dark times because it is that very word that will be used by the Holy Spirit to enlighten them. For this reason, we are assured that the path of a righteous man is as a shining light that shines brighter and brighter unto the perfect day [Proverbs 4:18]. Regardless of the prevailing conditions a righteous person has visibility. They may go through pain and suffering that brings tears to their eyes but will always keep their focus. They have learnt through many tests and trials that tears may endure for a night, but joy comes in the morning [Psalm30:5].

We are taught that Joseph was hauled into slavery by the will of God. It was not His brothers but God that sent him to Egypt to preserve his family and indeed the whole world from the worldwide famine [Psalm 105:16-22]. Joseph was sold as a slave and his sellers bruised his feet with fetters and placed an iron manacle around his neck. Until it was time for his promise to be fulfilled, God tested Joseph's character and integrity. Then he was set free and promoted to the position of number two official in all the Land of Egypt, exercising authority over all the Pharaoh's aides, counsellors, and his household. However, throughout his ordeal, Joseph never lost his form and never caved-in to the temptation to sin against God. His eyes were on God's promise and through the darkness, God's word was a lamp to his feet and a light to his path.

One acquainted with darkness was Jeremiah the Prophet. He had been called by God to warn the Nation of Judah about His forthcoming judgment because of the people's sin, but nobody took him seriously. He was derided by the king, the priesthood, other prophets, and the common man. In the eyes of the people, He lacked credibility. They preferred to listen to the prophets who promised them a prosperous future despite their sin. For years, he prophesied about the coming exile to Babylon and the series of invasions that would occur if the people did not repent of their sinfulness. Yet the people did not move away from their sin and Jeremiah was subjected to sustained physical and verbal assault. God had already distanced Himself from the false prophets, but they were more influential than Jeremiah because of their message.

Jeremiah was eventually thrown in prison, but even during incarceration he continued to prophesy. This made him deeply unpopular with the king's counsellors to the extent that they sought to have him executed. He was eventually taken out of regular prison and lowered into a dungeon which was essentially a pit in the ground with a surface covered in sludge. He stayed there for a period, starving and thirsty because no one bothered to feed him. But God was merciful, and Jeremiah was eventually transferred back to regular prison. Yet, despite the inhospitable treatment, Jeremiah's message did not waver. He shared exactly what he had been asked to share with those he had been asked to share it with. For Jeremiah, these were dark days when his life was constantly at risk and there was a strong temptation to compromise but he never gave in. When the invasion eventually took place Jeremiah was freed from captivity and allowed to reside as a free man within the land whilst other prophets were either slain or taken captive along with the rest of the population to Babylon.

Most of us may know the story of Apostle Paul and his protégé Silas who were thrown into prison for casting-out a demon from a young fortune teller. They were first beaten before being hurled into the jail, bruised and aching. They could have given in to self-pity and bemoaned their fate but instead at the midnight hour – the darkest phase of any crisis, they began to praise God; because they had the spiritual capacity to see the light, they were not ensnared by the darkness. The atmosphere changed and an earthquake shook the foundations of the prison loosening their chains and opening prison doors. Paul and Silas could have made a run for it knowing that they were innocent and feeling justified, but instead they remained where they were. They knew that God wanted to catch the prison warden's attention so that he and his family could receive salvation through Jesus Christ. In the midst of the darkness, they could still perceive God's purpose. Light always cancels darkness [John 1:5] and the light of Christ within us is greater than the darkness around us.

As we meditate on God's word in our midnight hour, we are called to arise and shine because God's glory has been bestowed on us [Isaiah 60:1].

Celebrating before the event

Faith is celebrating before the event. When we celebrate before the event that we are waiting to happen, it is a measure of our faith – our confidence in God and His faithfulness. The ability to get excited before manifestation is the evidence of a believing heart. When our minds are not on the facts of our situation, we are able to see more clearly through the eyes of conviction that see outcomes in advance of their physical emergence. Like a farmer who is expectant for a good harvest and rejoices over the land before the first shoot emerges, we are called to rejoice upon receipt of God's word. God's word meshed with our faith produces God's desired outcome.

Many times, we set about trying to work out how God's promises will be established in our lives and rather than celebrating possibility we mourn impossibility. Some of us, however, tend to count the natural or material opposition more worthy of our conviction than the word that was spoken. But Jesus says blessed is the person who has not seen yet believes [John 20:29]. In effect, we have to learn to see before we see.

When King Jehoshaphat of Judah was facing an invasion by a coalition of enemy nations, he was at his wits end [2 Chronicles 20]. What was he supposed to do against the might of three vastly superior armies? How was he supposed to defend the nation against this invasion and all the devastation that would accompany it? In our world it may not be an invasion by enemy armies but rather the overwhelming series of challenges such as health, financial, emotional, professional etc.

When circumstances invade us at the same time it feels as if we are drowning. We are not equipped to deal with a multitude of problems at the same time and soon feel out of our depth.

The king did what many of us would do in the circumstance and turned to God. But rather than approaching Him with complaints, he began to extol God's majesty and greatness. By so doing he was elevating God above his problem. He also reminded God of His promises knowing that God was a covenant keeping God. After elevating God to the pinnacle of his mind, he presented his petition regarding the pending invasion from treacherous nations. Jehoshaphat points out that Judah had no means of defending itself against the coalition and even if they did have the numbers, they did not know what to do. He rounds-up by telling God that the nation's eyes are on Him.

In response, God tells Jehoshaphat not to be afraid of the size of the opposition because the battle was not theirs but His. God informs Jehoshaphat that the people will not need to fight in this battle and tells him to stand still and witness God's miraculous deliverance. Assured by this promise, Jehoshaphat and the people start worshipping God and giving Him praise. The following morning the people all rose early and headed to the battle front praising God in advance for the successful outcome of the situation. As the people praised God, He intervened causing the coalition to turn on each other until there was none of them left alive. Jehoshaphat and his army did not have to lift a finger to secure the victory; just by praising God in advance of their victory, they received it.

Today, many of us treat Him like a God of last resort. We start off with self-help and when that fails to achieve the desired outcome we turn to God for help. But note Jehoshaphat's example; he did not start-off executing a plan in his head but sought out God. When he reminded God of His promises he was speaking to a covenant-keeping God, who had promised that He would not break His covenant nor alter what He had spoken [Psalm 89:34]. The covenant-keeping God responded to Jehoshaphat's invitation by giving words of assurance which formed the basis of the praise as the people headed towards the battlefield. They did not know what to expect but just kept praising God until they reached the arena where the fallen bodies of their enemies were spread out beneath the scorching sun awaiting the birds of prey.

Apostle Paul urges us to rejoice in the Lord always [Philippians 4:4-7] and to be careful for nothing. With prayer and supplication with thanksgiving we are advised to make our petitions known to God and in so doing the peace of God which surpasses all human understanding will keep our hearts and minds through Christ Jesus. This is what Jehoshaphat did thousands of years before Apostle Paul disclosed the strategy. It is clear that Jehoshaphat and the people were operating under a level of grace that was extra-terrestrial. The evidence of its presence is peace. Because he was utterly convinced that God had secured them the victory, Jehoshaphat did not prepare for war even though he sent his army out. The king's faith in God's faithfulness empowered him to take a risk. Rather than working on military formation, he arranged an orchestra of praise to God, glorifying Him for what He had done, even though Jehoshaphat had not yet seen the dead bodies of his adversaries in the natural.

Jehoshaphat's brand of faith that rejoiced before even seeing the manifested promise is the variety that Jesus commended when speaking to his disciple, Thomas, who had demanded proof that he had risen from the grave. Apostle Paul speaks about Abraham's reaction to God's promise and makes an emphatic statement which is important to know [Romans 4:10-24]. He says that Abraham staggered not at the promise of God through unbelief, but was strong in faith giving glory to God, and was completely persuaded that God would do what He had promised.

When the Bible says that the things that are revealed belong to us [Deuteronomy 29:29] it is a reminder that we are to take ownership of them. God needs us to take ownership of His promises and meditate on them until our minds are saturated with the possibility of receiving them. It is at this stage that we start rejoicing and praising God in advance of receiving manifestation of what He promised.

51

A scary assurance

Faith is often a scary assurance. All your senses tell you it's not going to work but something deep within provides a soothing reassurance that all things will work together for your good. Faith is not the total absence of uncertainty. It is perfectly normal for faith to sit alongside uncertainty. The reason for this is because faith comes from your spiritual perspective whilst uncertainty comes from your five senses. Now, provided your five senses do not rule your mind and dictate your decisions, you can manage the presence of uncertainty.

For as long as we function within the confines of a human body, we will juggle these contradictions – faith and uncertainty. Why? I believe it is because no one fully knows the mind of God. Apostle Paul says that in this life at best we only have partial knowledge and even our prophecies are incomplete because we do not see the big picture. He clarifies that all we see is a reflection of what really is, as if looking at a mirror. As a result, none of our information will be totally accurate [1 Corinthians 13:9-12]. As we mature in our Christianity, we know more but never the full picture. This is because the things that are revealed (whether by way of prophesy or manifestation) are for us but the things that are not revealed belong to God [Deuteronomy 29:29]. God never shows us the full picture. Moses never saw the full picture even though he saw more than any other prophet that has ever lived [Deuteronomy 34:10-12; Psalm 103:7]. Moses embarked on his assignment convinced that he would lead the children into the Promised Land and all along the way as he witnessed the might of Almighty God he grew in faith; yet he never knew the full picture.

When the floods hit the earth and wiped out all of humanity, only Noah, his family and a selection of animals were preserved. Noah had constructed the ark by faith in accordance with God's design [6:13-22] but he did so even though he had never seen a flood before and had no idea what to expect [Hebrews 11:7]. It is also possible that he had never seen torrential rainfall before and so one would expect him to be full of trepidation. The time in the ark could not have been completely free of apprehension. Imagine being confined to a limited space with no exit routes with some of the most dangerous wild animals and reptiles on earth. Also imagine the turbulence of the waters as the ark carved its ways through the waves to an unknown destination. Noah was not steering the ark as far as we know. How could he when he and his family were locked within the vessel? He had no navigational directions and did not know whether he was coming or going. There was such a level of uncertainty during that scary voyage. Yet Noah had a scary assurance that he and his family would be all right. How did he know this? He knew this because God had been merciful enough to forewarn him and give him a strategy for preservation.

We have explored the fascinating life of Joseph elsewhere within this book and the story is one of the best loved and most encouraging in scripture because of the hope it brings to many. Joseph was constantly in situations that were intimidating enough to induce uncertainty in his mind. He had no idea of the big picture and how it was all going to work out. All he had were his dreams and a quiet but scary assurance of God's faithfulness. Was he terrified when thrown in the pit by his brothers? Yes, he was. Was he terrified when placed in chains and taken many days journey away from his family home to be sold into slavery? Yes of course he was. Was he discouraged and weary whilst in prison? Naturally, otherwise he would not have appealed to Pharaoh's Butler the way he did. He had no idea how it was all going to end even though he trusted God. Yet Joseph had a scary assurance through all this because he knew that God would never fail him [Genesis 37 – 50].

What about Ruth who left her family and country to travel with her mother-in-law, Naomi, to a country hostile to people from her culture? She was taking a significant risk despite her bold proclamation that Naomi's people would be her people. She could have been assaulted and murdered because this was a time of great lawlessness in Israel where everyone did what seemed right in their eyes. Undoubtedly, she was functioning under a scary assurance that she would be kept safe and that the God of Naomi would preserve her. By submitting to Naomi and obeying her in all things, Ruth was not only preserved but she prospered in Israel becoming the great grandmother of King David [Book of Ruth].

David the shepherd boy knew that he had been anointed to be the next king of Israel but there was enough uncertainty in the intervening period to introduce an element of uncertainty. Many times, he had to flee for his life from King Saul or those loyal to him such as Doeg the Edomite. David lived in caves and hid in the wilderness to avoid capture, many times he barely escaped with his life but throughout this experience he had a scary assurance that God would come through for him and fulfil His promise [1 Samuel 16 – 31; 2 Samuel 1 – 5].

Can we forget Joseph, the husband of Mary and surrogate father of Jesus Christ? He had to overcome the stigma of Mary's culturally controversial pregnancy and trust in God who revealed Himself to him in a dream. With a scary assurance, he had to oversee the security of Mary and the new-born child, knowing that the child's life was in danger. He had to flee to a foreign country as part of that experience, all the while trusting in God. Even after he was given a green light to return to his country, he was still full of trepidation and settled somewhere unobtrusive. Throughout this experience Joseph was propelled by a scary assurance to obey God whilst dealing with the scary facts of his situation [Matthew 1:18-25; 2:1-23].

A scary assurance is not the same thing as doubt or unbelief. A scary assurance is all about obeying and serving God faithfully whilst addressing the uncertainty of the scary circumstance. Provided our eyes on Him, we will always prevail despite the presence of that scary assurance.

52

Obeying an instruction to go somewhere you have never been

Faith is obeying an instruction to go somewhere you have never been before. It is a risk. Every day we hear stories about Christians who quit their jobs and decide to join the mission fields. Many times, the places they choose to serve are remote and off the beaten path. They reside with local communities and share the gospel or get involved in diverse infrastructure and regeneration projects to improve the lives of the people there both spiritually and materially. These are laudable achievements as many are stepping into the unknown. Many have embarked on these trips and never returned, either because they were murdered for their faith or succumbed to terminal effects of certain sickness and disease. Many of these heard the voice of God and ignoring the voices of reason flowing from friends and family they set-off on the adventure of a lifetime to places they had never been before in total obedience to God. This chapter salutes their faith.

Like modern day missionaries who embark on missions driven purely by faith, their Biblical forebears did exactly the same thing thousands of years ago although with less certainty. There were many in the Bible who travelled to places they had never heard off before and for the simple reason that they had been told to. So, most Christians have heard about Abraham's faith in leaving his father's household and travelling to a land he had never been before. He had spent over seventy years in that community before he heard the summons from a God he had never worshipped (he was an idol worshipper – see Joshua 24:2). He was told to leave the familiar and step out of his comfort zone into the unfamiliar. Propelled by his conviction in this unknown God he abandoned his idolatry and travelled from his homeland but with his father and nephew in tow. He travelled to Canaan burying his father along the way and eventually separating from his nephew [Genesis 11:31-32; 12:1-9; 13:1-18]. It was not a smooth journey, as they were many lapses in judgment along the way, but God was with him regardless. That single act of obedience is the reason why we have the nation of Israel today and even more emphatically – the Church.

Over four hundred years later, a man called Moses who had been living in exile was called to leave the familiarity of his career as a shepherd and return to Egypt to lead the Children of Israel out of captivity. At the time he was eighty years old and a pensioner in today's terms. Like Abraham, he had been summoned forth in old age to go somewhere he had never been before. Although he knew the wilderness well, he had never experienced the challenge of not only confronting the leader of the most powerful nation on earth and then leading out a multitude of over a million people and livestock across hostile terrain to a land he had never been – the Promised Land [Exodus 2 – 14]. The first journey Moses had to embark on was the journey of faith in a God he had never directly related with or experienced. This is the start of faith, where we surrender our lives to Him even though He is initially a stranger. This was a challenging journey for Moses who had previously tried to launch his ministry of redemption without consulting God. He had killed a man in the process of trying to fill the shoes of a redeemer and been forced to flee Egypt, rejected by his people, and hunted by his adversaries.

The call to lead Israel out of captivity was a challenging one for a man whose self-esteem was already bruised by his previous brush with the ministry of redemption. It was a daunting task for anyone but for Moses it was an impossible one and he duly tendered his retinue of excuses for why he was not well suited for the role. For him the journey to the unknown was not one for someone who was insecure and lacking in the necessary eloquence. I am also convinced that deep within he believed he was too old for the job. The route to the Promised Land would involve confrontation and warfare, something that was now alien to him. Yet God did not let him off the hook because as with all journeys of this nature, man's role is confined to his willingness and obedience whilst God does all the rest. Every call to embark on a journey to somewhere you have never been before is grace-laden; the grace is only released as we faithfully take the first step. Although Moses never took the people all the way into the Promised Land, he got them as far as the boundary between it and the wilderness by the grace of God.

When Peter was told that he would become a fisher of men, he had no idea what that meant. It was a step out of the familiar into the unknown. How could Peter have known that the simple act of loaning his fishing boat to Jesus Christ as a platform for preaching the gospel would culminate into the astounding miraculous experience that ultimately birthed the Church as we know it today? For, as Peter honoured Jesus' request to use his boat, he had unwittingly signed up for discipleship. Overwhelmed by the boat-sinking catch of fish that followed his act of obedience, Peter must have sensed that his life would never be the same again. He had been a competent but not particularly successful fisherman because of the prevailing conditions. He caught more fish in one day with Jesus than he had probably caught in his entire career. This was however merely a sign of greater things to come because Jesus used the catch of fish to catch Peter's attention and reveal to him who he was meant to be and what he was meant to do. He was called to embark on a journey to somewhere he had never been before [Luke 5:1-11]. He was called to follow Jesus and forsake all that was familiar so that he would become a fisher of men. Fast forward three and a half years to the Day of Pentecost and we see the arrival of Peter at this Promised Land where in one day three thousand people became believers in Jesus Christ [Acts 2:1-47]. This was the beginning of the Church – a destination Peter could never have imagined when he first responded to Jesus' summons.

53

Ignoring all the warning signs

Faith is ignoring all the warning signs. How many times have we ignored all the warning signs and gone ahead with a decision or action that looked doomed for failure or risky in the extreme? Experts warn us about the risk of investing in a particular sector or industry, but we press on regardless; consular authorities warn us about the risk of travelling to certain countries, but we ignore the prevalent dangers and go there anyway. We are warned of the dangers of not complying with a particular law or edict, but we refuse to comply. These analogies are examples of the brand of faith that does not shirk back from risks or danger. This faith does not submit to the dictates of the five senses but is firmly anchored to trust in God.

When I think about one who persistently ignored all the warning signs, Apostle Paul comes to mind. This was one of the most stubborn individuals in all of scripture. He frequently displayed a complete disregard for danger however it came packaged. In one incident that never ceases to fascinate, Paul was in a city called Lystra where the Holy Spirit had just used him to heal a crippled person, but some Jewish opponents persuaded the people to stone him to death [Acts 14:19-20]. He was left for dead on the outskirts of the city, however, when other disciples showed up and gathered around his body, he rose up. Now rather than running away from the city as he had done elsewhere when faced with persecution, he did something bizarre; he headed back into the city. It is not clear whether he was actually dead or merely unconscious, but he would undoubtedly have sustained severe injuries, yet he defied the risk and went back into the city. This incident defines Apostle Paul for me.

Paul's ministry was continuously fraught with all manner of danger, but he never relented in his fervency as he travelled from place-to-place preaching, teaching, and establishing new church branches amongst the Gentile nations. He was relentless. This nature presented all sorts of challenges to his adversaries who opposed the preaching or teaching of the gospel. Even though they had no answer to the miracles he was being used to perform, they still sought to kill him. The devil's hope was that by intimidating Paul he would shut down the rapid spread of the gospel. We are told that Paul had a thorn in the flesh that weakened him [2 Corinthians 12:7] but it is clear from his ministry that he was the biggest thorn in the devil's side. The person Satan fears the most is one that cannot be bought and who is not afraid to die. Paul was that kind of a person.

A defining moment in Apostle Paul's ministry came when he informed some of the Ephesian church elders that he was going bound in the spirit to Jerusalem knowing what things would befall him there [Acts 20:17-25]. This was quite an ominous message, and it is easy to imagine them wondering why he would voluntarily head to possible death. Even more troubling, Paul informed them that the Holy Spirit had been witnessing in every city he had passed through (most probably through prophets and members of the churches) that bonds and affliction awaited him. However, as Paul made clear, none of these things moved him; neither did he count his life dear to him, so that he might finish his course with joy and the ministry which he had received from Jesus to testify the gospel of the grace of God. Paul then informed the elders that they would not see his face anymore and this caused great sorrow in their midst. Apostle Paul was making clear that he knew the risks, had seen all the warning signs but was not dissuaded from his course.

At another town called Caesarea, a Prophet from Judea named Agabus showed up and used Paul's girdle to bind his own hands and feet and then prophesied under the power of the Holy Spirit that in like manner the Jews in Jerusalem would bind the owner of the girdle and deliver him into the hands of the Gentiles. Now, when the other disciples heard this prophecy, they begged Paul not to make the trip to Jerusalem. However, Paul asked them why they were weeping in a manner that was breaking his heart. He then proclaimed that he was ready not only to be bound but also to die at Jerusalem if it came to that for the name of the Lord Jesus [Acts 21:8-14]. When it was clear to the disciples that Paul's mind was set and that he would not be dissuaded they ceased imploring him and said, 'The will of the Lord be done."

When Paul eventually arrived in Jerusalem, he was seized by some of his adversaries who saw him in the temple and stirred up the crowd to mob him [Acts 21:27-40; 22]. He was not killed in Jerusalem at that time, but it set in motion a train of events that culminated in him being transferred to Rome. It was Paul's determination to walk in faith that empowered him to defy the warning signs that would have choked the life out of his ministry. Because of Paul's faithfulness many Jews and Gentiles in Rome came to know Jesus Christ as their Lord and saviour. There was a purpose which he might not have fulfilled if he was dissuaded by warning signs. Even when God tested his heart by sending him all those prophecies,

Paul's mind was made up because he knew that it was the will of God for him to go to Jerusalem.

How many times have we been discouraged from following through or fulfilling God's will because we are walking by sight and not by faith? The warning signs often come to distract us and dissuade us from following through, but our inner witness should be more potent that the external witness. We are assured that greater is He that is in us than he that is in the world [1 John 4:4]. Greater is the power of the Holy Spirit in us than the power of darkness around us.

54

Walking in love with those you want to hate

Faith is often about walking in love with those you want to hate. Jesus commands us to love the Lord our God with all our heart, soul, strength, and mind, and to love our neighbour as we love ourselves [Luke 10:27]. The question then arises as to who our neighbour is. Jesus answered this question by sharing the Parable of the Good Samaritan. This idiom has become popular in everyday language as we speak about a Good Samaritan being anyone who shows up to assist us in our hour of need. However, when Jesus taught this parable, it was very controversial because the two protagonists were from tribes and cultures that were diametrically opposed to each other. In fact, these were arch enemies. The Jews and Samaritans did not dwell in the same towns or share the same facilities; they did not intermarry or trade with each other and did not visit each other's towns. Yet Jesus' parable cut right through the manmade conflict to firmly establish God's perspective on the issue.

In the parable [Luke 10: 30-37], Jesus taught about a man travelling from Jerusalem to Jericho when he was attacked by robbers who stripped him off his clothing, beat him up and left him half dead. Whilst the man lay bleeding to death and in agony, a priest who happened to be travelling along the same road saw the man and passed by on the other side of the road. Shortly after a Levite came along but on seeing the victim chose to pass him by and cross to the other side of the road. Eventually a Samaritan who was travelling along that road came to where the victim lay and took pity on him. The Samaritan treated the man's injuries with oil, gave him wine to revive his strength, and bandaged his wounds. The Samaritan then placed the man on his donkey and brought him to an inn where he took care of him. The next day the Samaritan gave some money to the innkeeper and asked him to look after the victim, promising to reimburse any extra expense on his return journey. Jesus then asked his audience which of the three people was a neighbour to the victim of armed robbery. In response, a lawyer said it was the one who had mercy on the victim and Jesus told him to go and do likewise.

Jesus commands us to love our enemies, bless those who curse us, do good to them that hate us and pray for those who despitefully use us and persecute us [Matthew 5:48]. Jesus clarifies that we need to live this way so that we may exhibit the traits of children of our heavenly father – God who causes the sun to rise on the evil and the good and sends rain on the just and unjust. This is about producing the fruit expected of children of God, so that we may be in alignment with our father. Jesus goes on to question the value of love if we only love those who love us when even sinners love those who love them [Luke 6:32-36]. If we lend to those from whom we expect repayment, Jesus points out that there is no reward in that because even sinners do this. But we are called to love our enemies and do good to them; lending to them without expecting anything in return. Jesus says that when we live like this our reward will be great. He calls us to be perfect even as our heavenly father is perfect [Matthew 5:48]. Loving our enemies and treating them well is the evidence of our perfection.

Apostle John challenges us when he says we should not love in word alone but in deeds and in truth [1 John 3:18]. In John's view love is action and this aligns with Jesus's teaching. As a mark of our faith, we need to love everyone not only in word but more so in deed. We are to respond in love to acts of hatred because this is the evidence of the love of Christ which is demanded of us in this new life. We have been given a spirit of love, power, and a sound mind [2 Timothy 1:7]. That spirit of love compels us to walk in love towards our neighbours.

Some fallout with those they are supposed to love particularly within the church and when this happens, hatred can quickly seep in if allowed. But, if we say we love God, but hate our brothers and sisters, the Bible says we are liars [1 John 4:20-21]. After all, how can we claim to love God whom we have not seen and hate our brothers and sisters whom we have seen? Whenever we find ourselves falling out with other members of our Christian community and having negative feelings towards them, we need to check ourselves and repent by seeking to make peace from the place of humility. Faith says sorry and makes peace because of the love and Christ. The gateway to peace is often a realisation that by hating our brother or sister we are in the wrong. Refusal to compromise or make peace is often the fruit of pride and arrogance. God gives grace to the humble but resists the proud [James 4:6; 1 Peter 5:5].

King Solomon presents the issue of how to respond to our enemies in a more satisfying way for those who struggle in this area. He says if our enemy is hungry, we should give him food to eat, and if he/she is thirsty we should give him/her water to drink for in doing so we will heap hot coals on his/her head and the Lord will reward us [Proverbs 25:21-22]. God will reward you because of your faith because love is action and when we show love to our enemy, we catch God's attention.

55

Speaking about things no eye has seen

Faith is speaking about things no eye has seen. You cannot speak about things that no eye has seen if you are confined to a five-sensory perception. No eye has seen the things we are speaking about because they are located in an invisible realm not accessible by the five senses.

The moment we start speaking with conviction about things that God has revealed to us, we are walking in faith. Walking in faith will often see us making declarations about things that natural senses cannot see. These words are often prophetic because they speak about future events or provide insight into current events and situations. At other times a person may testify about things that have already taken place in a way that unveils mysteries. All around us there are events taking place, but our five senses are unable to comprehend the source or meaning of these things. This is where such testimonies are valuable for providing insight. This sort of narrative flows from a mind being drip-fed from the spiritual realm. The Holy Spirit who dwells within us communes with our spirits sharing things that no eye has seen neither any ear heard. These matters are processed through our minds and overflow out of our lips.

When Paul emphasises that our conversation is in heaven [Philippians 3:20], it speaks about our focus. Because we are spirits who have a soul and live in a body, we cannot and should not be rooted in the earth realm alone. We are called to fix our thoughts on the realm where God our father resides – the spiritual realm. This is why our conversation, our sense of being or belonging, is in that realm. Some versions of the Bible use the word "citizenship" which is perhaps closer in meaning to the original Greek word. Therefore, Jesus urges us not to store up treasure in the earth but in heaven (Matthew 6:19-21]. He knew that where our treasure was there also our hearts would be. If our conversation or citizenship is in heaven, then our treasure will be there – in the invisible spiritual realm. This is because we place higher value on things invested in the spiritual realm than in the earth realm.

Dreams are the windows to the spiritual realm [Numbers 12:6]. God informed Aaron and Miriam, Moses' siblings, in the presence of Israel that if there was a prophet amongst them, the Lord would reveal Himself to them in a vision and speak to them in a dream. Dreams are often God's way of communicating things to His children. There are many examples of characters in the Bible who received dreams from God; perhaps the most famous of these was Joseph, the son of Jacob who became the Grand Vizier in Egypt.

Joseph had two dreams [Genesis 37]. In the first dream, Joseph dreamt that he was binding sheaves of wheat in the fields when suddenly his sheaf rose up and stood upright while his brothers' sheaves gathered around his and bowed down to it [Genesis 37:5-7]. When he shared the dream with his brothers, they hated him for it because the literal interpretation was that he would reign over them (which as we know is what eventually happened). In Joseph's second dream [Genesis 37:9-11], he saw the sun and moon and eleven stars bowing down to him. This time he told his father as well as his brothers and Jacob told him off for even suggesting that they would all bow down to him. However, whilst his brothers expressed their hatred and jealousy, Jacob dwelt on the dream and its meaning.

All the prophets in the Bible relied on revelation from the Holy Spirit to share what God had deposited in their hearts; but not everything they said was revelatory, hence the presence of false prophets. One prophet often spoke under the unction of the gift of the Word of Knowledge. Prophet Elisha received revelation of current events from God and had access to information he should not have known about. There is an account in the Bible where Elisha was revealing to the King of Israel what his adversary the King of Syria was plotting in private [2 Kings 6:8-12]. As a result of Elisha's intelligence, the King of Israel's life was spared on many occasions. The King of Syria began to suspect that he had a spy in the midst of his counsellors and began to interrogate them. But one of the Syrian king's servants clarified that the culprit was Elisha who was sharing with the King of Israel everything the Syrian king discussed in the privacy of his bedchamber. Elisha did not live in Syria and so the only way he could have known what he shared with the King of Israel was by way of revelation – the word of Knowledge.

When the King heard about Elisha's involvement, he sent a large army of men and chariots to abduct him [2 Kings 13-17]. At the time, Elisha was in the City of Dothan and the army surrounded the city sealing all means of escape. Elisha's servant seeing the threat panicked and cried out to him asking what they should do. Elisha however asked him not to fear for those who were with them were more than the army that had come to arrest them. Then Elisha prayed that God would open his servant's eyes that he might see, and immediately the servant saw that the mountains were full of horses and chariots of fire all around Elisha. This was God's divine protection which Elisha was aware of, but his servant could not see due to his limitations.

Jesus Christ never shared anything without it coming from the place of revelation. In one account, He was on His way to the house of Jairus, a ruler of the local synagogue, whose daughter was lying ill at the point of death [Mark 5:21-43] when people came from Jairus' house to announce that his daughter was dead and advised him not to bother Jesus any further. However, Jesus asked Jairus not to be afraid but only believe. On arrival at the house, He bypassed the mourners and informed them that the girl was only sleeping but they laughed at him scornfully. So, Jesus shut them out of the house and then taking the child's parents and His disciples into the girl's room, He took her by the hand and asked her to arise. Immediately, the girl rose up and began to walk about to the amazement of those around. Jesus had a perspective that flowed from His connectivity to heaven and the counsel of the Holy Spirit. When others saw death in the natural realm and confessed it, He on the other hand perceived life and so spoke it. This is the work of faith.

56

Leaving your comfort zone

Faith is all about leaving your comfort zone. Our comfort zone is our place of convenience. It is familiar and reassuring to its long-term residents who are in no hurry to vacate it. However, to enlightened observers it is restrictive and disempowering, providing shelter for stagnation and mediocrity. Today, it has become part of the mainstream to speak about stepping out of your comfort zone and pursuing new or risky opportunities. Motivational speakers thrive on what has now become a well-worn cliché having wrung every last ounce of lucrative juice out of it. However, for our context it is all about stepping out by faith.

God never created comfort zones; these are manmade. Comfort zones provide certainty and suppress the risk appetite. Residents robustly defend their right to reside in these zones and rarely venture outdoors. They justify their right to remain within the zone, peddling a strategy of self-preservation, but never encountering faith. They refuse to raise their heads over the imaginary parapet, held hostage behind the bars of vain imaginations, that produce strongholds in the mind. Those who cleave to their comfort zones will almost certainly never fulfil their destiny unless they have a change of heart. God's will is rarely, if ever, fulfilled within comfort zones.

One who was well acquainted with the detriments of a comfort zone was Abraham who lived within his family community until he was summoned by God to get out of it. We have explored bits of his biography elsewhere in this book but the key points to consider here are (i)

Abraham's strong loyalty to family; (ii) his devotion to his barren wife; (iii) his acceptance of mediocrity; and (iv) his poor self-image. God however called him out of obscurity, mediocrity, barrenness, and ignorance into prominence, excellence, fruitfulness, and insight [Genesis 12:1-3].

Abraham was advanced in age when he received the summons and was already established in the family culture, religion, and business. His family were from a place called Ur of the Chaldees region believed to be in Mesopotamia. The family practised idolatry like many others in the region and were believed to be traders in livestock and other goods. They had a tradition of remaining in the homestead living in extended family groupings. This explains why Abraham would still be living with his father and nephew well into late middle age. The Bible records that he was seventy-five years old when he left Haran in the land of Canaan [Genesis 12:4] which means he was probably well into his sixties when he left Ur of the Chaldees. The pattern of life indicates communities built around large households and even after Abraham married, he brought his wife Sarah into the extended family. There was nothing overtly wrong with the lifestyle other than the fact that it was Abraham's comfort zone. It was the familiar; what he was used to.

If Abraham had not heeded the voice of God and stepped out of the known into the unknown, he would never have fulfilled his place in history. There probably would have been no nation of Israel as we know it and his incredible journey of faith which has inspired hundreds of millions over the years would never have been recorded.

When God called him out of that familiarity, he did not completely obey. Such was the strength of his family ties that he carried along his father and nephew even though God had called him to leave the family behind. The Bible says he was called alone [Isaiah 51:2], this is why his father died along the way at Haran [Genesis 11:32] and he was forced to part company with his nephew for the sake of peace [Genesis 13:8]. When God calls us to step out of our comfort zones by faith, He calls us to do so alone because it is a very personal experience. It is not a communal or group experience because faith is a very personal experience.

When a young man named Elisha was anointed by Prophet Elijah, he quit his career and followed the man of God [1 Kings 19:20-21]. Elisha was a successful farmer who ploughed people's farmlands for a living with the aid of twelve pairs of oxen – this was a large plough (twenty-four cows) and most likely used for large fields. He was engaged in his profession when the Prophet placed his mantle on the young man's shoulders which was the means of transfer. Elisha recognising the summons quickly abandoned his oxen and ran after the prophet. On catching up with him Elisha sought permission to go and bid farewell to his parents before following the prophet. But Elijah downplayed the event and told Elisha to go back. However, Elisha went back and slaughtered his oxen then cooked the meat with the broken wooden ploughs. He served the meat to the people within his community and thereafter he followed Elijah becoming his servant. Like Abraham, Elisha was called to leave the familiar and step out by faith and he did so in spectacular fashion. By slaughtering the oxen and burning the ploughs, Elisha was closing the door to his old life. He could never return to that way of life ever again.

When Jesus called His disciples, they all left their careers and livelihoods behind them and followed Him [Matthew 19:27; Luke 18:28]. They left their families and friends and detached themselves from the familiar and stepped out into the unknown. Although they left one community for another, they had each been called individually. Their faith was not great, but it was enough to get them out of their comfort zones. It is one thing to hear the call but another to obey it. For those who hear and obey the rewards are great.

57

Jumping without a parachute

Faith is jumping without a parachute. In the ordinary scheme of things, nobody jumps without a parachute. Imagine you're in a plane flying thousands of feet above the earth's surface and then suddenly felt the urge to jump out of the plane without first strapping on a parachute. This is what faith is like. It doesn't conduct endless due diligence sessions to determine the likelihood of survival from a jump at thirty thousand feet without a parachute, it just jumps. In most communities that sort of behaviour would be deemed reckless and attract widespread condemnation. But in the Church, for those who walk by faith this is meant to be the norm.

Jumping without a parachute is a matter of trust. Faith is not scared of heights. It just trusts. Fear on the other hand is evidence of the absence of trust. When we give in to fear we start looking for a parachute. Fear never jumps without a parachute, if at all. However, jumping with a parachute is incomplete obedience. Jumping without a parachute is not an act of self-will; it is an act of obedience. It is our response to the summons of the Holy Spirit. If we were confident that there were angels waiting to catch us, we would most likely jump. So why don't we? Because of fear.

In one of the most profound accounts in scripture, Satan invites Jesus to jump off the pinnacle of the temple [Matthew 4:5-7]. In the encounter, Satan challenges Christ to prove that He is the Son of God by throwing Himself down from the temple. The tempter then quotes scripture [Psalm 91: 11-12] telling Jesus that God would give His angels charge concerning His safety and that they would bear Him up in their hands to prevent Him from dashing His foot against a stone. This was an invitation for Christ to jump without a parachute. However, Christ resisted the temptation by reminding the tempter that he should not tempt the Lord his God [Deuteronomy 6:16]. Had Christ succumbed to the temptation He would have played into Satan's hands. The tempter's objective was to get Christ to act in obedience to him rather than the prompting of the Holy Spirit. That would have been a sin. Every child of God should only obey the voice of the Holy Spirit. Apart from the fact that Christ would have been jumping in the flesh – to prove a point, He would have lost His righteous status and the sinless nature required for the fulfilment of His assignment on the cross. There was a lot at stake and Jesus was mindful of this.

The parachute represents something of safety that we cling to instead of God. When the rich young ruler approached Christ seeking to know what he must do to earn eternal life, he had no idea that he would be told to jump without a parachute [Luke 18:18-25]. His parachute was his wealth and he had obeyed God's commands whilst clinging firmly to his parachute. Christ effectively tells him to jump without a parachute, but he departed in sorrow because he was not prepared to do so without his parachute. From the moment you jump without a parachute, you are losing your life. Jesus makes clear that whoever tries to save their life will lose it but that whoever intentionally loses their life shall save it [Luke 17:20-21].

The problem with parachutes is that they prevent us from losing our earthly lives and fully crossing over to the new life. The person who clings to a parachute has never learnt to totally depend on God. With them, it is always God and something else, never just God alone. God and career; God and wealth; God and social network etc. Yet, He calls us to that place of total dependency. He makes clear that no-one can serve two masters without hating one and loving the other. We may think we are loyal to God but our refusal to let go of the parachute reveals our lack of trust in Him.

When jumping, the most important objective is a safe landing. It might not be a soft landing, but we all desire it to be a safe one. So, a broken ankle is not desirable because having landed, our mobility is impaired. The idea is to land and serve – land in a way that doesn't impair your capacity for service. The reason being that jumping without a parachute is ultimately about service and others are almost always the beneficiaries of our bravery. It takes bravery to jump without a parachute and the righteous are as bold as a lion [Proverbs 28:1]. To ensure that we remain safe enough to carry on serving, we have a guarantee of God's protection. The Bible makes clear that the eternal God is our refuge, and underneath are His everlasting arms [Deuteronomy 33:27]. His everlasting arms are there not only to catch us but to drive away our adversary from before us because the devil who seeks to steal, kill, and destroy is always waiting on standby to thwart our leap of faith.

Apostle Peter, Jesus' most exuberant disciple was famous for jumping without a parachute. He was a man of faith regardless of his bloopers and propensity for putting his foot in his mouth. For instance, Peter was the only one of Christ's disciples to physically walk on water. He had a hunger for the things of the spirit despite his character flaws and that zeal was often rewarded. Those who jump without parachutes also experience fear on occasion and Peter's denial of Christ is a prime example.

When Peter decided to follow the arresting party, who had taken hold of Jesus, Peter was jumping without a parachute. Although Peter jumped without a parachute, he was not led by the Holy Spirit but rather by his zeal. When he jumped on this occasion he landed badly and twisted his ankle – for this reason he was not able to continue with service for a season. He even considered returning to his less than stellar career as a fisherman which initially became pear shaped until Christ intervened. However, his love for Christ facilitated his restoration and elevation.

Those who jump without a parachute are those whose obedience is immediate. They receive an instruction to jump, verify its source and then jump. We can think of the example of Abraham who was called to sacrifice his son Isaac to God and rose early in the morning to execute God's command. He believed that even if he killed his son, God was able to bring him back to life. He literally killed his son before God intervened. By his actions he had jumped without a parachute but landed safely because he trusted God. I pray that we may emulate his example of faith and jump without a parachute so that we too may experience the benefits of landing safely.

58

Not assessing circumstances from the facts

Faith is not assessing circumstances from the facts. When we assess the quality of our lives from the facts we disconnect from God's perspective. God never sees our lives through the lens of facts because He knows from His omniscient perch that facts are subject to change. Facts are never constant; if they were, we would have no history.

When Elijah discovered he had a death warrant on his life, he panicked and fled into the wilderness terrified of what Queen Jezebel would do to him for having the effrontery to murder her prophets 1 Kings 19:1- 4. He despaired of life and prayed for death to take over as he did not consider himself any better than his forebears. This was a man who had just summoned the presence of God in such a mighty way, calling down fire from heaven to burn a sacrifice placed in a water-filled trench. He was also the one who orchestrated the demise of four hundred and fifty prophets of the pagan god Baal and then prayed for rain to fall after a three-and-a-half-year drought. In torrential rain, he outran a horse drawn chariot – something impossible in the ordinary state of affairs. [1 Kings 18:21-41]. Elijah had experienced the presence of God and possessed a fearsome reputation even amongst his adversaries. But, in his weary state he fled from a threat of death forgetting about the God who had been working through him.

Elijah's example is not unusual, as many of us have a tendency to view our lives through the lens of the facts. This same proclivity was responsible for the Children of Israel's forty years of aimless wandering in the wilderness. The people forgot the God who had rescued them from Egypt with a mighty hand, inflicting exacting conditions on their enemies through gruesome plagues; they forgot how He had parted the Red Sea and created a dry pathway for them to walk along. They grumbled any time they were thirsty and even though He addressed their hunger with manna they disdained it and craved for meat, such as they had eaten in Egypt. The people were ungrateful and constantly viewed their lives through the lens of the facts [Exodus 16:1-36; 17:1-7; Numbers 11:4-33]. Was the wilderness inhospitable? Yes it was, but God sustained them in an environment where no person dwelt, or man passed through [Jeremiah 2:6]. Because they viewed life through the facts, when their leaders were sent to spy the Promised Land, they came back with a negative report based on their facts-based perspective. They said the land was indeed good with lots going for it but the inhabitants of the land were too strong for them to dislodge and so it would be impossible for them to occupy [Numbers 13:17-33]. Therefore, God was upset with them and caused them to wander about for forty years – a year for each day they had spent assessing the Promised Land [Numbers 14: 28-34].

The facts are always misleading, and this is why we are instructed not to walk by sight [2 Corinthians 5:7]. Our five senses represent our sight in this context. The sight of Jesus on the cross was a moment of victory for the gloating Pharisees and religious rulers [Matthew 27: 39-43; Mark15:29-31; Luke 23:35]. They saw their enemy defeated and dying and celebrated his demise. Little did they know that on the cross Jesus obtained for us the greatest victory in all of humanity. On the cross, He was victorious [2 Corinthians 2:6-8]. Had they known what manner of victory was coming their way, they would not have crucified Christ. However, they were blindsided by their hatred and bitterness and restricted by their five senses. The one who was the object of their loathing was the very one sent to save them from God's wrath on all humanity, but they did not realise this. They thought they had killed Him without realising that they were playing into the hand of God.

How many times are we blindsided by the facts? King Saul was anointed to be king of Israel but never fully embraced the opportunity to walk by faith and not by sight. During a ferocious battle with the Philistine army, Saul encountered a problem [1 Samuel 13:5-15. The adversary was far greater in size and more advanced technologically. Saul's army was minuscule by comparison. The sight of the Philistines caused the soldiers within Saul's army to panic, and many went into hiding. Believing that death was inevitable and seeing that Samuel the Priest's arrival was delayed, Saul took it upon himself to step into the office of the Priest and offered a burnt offering. But as soon as he finished offering the sacrifice Samuel turned up and berated him for breaking God's command – only priests could perform the offering of a sacrifice. It was a holy activity. What was Saul's real crime? He had been deceived by the facts into disobeying God. By allowing fear and desperation to govern his actions, he destroyed his destiny.

God gave us the Holy Spirit so that we would not be wholly governed by our five senses. As we meditate on God's word, we find ourselves developing a different perspective. When Paul urges us not to be conformed to this world but to be transformed by the renewing of our minds he is saying that we should not function by our five senses alone. It is absolutely critical, because the things of God cannot be received by a person limited to their five senses because they are foolishness to him, neither can he discern them because they are spiritually discerned [1 Corinthians 2:14]. But we have the spirit and so can discern things spiritually and know the mind of God through the gateway of revelation [1 Corinthians 2:12 and 2:16]. When we are in the spirit we will not be constrained to a one-dimensional perspective.

59

Diligence in spite of results

Faith is diligence in spite of results. Faith is not primarily about successful results or outcomes; faith is about commitment. What are you committed to? What cause demands all your attention and investment? Faith does not run out of steam just because a particular desired outcome has not been achieved. Faith carries on regardless of results because it has become a way of life. In fact, faith is a lifestyle not an activity or an event [Habakkuk 2:4; Romans 1:17; Galatians 3:11 Hebrews 10:38].

The Bible teaches that without faith it is impossible to receive anything from God and that those who come to Him must believe that He is and that He rewards those who diligently seek after Him [Hebrews 11:6]. Diligently seeking Him is the key to obtaining a desired outcome from God even though this is not the bedrock of faith. So how do we diligently seek Him? We do so by seeking (and acting on) His will. How do we know His will? We know His will through His word and the revelation we receive from His Holy Spirit. As we meditate on His word (something I have reiterated throughout this book) we gather insight and that in turn yields revelation of His will [Psalm 119:130]. God's word yields light.

The challenge of faith however is that despite our best efforts and good intentions we may often not receive an outcome we desire. The Bible is clear that many of the heroes of faith we read about never received what they were expectant for [Hebrews 11:13]. Many of them died in faith, having not received the promises, but having seen them in the distant future they were persuaded of their reality and possessed them. Some of us may struggle with this because we have probably believed or been taught that faith always yields the outcome and results we desire. The most popular scripture at the root of that belief is Mark 9:23. This passage assures us that if we can believe, all things are possible to them who believe. Another scripture that some latch on to is Mark 11:24 which teaches that whatsoever things we desire when we pray, we should believe that we have received them, and we shall have them. For those with red letter Bibles, these words will be in red because they are the words of Jesus Christ, and their truth is indisputable.

However, these have to be understood in the context of God's sovereignty. To put it another way, is what you believe or trust God to do for you in line with His will for your life? Are you praying in line with His will? Apostle John clarifies this point when he says we should have confidence that when we pray in accordance with His will He hears us and if we know that He has heard us then we know for sure that we have received the subject matter of our prayer [1 John 5:14-15]. Why is it important to know the will of God for you when you pray? It is so that you don't pray and exercise faith for something you may never receive. God says that His thoughts are not ours and His ways are not ours; as far as heaven is above the earth that is the distance by which His thoughts are above ours [Isaiah 55:8-9]. This speaks about the chasm between the spiritual and earth realms.

Now I need to make a distinction between a situation where we diligently act on a perceived promise of God without seeing results (because we are not praying in His will) and one where we are diligently acting on a promise that we know is from God but do not receive a favourable outcome. The distinction is simple. When we pray and act on a conviction that is not linked to God's will we are acting on our imagination. We imagine what God's will is and then act on it without verification. Just because we believe that we are acting on a promise from God does not mean we are. Apostle Paul says the devil disguises himself as an angel of light [2 Corinthians 11:14] and we know from his encounter with Christ in the wilderness that he knows scripture and often quotes it out of context. There are many false prophets out there prophesying falsehoods and leading many astray. The only way to be absolutely sure that we are diligently acting on God's will, is by meditating on scripture and feeding our spirit man within. The stronger our spirit is the greater our capacity to discern between the voice of the devil and the voice of God [Hebrews 5:12-14].

Now I distinguish this from the scenario where we are diligently acting on a promise that we are confident is from God but still do not receive the desired outcome. The reason for this is the sovereignty of God. What is the sovereignty of God? It is the will of God which He often does not reveal to us. He says that the things which are revealed are for us but the things that are not revealed are for God [Deuteronomy 29:29]. There are secrets that God has reserved for Himself and unless He reveals them, we will never discover them. This is perhaps the dilemma of science. But we are assured that God does reveal secrets to those who find favour with Him [Psalm 25:14; Colossians 1:26; and Ephesians 3:5].

However, under the umbrella of God's sovereignty also lies His timing for the fulfilment of promises. For the prophetic promises that are not meant for us alone, but the wider community, God will only bring them to pass at the appointed time when everyone can partake [Hebrews 11:39-40]. For instance, Abraham was promised that he would be a Father of Many Nations (which includes the Gentile nations), but he never witnessed this event in his lifetime. This is because Christ had to be born, die and resurrect before that event, and the birth of Christ was for an appointed time. That is why Jesus said rather controversially that Abraham rejoiced to see the day of His birth and ministry [John 8:56]. He saw it by faith and was glad even though he never witnessed it in his earthly lifetime.

So how does one remain diligent despite the results? We remain diligent by acting on what has been revealed to us by God in the place of meditation or authentic prophetic unction. Not every desire we have comes from God and not every promise in our heads is from him. Not every preacher or evangelist is speaking the truth. When Apostle John calls us to test the spirits [1 John 4:1-6], he is asking us to verify the source of our conviction. Where are those voices in our head coming from? Is it God or the devil? We can only ever be sure by meditating on God's word.

60

Craving what no man can provide

Faith is craving what no man can provide. Humanity is limited to the scope of authority that God has permitted it. From the moment Adam and Eve lost their divine authority to the moment Jesus Christ restored access to that authority by His death and resurrection, humanity has been limited. In Christ there is less limitation, but we find expression for our authority through submission to the Holy Spirit even as Christ did during His earthly ministry. When God observed a global community galvanising their collective will, talents, and ability to build a tower that would reach to the heavens, He acknowledged that where humans are united nothing is impossible for them [Genesis 11: 6-9]. However, despite their decadent unity built on the depraved platform of arrogance, God was still able to intervene and establish His will.

Whatever is impossible with man is possible with God [Luke 18:27]. There is something that only God can give or achieve. Despite man's resilience and creativity which has yielded astounding achievements in the fields of science and technology, man is still limited. Man cannot pass certain boundaries and achieve certain feats. In this vein, there are gifts that man will never possess except God grants them to him. Only two men in this life have ever walked unaided on water without sinking – Jesus Christ and Simon Peter, His disciple. Only one woman has ever conceived without the introduction of a man's semen to fertilise an ovary either in her womb or via IVF – Mary the surrogate mother of Jesus. How many ninety-year-old women have given birth to their first child? Only one woman – Sarah. How many centenarians have successfully impregnated a ninety-year-old woman? Only one man ever did – Abraham. Who knows anyone that has brought water forth from a rock just by striking it with a staff? Only one man ever did – Moses. No magic or occultist practises can ever replicate these things.

During the last days of Israel's captivity in Egypt, when God unleashed plague after plague against the Egyptian people, the magicians and occultist practitioners in that city tried to replicate the plagues. They did succeed up to a point, but only because God permitted them most likely to boost their false sense of accomplishment and foolish pride. So, they were able to turn their staffs into serpents (although Aaron's serpent swallowed theirs) [Exodus 7:11-12]; they were able to with their enchantments turn water into blood [Exodus 7:22] and they were also able to bring forth frogs from the rivers [Exodus 8:7]. However, when God through Moses miraculously produced lice which settled on both humans and animals the magicians tried and failed to replicate the plague. With their tails between their legs, they admitted to Pharaoh that the plagues were the "finger of God" [Exodus 8:18-19].

Apostle Paul makes clear that the things of God cannot be received by the naturally minded (fallen) person because they are foolishness to them neither can that person discern these things because they are spiritually discerned [1 Corinthians 2:14]. There are gifts that only God can give and those who know Him crave them.

The blessings of God make a person prosper and He adds no sorrow with them [Proverbs 10:22]. God's blessings come with a guarantee. The origin of the gifts however is spiritual not earthly. So even though the blessings may manifest in the natural, their origin is in the unseen spiritual realm. As the Bible makes clear, God has blessed us with all spiritual blessings in heavenly places in Christ [Ephesians 1:3]. The Bible describes some of these blessings. For instance, we are told that he who finds a wife finds a good thing and obtains favour from God [Proverbs 18:22]. Elsewhere, we are taught that houses and riches are the inheritance left by parents but that a good wife was of the Lord [Proverbs 19:14]. Therefore, a good marriage is a gift from God. What about contentment? Apostle Paul spoke about learning to be content regardless of whatever state he found himself in because he was able to do all things through Christ who strengthened him [Philippians 4:11-13]. Therefore, contentment is a gift and God is the one who bestows it. Many today do not have contentment despite the abundance of their possessions.

God says he will keep in perfect peace any person whose mind is focussed on Him [Isaiah 26:3]. Therefore, peace is a gift from God. There are many in our world who are not enjoying peace no matter how much they possess or how much they have accomplished. Apostle Paul speaks about a peace that surpasses all (*human*) understanding [Philippians 4:6-7]. We cannot buy this brand of peace. We also learn that children are a gift of the Lord and that the fruit of the womb is His reward [Psalm 127:3]. This is because it is God who grants fertility [Psalm 113:9]. And some may point out that many unbelievers who don't know God or accept Jesus Christ are enjoying fertility whilst many Christians are experiencing barrenness. However, this is a wrong comparator because God showers His mercy and goodness on the Christian and the unbeliever [Matthew

5:45]. I believe that every child born is a gift from God who blesses people with fertility.

Joy is another gift from God which many in our communities lack. Many are happy but fewer are full of joy. Real joy comes from God – it is a gift. When the joy of the Lord is our strength [Nehemiah 8:10], we find ourselves able to rise above depression and other maladies that plague the human soul. Jesus in his epic prayer to God regarding the welfare of the disciples and the church to come desired that we might have His joy fulfilled in ourselves [John 17:13].

The gifts of the Lord make us more prosperous and add no sorrow to us. These are the true gifts that we should crave because everyone desires them but only a few experience them.

61

Being encouraged in the midst of discouragement

Being encouraged in the midst of discouragement is the evidence of faith. We get upset with personal circumstances whether financial, professional, or emotional, and this produces discouragement which in turn could foster psychological challenges. We get discouraged when we either don't hit our goals or achieve our desires as quickly as we want. Most discouragement is a by-product of competition or comparison. Regardless of how the discouragement was produced, it impacts us.

Real faith thrives in atmospheres where discouragement is present. Something prompts a person of faith to look beyond the discouragement and embrace hope. We are told that against hope Abraham believed in hope or to put it another way when having hope was pointless, Abraham still chose to hope [Romans 4:18]. What was Abraham believing in hope for and why was his situation so hopeless? Well, he was almost a hundred years old, and his wife was almost ninety. He was infertile and impotent, and she was barren. Abraham's hope was in the promise of God that he would become a father of many nations. God had shown him the twinkling sparkles in the night sky and said that his children would be as numerous as the stars. Abraham believed this and clung firmly to it in the midst of his discouraging circumstance.

The Bible gives an account of an episode in the life of David where he had every reason to be discouraged [1 Samuel 30]. David was in exile at the time hiding from

King Saul who had issued a death warrant for his execution. David returned to his camp located in a place called Ziklag to find that the Amalekites had invaded the place, burnt it to the ground, and taken all the women captives. None of the people were murdered but the women and children were gone. David and the men with him began to mourn their situation, weeping until they had no more strength to cry. David had lost his wives and was equally discouraged by the state of affairs. However, his discouragement escalated to great distress when his men turned on him and wanted to stone him to death for their loss. However, the Bible tells us that David encouraged himself in the Lord his God. At a time when he should have caved in and begun to beg for his life, he sought the Lord through Abiathar his priest and enquired what he should do [1 Samuel 30:6-9]. Suffice to say David was asked to pursue his adversaries and promised that he would recover all that he had lost.

When David and his men set off in pursuit, they had no idea which direction the invaders had gone and were most likely relying on their trackers to navigate the way. Along the way David experienced a setback. Two hundred of his men – a third of his army – were too fatigued to continue the journey but rather than giving in to discouragement, David showed compassion and left them to recuperate at a Brook called Besor. Continuing in his pursuit with four hundred men, they chanced upon an Egyptian man who had been left to die in the wilderness by the invaders because he had fallen ill. David showed great compassion again in caring for the man, giving him food and drink without realising that he was the key to their problem.

When the Egyptian had recovered his strength, he informed them that he was the servant of an Amalekite who had been part of the army that burnt Ziklag. After extracting a promise from David that they would neither kill him nor hand him over to his master, he showed them the way to the invaders' camp. David and his men defeated the Amalekites, catching them unawares whilst they were celebrating, and they recovered everything they lost and more besides. By encouraging Himself in the Lord, David was able to overcome the weight of discouragement and focus. That focus enabled him to receive assurance from God and form a strategy.

In the heat of a discouraging situation, the wisest thing we can do if we are able is to focus on God. For those who struggle to focus on God in the midst of discouragement it may because they have not cultivated a close enough relationship with God. David had the advantage of a close relationship with God which gave him an outlet when the situation escalated. Discouragement can sometimes produce a fight or flight situation where a person either lashes out with misplaced aggression or sinks into depression. David did not however succumb to either of these negative outcomes because of his relationship with God.

The evidence of who we are on the inside will always show up in the middle of a discouraging situation. Like the children of Israel who resorted to mob psychology every time they encountered a challenge, those who pay lip service to their Christianity sag like an empty sack in the face of discouragement. Apostle Paul and his protégé Silas could have given in to discouragement when they were beaten up and thrown into prison for casting a demon out of a fortune teller [Acts 16:18-34]. But rather than give in to discouragement, at midnight they started to sing praises to God in the hearing of the other prisoners. Their divine exuberance caused an earthquake that shook off their chains and caused the prison doors to be flung open.

There is a grace-filled reaction that produces a miraculous outcome in the middle of discouragement, and we should learn to embrace it. This is the brand of faith we are speaking about.

62

Setting goals not based on ability

Faith is setting goals not based on ability. For clarity, we are concerned here with the sort of matters that require strategic planning. Brushing your teeth or cooking a meal for instance does not require faith. An example of our context would include life goals such as career and marriage. Faith does not conduct a skills or talent audit before it sets its targets and puts in place the plans to achieve them. Faith's strategy does not assess its strengths but rather it focuses on its aspirations. If setting goals is largely reliant on natural ability and experience, then the very spiritual concept of faith is redundant. The premise of faith is that those who live by it do not rely solely on their own ability, talent, and skills. The challenge for the gifted and talented is resisting the temptation to achieve their goals without total or large reliance on self.

The important thing to remember regardless of our IQ scores is that every gift and talent was bestowed by God; even our physical appearances are determined by Him. For those who believe, this is sobering as it robs them of a legitimate basis for pride. For those who are in denial, it doesn't change the truth of that position. God is the author of life, and all its colours and shades are determined by Him. By faith we believe that the worlds were created by God so that the things that can be perceived with five senses were created from things that cannot be seen by them [Hebrews 11:3]. Those who embark on goal setting without reference to God have no guarantees but those who place God at the centre of their plans rarely if ever miss a beat.

The Bible says that God has chosen the foolish things of this world to confound the wise and the weak things of the world to confound the things which are deemed to be mighty, and the base (despised) things of the world to undermine and terminate the things which are of value [1 Corinthians 1:27-29]. Why does He bypass the things the world rates highly? He does it so that no person should have a basis for glorifying themselves in His presence. The Bible makes clear that if anyone wishes to find a basis for self-glorification it should be in the fact that they know the Lord and have a relationship with Him [Jeremiah 9:24; 1 Corinthians 1:31].

God cautions the wise man against glorying in his wisdom, or the mighty man glorying in his might, or the rich man glorying in his riches. God emphatically states that if they must glory at all it should be that they understand and know Him – the Lord who exercises loving-kindness, justice, and righteousness in the earth [Jeremiah 9:23-24]. That means He is not obliged to assist anyone who seeks to accomplish anything in their own limited wisdom, strength, or wealth. Even if He summons us to serve Him, we have to approach the task from the place of faith and total dependency on the leading of His Holy Spirit. This is why in the leadership of the Church God often chooses people who may be unremarkable by worldly standards. Such people are usually humble and willingly submit to His plans.

The Bible is clear that whatever is not done from the place of faith is sin [Romans 14:23]. Sin in this context is anything that originates from and relies totally on fallen humanity. Because all of us have sinned and fallen far short of God's standard we are not qualified to deliver His projects in our own strength. In a similar vein, any plans we make for our lives which are wholly reliant on our understanding or ability will never be endorsed or relied on by him.

There was a Governor in Judah named Zerubbabel who was charged with the restoration of the temple after the nation's return from exile [Haggai 1:14]. As the project got underway, Zerubbabel was coming under pressure from the enormity of the task. So, God sent the prophet Zechariah a word for him to focus his mind and in fact it is a word for all of us who are fellow labourers in His vineyard. The prophet said that it was not by his might nor by his power that the project would be completed, but by God's Holy Spirit [Zechariah 4:6-10]. God promised to remove every obstacle (mountain) obstructing him and assured him that even as he had laid the foundations of the building, he would complete it. These must have been refreshing words for the governor who was possibly at his wits end.

Having begun with much zeal, as the Lord stirred up a desire within him, the governor was getting fatigued. As some of us do, he had defaulted to his own strength and capacity to solve problems with the project and was running out of steam because of his limited range of options. The timely reminder was a wakeup call. We should never become too caught up in trying to achieve things for God in our own strength.

Moses found himself in a similar position where he was trying to do too much by his own ability [Exodus 18:13-27]. Moses was judging every dispute that the Children of Israel brought to him without assistance. His father-in-law Jethro observed him judging the disputes from morning to evening and queried why he was administering in this way. Jethro warned Moses that if he carried on in that way he would not survive. He was then advised to delegate to different tiers of administrators from the tribes to deal with the disputes, men who feared God, who were truthful and were not covetous. These men were to be trained-up to support him in his role and ease his burden. Only the hardest matters would be referred to Moses for adjudication. Moses listened and obeyed because he recognised that it was God speaking to him through his father-in-law. The administrative arrangement was orchestrated by God and was for the purpose of preserving his life. If he had continued administering according to his own ability he would have died prematurely from exhaustion as has sadly happened to some in the church.

King Solomon urges us to trust in the Lord with all our hearts and not to lean on our own understanding, in all our ways we are called to acknowledge Him, and He will direct our paths [Proverbs 3:5-6].

63

Wanting to quit but showing up anyway

Faith is often revealed in a desire to quit but showing up anyway. How many times have we wanted to throw in the towel but showed up anyway and carried on with the task ahead of us? Everything tells us we are wasting our time and to quit whilst we have the opportunity, but we still carry on; this is the heartbeat of faith. At its core is integrity. We often hear people speak about hope in relation to faith but not much about integrity. Without integrity, hope is worthless. The smallest denomination of faith is a mustard seed faith, and this always contains integrity and a modicum of hope. So propelled by integrity, packaged in our mustard seed faith, we soldier on. We may feel like quitting because of a sense of inadequacy but remain submitted to God.

Gideon was a reluctant agent of change. He deplored the oppressive conditions in his country – Israel – where the Midianites invaded at will and took what they wanted [Judges 6:1-8]. This was the era of the Judges where everyone in Israel did whatever they pleased. Joshua, the warrior-leader, who had brought them into the Promised Land and driven out the inhabitants was long dead as were those men of his generation who recalled God's deliverance on the field of battle. The population of Israel comprised a generation born long after the conquest of Canaan who had turned to idolatry and other forms of pagan worship. They no longer served God and their disobedience had separated them from His presence. In this climate, God summoned Gideon a young field worker who was aggrieved about the state of affairs, but too fearful to contemplate confronting the oppression.

Gideon was enlisted by an angel who called him a mighty man of valour and informed him that he had been chosen by God to liberate Israel. Prior to the issuance of this summons, Gideon had been bemoaning the fate of Israel and recounting all the stories he had heard about God's deliverance in the past. If Gideon lived in our day and age, he would have been part of the chorus querying where God was after each terrorist attack, or natural disaster, or outbreak of civil war, claimed multiple lives. But when he was called to take up arms, he began to give excuses as to why he was not the most qualified for the task because his family was the poorest in his community (Manasseh) and he was the least in his father's house. Many years earlier, Moses had disqualified himself as being fit to lead the Children of Israel out of captivity, because he didn't consider himself to be eloquent due to a speech impediment. He had previously revealed his lack of confidence, claiming that the people would not believe him if he said God had sent him. Like Gideon he was full of excuses, but like Gideon he went, even though his mind was telling him to quit.

Gideon was given the assurance that God would be with him and that he would defeat the Midianite army and deliver Israel. However, when he was given his first task to destroy the altar of the pagan god Baal, he was so afraid he executed the task under the cover of darkness [Judges 6:16-32]. Gideon obeyed God but a part of him wanted to quit if he had the chance. What committed him to the task was his integrity and this is what I believe God had seen in him.

Gideon remained reluctant for most of this Biblical account, but God did not give him an easy exit because with Him there is no plan B. Gideon obediently gathered an army together, though his mind was still riddled with insecurity, and he would gladly have quit if given the opportunity. When Gideon put God to the test with the fleece of wool, God was patient with him. He knew that Gideon required further assurance because it was a daunting task to face the fearsome hordes of Midian. When Gideon requested that there should be dew on the fleece only but the ground beneath dry, God complied. When he tested God further and asked for the fleece of wool to be dry but the ground beneath it wet, God again complied [Judges 6:36-40].

Gideon went through the motions of assembling the army. When God said that thirty-two thousand men was too large a number for Him to use, Gideon suppressed his apprehension and obeyed God's instructions reducing the army through a process of elimination till he was left with three hundred men [Judges 7:1-7]. Recognising Gideon's suppressed apprehension, God got him to carry out reconnaissance in the Midianites' camp where he overheard one of the Midianites narrating the details of a dream to another. The other gave an interpretation of the dream which indicated that Gideon would be victorious over them. Hearing the dream's interpretation, vanquished the residues of fear, and he went courageously into battle. With God's help he overcame the invaders.

Despite the cowardice and fearfulness, God who looks at the heart of men saw something within Gideon that he could use [1 Samuel 16:7]. God knew that Gideon was faithful and that he could be used regardless of any weaknesses. God's strength is always made perfect in our weakness and His grace is sufficient for us [2 Corinthians 12:9]. The Gideon we subsequently see overcoming one hundred and thirty-five thousand Midianites with only three hundred men is a completely different man from the one who was approached by the angel at the start of the account.

64

Sowing all you have

Faith is sowing all you have. This is probably the most challenging faith principle because it hits where it hurts. The purse strings have always been a target when faith is tested because it's an open secret that our relationship with our money and possessions determines to an extent the nature of our relationship with God.

Jesus was emphatic when He said that we should not accumulate treasure in the earth where moths consume and rust destroys, and thieves can break in and steal. He said instead that we should store our treasure in heaven where it is not exposed to consumption or destruction or theft, because where our treasure is there also will our hearts be [Matthew 6:19-21]. This has been a very controversial piece because it conflicts with the principles of capitalism which encourages the opposite. Jesus was plain about His position. If we store treasure in the earth our hearts will be fixed on earthly things but if we store treasure in heaven our hearts will be fixed on spiritual things. Faith is concerned with the spiritual and so if we are hooked on earthly things we are not walking by faith.

The encounter between Jesus and the rich young ruler has been documented elsewhere in this book but bears repeating because of its relevance to our context [Luke 18:18-30]. The rich young ruler approached Jesus seeking clarity on what he needed to do to inherit eternal life. Like many religious observers he genuinely wanted to secure his eternal destiny. In response, Jesus told him to keep the commandments such as not committing adultery, not killing, not stealing, not bearing false witness and that he should honour his father and mother. However, the young man said he had kept all these commandments from his youth, which was in itself impressive from a religious standpoint because of the discipline involved. But then Jesus pointed out to his chagrin that there was one thing he lacked.

One can imagine at this stage the young man's ears pricking-up in earnest expectation for another commandment to keep. But, when Jesus told him to sell all he had and give to the poor so that he could have treasure in heaven and thereafter to follow Him, the man became sorrowful. Why was he sorrowful? The Bible says he was mournful because he was very rich. The thought of having to give away all his wealth dismayed him, and he instantly revealed where his heart was. Jesus made it clear that it was virtually impossible for a rich man whose heart was fixed on earthly things to make it to the Kingdom of God. The rich young ruler was not walking by faith even though he had kept all the commandments. He was religious and had no appreciation of spiritual things. Anyone who has no appreciation for spiritual things will struggle to live a victorious Christian life. Apostle John says we are not to love the world or the things that are in the world [1 John 2:15-17]; the reason being that if we love the world the love of the father is not in us. Those who prioritise storing treasure on earth love the world and will find it impossible to walk by faith, and without faith it is impossible to please God [Hebrews 11:6].

Jesus makes clear that a person's life does not consist in the abundance of their possessions [Luke 12:15] because that is the essence of greed. The King James Version uses the word "covetousness". The alarm bells about amassing wealth are all over scripture particularly in the New Testament of the Bible. God has nothing against the rich, but He is against those who horde wealth and are not rich towards Him [Luke 12:16-21].

How can a rich person be rich (generous) towards God? The Bible makes clear that those who give to the poor lend to God and He will reward them for their generosity [Proverbs 19:17]. God also promises that those who give to the poor shall not lack 'Proverbs 28:27]. Jesus was not inviting the rich young ruler to a life of penury but was giving him an opportunity to be delivered from the stranglehold his wealth had over him. Call it deliverance if you will. By giving it away the rich young ruler would have lent to God and stored up treasure in heaven where his account was in the red. In addition, God would have rewarded him on earth with the things money cannot buy. This principle explains why the rich man who bypassed Lazarus every day without addressing the poor man's needs went to hell [Luke 16:19-31].

Those folk who refuse to show kindness to the poor are not walking by faith and because of this they do not store up treasure in heaven. By way of contrast one can read about a tax collector named Zacchaeus who repented of his corrupt behaviour. When Jesus visited his home, he gave back four times what he had illegally obtained and then gave away half of his wealth to the poor [Luke 19:1-10]. Jesus observed that salvation had come to his house because of his actions – repenting of storing up treasure on earth and his fraudulent practices. Zacchaeus had discovered the secret that those whom God blesses with capacity for making wealth are supposed to be treasurers in His kingdom. They make wealth and then sow it in accordance with His instructions to them about the areas of need. They do not horde it.

We can also read the account of the widow who gave two mites in the temple treasury which was all she possessed. Jesus upon seeing her remarked excitedly that she had given more than all the others who had given from their wealth. The widow had given out of her penury what amounted to all she had to live on [Luke 12:1-4].

With the abundant evidence cautioning against us amassing wealth on earth, why would anyone wish to risk it? It is clear that one whose treasure is in the earth has their heart fixed on earthly things and that such a person cannot be walking by faith.

65

Walking in authority regardless of earthly status

Faith is walking in authority regardless of earthly status. There are two types of authority – spiritual and natural. The brand of authority we are concerned about is spiritual authority. Spiritual authority has absolutely nothing to do with earthly status. Natural or material authority has to do with one's status in society and level of influence but does not spill over to the spiritual. Spiritual authority on the other hand has to do with one's status in the spiritual realm and it spills over into the earth realm. By way of analogy, you could be a CEO of a corporation with a lot of clout but be subject to a janitor in that same organisation who is walking in spiritual authority. The CEO earns more and exercises more authority in the natural, but the janitor has access to the throne room of God where in prayer he or she can by faith establish the will of God in the corporation.

Jesus sent out seventy of his disciples in pairs of two to visit every town and city He planned to visit eventually [Luke 10:1- 20]. He instructed them to go forth as lambs amongst wolves and told them not to carry a purse, or cloak or footwear and they were not to greet anyone along the way. Presumably, Jesus did not want them to be discussing their assignment with those who might either derail them or oppose their presence in those towns. By not carrying any purse or cloak or shoes they were walking by faith, trusting that God would supply all their needs along the way. They were told to accept whatever hospitality was extended to them and where they were rejected to shake the dust of that city off their shoes. They were asked to heal the sick and share the message about the arrival of the Kingdom of God.

The seventy returned from the mission fields rejoicing at the level of authority they had been operating in and recounting how demons were subject to them in Jesus' name. However, Jesus informed them that He had observed Satan fall like lightning from heaven. Jesus then said He had given them authority to tread on serpents and scorpions and over all the power of the enemy and that nothing would by any means harm them. Then Jesus stated emphatically that rather than rejoicing about demons submitting to them they should rather rejoice that their names were written in heaven.

This piece of scripture brings clarity to the whole concept of authority. The difference between power and authority is that power acts in its own capacity but authority acts in another person's capacity. Jesus sent them out with authority in His name. He gave them clear directions regarding their assignment and then sent them out. They obviously followed His instructions to the letter and returned rejoicing. They had subdued demonic forces in Jesus' name and cast them out of the lives of tormented people in the name above all names in this world and the world to come. God never gave humanity spiritual *power* but rather He gave them spiritual *authority* to act in His name. This authority when exercised unleashed God's power. The reason for this was to ensure that humanity (Adam and Eve) had access to the highest power in the universe so that they could govern the earth realm and all the creatures in it.

Jesus clarified that He had witnessed Satan fall like lightning from heaven. He was most likely making the point that Satan was operating at a lower level spiritually in the earth realm [Job 2:1-2] and that when God's authority is exercised by us, all the demons under Satan's command are neutralised. That authority is triggered when a Christian stands on the word of God and declares it in the name of Jesus Christ. Jesus however emphasised that even though He had observed Satan fall like lightning out of heaven, He was not rejoicing over that fact. What mattered ultimately was that a person's name was written in heaven (in the Lamb's Book of Life). Jesus knew that many who used His name to perform mighty miracles would not make it to heaven [Matthew 7:21-23] which defeated the whole purpose of their earthly ministry.

The seventy disciples were elevated to the level of Jesus Christ in spiritual matters just by using His name. By having their names written in heaven, Jesus was now able to bestow authority on them that went beyond their specific assignment and its geographical confines. They could now trample on the power of the enemy that transferred poison whether through a bite or a sting with the confidence that in doing so they were protected from harm.

The authority of the church is captured in Apostle Paul's epistle to the Ephesian church [Ephesians 1:19-23; and 2:4-10]. Apostle Paul describes how the power of God raised Christ from the dead and set Him at God's right hand in the heavenly places far above all principality and power and might and dominion and every name that is named in this world and the one to come. Paul also explains that God has put all things under Christ's feet and made Him the head over the church which is His body. This means that the church is also elevated to God's right hand in heavenly places above all principality, power, might, and dominion of Satan. Paul subsequently confirms this when he teaches that we have been raised together with Christ and seated together in heavenly places in Christ Jesus. This is the root of our authority in Christ and when we were saved by grace through our faith, we instantly had access to it by virtue of our location in Christ.

This means that as a Christian when we exercise our authority we are walking by faith. The authority has one purpose and that is to subdue Satan and his hordes of fallen angels who unleash demonic forces against humanity. We need to exercise this authority as we battle against these forces because we do not wage war against human beings but against principalities, against powers, against rulers of darkness of this world and spiritual wickedness in high places [Ephesians 6:12]. Without authority we cannot exercise dominion over these forces of darkness and our weapons are useless. We need authority to underpin our prayers and declarations so that we get results.

If we are walking in our authority, Satan and his demons are subject to us in Jesus' name. We will decree a thing and it shall be established and will also bind demons and loose captives from their strongholds. Christians cannot walk by faith without exercising authority because they will be undermined. It has nothing to do with earthly status but spiritual status and since the spiritual realm is superior, we will exert influence in the world.

66

Believing things will change

Faith believes things will change. There is a grippy kind of hope that clings tenaciously to the truth, refusing to let go even when the surface becomes slippery. Truth becomes slippery when our ability to hold on is challenged. Faith never lets go because of the expectation that things will change. Faith knows that the facts must change like the seasons of the year, and it invests a lot of energy in holding on. The enemy's strategy is to project the future based on today. So, he will project a mindset that says the current facts will never change and that the future will be bleak. This promotes fear and apprehension wrecking the ozone layer of righteousness. Faith in God's promises, however, overthrows this mindset by dwelling on and confessing the relevant word.

The classic definition of faith informs us that faith is the substance of things hoped for, the evidence of things not seen [Hebrews 11:1]. The substance of things hoped for refers to a degree of tangibility – where what is hoped for is as good as real. Although there is no physical or visible evidence, there is a belief that establishes the truth of it. Buoyed by the weight of expectation we start to act on what we believe. The facts, no matter how deep-rooted they may seem, are considered temporal and subject to the winds of change blowing in your direction from the throne of God. Those who know God do not accept the facts when they don't line-up with God's word no matter how harrowing they are.

It was a fact that the inhabitants of Canaan lived in fortified cities and that the sons of Anak who occupied part of the territory were giants. Neither Joshua nor Caleb disputed this. What they did dispute was that the fortified cities and the giants could prevent them from possessing the inheritance God had given to Israel [Numbers 13: 28-30]. Twelve spies went into the Promised Land to survey it for forty days; they all saw that it was a land flowing with milk and honey, very fertile and well-endowed. But the fear in the hearts of ten of them prevented them from visualising themselves living in the land instead of the current inhabitants. In other words, the ten apprehensive spies could never see themselves living in the Promised Land because of their perspective on the facts. Joshua and Caleb however saw the potential for the facts to change because of the presence of God with Israel.

Believing that facts will change starts off by visualising the altered state of affairs and then doing everything to bring about the change you see. Joshua and Caleb were ready to instantly possess the land because they saw themselves in possession. They believed that if God delighted in them, He would bring them into it and give it to them. They however cautioned the people against rebelling against the Lord or fearing the people in the land because they were an easy defenceless target and Israel had God on their side [Numbers 14:9]. Joshua and Caleb believed that if God was for them nothing could be against them [Romans 8:31]. Fact-altering Faith builds its conviction on the word of God and His presence with those who believe it.

The people however believed the negative report provided by the ten spies and wanted to stone Joshua and Caleb for trying to give them hope. This reaction reflects the mindset of the people within the camp [Numbers 14:10]. The only thing that prevented them from carrying out their cowardly plan was the arrival of God's presence in the camp. The people were clearly not prepared to fight for what God had already given to them. They did not see themselves in possession and it is a spiritual principle that anything you cannot see, you cannot have [Mark 11:23-24]. This is because believing that change will happen is dependent on your capacity to see the change happen. We know the rest of the story; the rebels all died in the wilderness but only Joshua and Caleb from that generation physically possessed an inheritance in the Promised Land.

When Elisha informed the King of Israel that Israel's economy would change within twenty-four hours, he presented the people with a challenge [2 Kings 6:24-25]. With Samaria besieged by the Syrian army and a great famine within the city, people had turned to cannibalism. There was a food crisis of epic proportions, and nobody had a solution. Even if they could have imported food into the country through some secret passageway undiscovered by the invaders, it would be nigh on impossible for the price of food to drop significantly to be (a) affordable and (b) available to all. However, Elisha received a word from God which he shared with the king and his court. He informed them that by the same time the following day, a measure of flour would be sold for a shekel and two measures of barley for a shekel. Then one of the king's counsellors sneeringly responded that even if God made windows in heaven to pour down food it would be impossible. Elisha however informed him that the facts would change but that he wouldn't partake of the blessings associated with it [2 Kings 7:1-2].

Change did happen; God did intervene and break-up the siege; food did drop in price because the invaders fled away leaving all their food supplies and livestock behind;

the prices of a measure of fine flour and two measures of barley dropped to a shekel; and just as Elisha prophesied, the pessimistic counsellor who did not believe that the facts could change did not partake of the blessing. He was trying to organise the crowds, but in the process got trampled upon and died.

Faith believes that facts can change because it can visualise the change it is expectant for before it happens. As the two scriptural accounts demonstrate, those who do not respond by faith to God's promises will not benefit from the change when it occurs. I cannot think of a stronger argument for a person intentionally deciding to walk by faith.

67

An eternal mindset

Faith is an eternal mindset. This is an inalienable fact. Faith looks beyond time. Actually, faith transcends time. Faith is a superior spiritual law to time because it either bypasses or transcends it when seeking results. Those who walk by faith operate a mindset that is not limited by time. This is because time does not exist in the spiritual realm – the domain faith derives from and operates in. Time connotes process, but faith produces results not tainted by time.

A good example of this can be found in the scriptural account of the wedding at Cana where Jesus Christ performed His first miracle on record by turning water into wine [John 2:1-11]. Jesus had been invited to a marriage ceremony at a town called Cana in Galilee. In attendance were some of His disciples and His mother. At some point the wine ran out and this was brought to His attention by His mother. Despite Jesus making clear that His hour (time for performing miracles) had not yet come, Mary told the servants to do whatever He said.

Now, I have often pondered over this point, wondering how Mary knew that Jesus was in a position to do something about the lack of wine at the wedding. My conclusion was that Jesus had probably already been performing such miracles behind closed doors and she had witnessed them. It is more than likely that she was a beneficiary of such miracles. There may have been times when due to shortage of food or drink within his home Jesus had replenished the expended supply miraculously. At such times, he may have cautioned them not to share this with anyone and the family had kept his confidence.

In a sense Jesus felt exposed by His mother's request but knew that he had to honour His mother regardless of His own feelings on the issue.

The account reveals that there were six stone water jars of the sort used by Jews for ceremonial purification, each one holding between twenty and thirty gallons. Jesus then asked the servants at the ceremony to fill them with water and they complied filling each one to the brim. On completing this task, He then told them to scoop water from the water jars and present it to the master of the banquet. The servants who had faithfully filled the water jars must have been surprised at this request, as they knew that it was water. After all they had fetched it themselves. None of them had a precedent regarding turning water into wine and so their action of taking the cup of water to the master of the banquet was an act of faith.

The servants presented the cup of water to the master of the banquet who after sipping its contents immediately summoned the bridegroom. He informed the bridegroom that it was the best wine he had ever tasted and then asked why he had chosen to bring out the superior wine last rather than serving it from the outset. The tradition was to serve the best wine first and the lower quality wine when men were sufficiently inebriated so that they couldn't taste the difference. However, the bridegroom was accused of reversing the tradition. The clueless groom is unlikely to have understood the background to the situation and would have subsequently tasted the wine for himself.

To understand the relevance of the miracle one needs to look at the timeline in the miraculous process; there was no timeline. The water was turned into wine instantly. To create wine there is a process. You need the right type of grapes, wine yeast, processed water, sweeteners, and other additives. The grapes need to be crushed with bare feet or a wine press, then the juice must be mixed with yeast, water, and the sweeteners; after this the resulting mixture must be left to ferment for a while (often weeks) depending. The fermented liquid must then be put through various processes to siphon the wine, and this must be bottled and then stored for a while. The very best wine is left for many years until it achieves its optimum quality. The whole process described above according to ancient standards would have taken over a year for basic – average quality wine and more than a decade for the very best wine.

In addressing the shortage of wine, Jesus bypassed the process and time involved in producing the very best wine. In an instant He converted ordinary water possibly fetched from a well into wine. The only way He could have achieved this was with the power of the Holy Spirit. In other words, this was a supernatural act which reveals the superiority of faith over the law of time. They are both spiritual laws but there is a hierarchy of laws and faith is the superior one. Every time Jesus performed a miracle where there was an instant outcome, He was transcending time. The fact that He performed these miracles in the presence of His disciples means that He wanted them to understand the necessity of operating by faith. We are told to walk by faith and not by sight for a reason. Walking by faith is a lifestyle where we look beyond the restrictions of time into the eternal realm. The answers we are looking for come from that realm and invade the earth realm. Because it is impossible to please God without faith [Hebrews 11:6], we cultivate an eternal mindset.

68

Thanksgiving at a graveside

Faith is thanksgiving at a graveside. Death is a period for mourning the deceased and for subdued or silent empathy with the loved ones of the dearly departed. When we lose someone close to us there is an indescribable pain that many feel and a sense of finality. Some struggle with denial and refuse to speak in the past tense about the deceased as in their minds the person is still very much alive. However, what you rarely if ever find is thanksgiving at a graveside. Thanksgiving at a graveside is an anomaly in mainstream society and could be perceived as insensitive or callous. Yet for those who walk by faith thanksgiving at a graveside can often be the evidence of the faith they have in God's promises.

Thanksgiving by itself is an act of worship. Apostle Paul tells us in all things to give thanks for this is the will of God in Christ Jesus concerning us [1 Thessalonians 5:18]. Apostle Paul says that we are to rejoice evermore, pray without ceasing, and in everything give thanks. The attitude we display flows from what is on the inside. How can we rejoice forevermore and give thanks in all things when we are sorrowful? Paul is not calling us to a place of thanksgiving at the graveside of the deceased but rather he is addressing the attitude we are called to have regardless of what situation we find ourselves in. We can mourn and yet give thanks because we understand that the graveside is not the end.

To understand the full context, we need to explore the premise of Paul's remarks. Earlier on in the same message, Paul says that we shouldn't be ignorant concerning those believers who have passed on (or are asleep) so that we don't grieve or sorrow like those who have no hope [1 Thessalonians 4:13-15]. Paul goes on to clarify that since we believe that Jesus died and rose again, even so those who believed in Him and passed on will be brought back by God along with Jesus. So, we understand that Paul is telling us to give thanks in all things because of God's greater plan for those who believe in Jesus Christ His son. Paul makes these remarks in the context of eternal life in Christ; he is speaking about the attitude those who know they're saved should have. Paul is also advocating a mindset that focuses on eternity and catches a glimpse of God's ultimate plan for humanity which extends beyond the grave.

When a believer passes away, Paul says they are only asleep; this is because as we know death has lost its sting and can no longer detain the believer in Christ whose sins have been forgiven and whose soul is reconciled with God the father. Yes, we miss the loved one but if they had been reconciled to God through Jesus Christ, we are still able to give thanks that they are not going to everlasting damnation and separation from Him. Thanksgiving at a graveside would be apt when we consider the thief who repented of his sins whilst being crucified next to Jesus [Luke 23:39-43].

This death bed conversion showcases the incredible measure of grace that God unleashes on us every day. Here we have a thief who was condemned to death for his numerous crimes. He has been crucified next to another criminal and a righteous man who had only preached a message of love and gone about doing good works. The thief recognises Jesus and knows within his heart that Jesus does not belong on a cross like him. So, when the other criminal started berating Jesus asking Him to prove that He was Christ by saving himself and them, the reflective criminal intervenes. Why? Well, as he sees it, himself and the other criminal were guilty of their crimes and deserving of the punishment meted out to them. Jesus on the other hand is innocent in his view. Having silenced the other criminal, he turns to Jesus and asks to be remembered when Jesus arrived in His kingdom. With what little strength He could muster, Jesus assures him that even before the end of the day the criminal would be with Him in paradise. We are not told the criminal's reaction to this assurance, but I am certain that he would have heaved a huge sigh of relief and begun to give thanks with his dying breath.

When we know where we are going, we do not fear death. The fact of death is never pleasant for those we leave behind. But if they are believers like us and know where we are going when we breathe our last, there is an expectation that they should be in thanksgiving. Death for these ones is a transition from illusion to reality.

This is also the attitude we must retain even when something we cherish dies. It might be a dream, a possession, or a favourable circumstance. When something we value dies, as Christians we give thanks. Job understood this, and when the devil murdered all his children and robbed him of his wealth, Job remarked that he came into the world naked and that he would die naked. He clarified that God had given him the children and wealth, but also permitted for them to be taken away and then he blessed the name of the Lord [Job 1:13-22]. To a casual observer this would appear to be an act of lunacy. Some may even say that he was psychologically unbalanced as a result of the losses he had suffered. His reaction was not natural. However, it is clear that he believed in the righteous nature of God and refused to give in to the lie that He was the architect of his sorrow.

I also believe that his praise was made at his children's gravesides as he surveyed their bodies being laid to rest. In that respect, we can argue that Job was walking by faith despite his insurmountable loss. This is an attitude worthy of emulation.

69

Taking a step

Faith is taking a step. The most difficult step is the first one; thereafter every other step is incremental. The first step is nerve racking because it requires the greatest courage to start something than continue with it. The great unknown that lies beyond the first step triggers apprehension as we wrestle with uncertainty. Once we have taken the first step without encountering all the fears we envisaged at the outset, we find it easier to carry on doing what we started even though we have no guarantees regarding the journey ahead.

When Peter walked on water, it began with him taking a step [Matthew 22-32]. After the miracle of feeding the five thousand men and their families, Jesus sent His disciples on ahead in a boat whilst He dispersed the multitude. Thereafter, He went to pray on a mountain where He could not be disrupted. However, the boat carrying His disciples encountered some rough weather and made very little progress due to the strong winds. In the early hours of the morning, Jesus went out to join them, walking on the surface of the water as if it were made of solid matter. When His disciples saw Him in the gloom, they exclaimed that it was a ghost and panicked. But Jesus calmed them down asking them to take courage and identified Himself.

Unconvinced, Peter immediately called out saying that if it was really Him, he should summon him to come to Him on the water. When Jesus called Peter to come, Peter got out of the boat and took a step. Peter took a step when the other disciples were huddling together in the boat. It was a daunting step, but he took it. He stepped out of his comfort zone and from the dubious safety in numbers that it afforded and headed into uncharted territory. Peter walked on water towards Jesus and the other disciples in the boat watched from their places of safety. With each step he took Peter would have grown in confidence, until from taking baby steps he was striding about on the water's surface to the amazement of his colleagues. As long as Peter kept his eyes on Jesus, he was safe and confident.

When the wind became boisterous and increased in intensity, he panicked and took his eyes off Jesus. Why did the wind become stronger? I speculate that it was probably Satan who engineered it. Having studied humanity for long enough the devil knew exactly what distractions to bring to make Peter switch to his default mode. The moment Peter took his eyes off Jesus he began to sink, and the reality of death kicked in. As he sank, he cried out to Jesus to save him and immediately Jesus stretched across a hand and caught him. Unsurprisingly, the first thing Jesus said was that Peter was a person of little faith, and then asked Peter why he doubted. With Jesus holding Peter's hand they walked back together and once they got onboard the vessel the strong winds stopped. It was clearly a manufactured scenario designed to test their faith but the only one who got any score was Peter who had the courage to take a step and leave the vessel.

Taking a step requires faith. Although in Peter's case this was assessed as being little faith, it was better than no faith which is the assessment on the other disciples. We have already explored the account of the four lepers outside the gates of Samaria who took a step. Motivated by the need to address their hunger they took a step towards the enemies' camp knowing that death very likely awaited them but grasping on to a small glimmer of hope that their fate would not be so morbid [2 Kings 7:3-8]. Once they had taken the first step, the other steps gradually became easier. What they did not know was that the Prophet Elisha had prophesied that food prices within Samaria would drop drastically by the following day. They also did not know that as they took those steps, God was amplifying the sound of them in the hearing of the invading force surrounding Samaria, so that each step sounded like a multitude of chariots, horses, and soldiers. God used the lepers' steps to drive fear into the hearts of the Syrian Army causing them to flee and abandon their camp and everything in it. It all began with a step.

We have also examined the life of David, in particular his encounter with the giant of Gath named Goliath. When everyone within the camp of Israel's armed forces cowered in fear, at the sight of the giant and the sound of his voice, David was indignant and defiant [1 Samuel 17:21-51]. David was more concerned with verifying the reward that would be given to the person who killed the giant. When King Saul who was the tallest man in Israel was taking refuge in his tent, afraid to confront the giant, David was preparing to take a step. David's step gave God the opportunity to give Israel a great victory over the Philistines and their gigantic hero. David killed Goliath in a matter of seconds, restoring dignity to Israel, but it all began with a step.

When Ruth took a step beyond the borders of Moab, she had no idea what God was going to do with her solidarity [Ruth 1-4]. She was taking a seismic risk going to Bethlehem, a city that was hostile to people from Moab. All she was doing was accompanying Naomi her mother-in-law, who had lost everything in Moab, to ensure that the woman was supported and cared for.

Ruth resisted the call for her to return home and instead took a step in the direction of Bethlehem. How could Ruth have known that God was going to use her step to establish the lineage of Jesus Christ? She was a widow and vulnerable just like her mother-in-law, but she was prepared to take a step even if it cost her, her life.

Those who take a step have a particular mindset that is not afraid of taking risk. In the domain of faith, taking a step and taking risk go hand in hand. Standing still was not an option for Ruth, David, and the four lepers, neither was retreating. The only option for them was to take a step; not a backward step but a forward one. This is faith.

70

Calling out the result before the game

Faith is calling out the result before the game even starts. There is a difference between being able to predict the outcome and actually knowing it. Professional betting and gambling (used interchangeably) rely heavily on predictions based on complex algorithms that analyse patterns of conduct, behaviour, prevailing conditions, past performance and so on to assess outcomes. Generally speaking, however, most gambling is the product of guess work. It is a rule of thumb with no underpinning scientific analysis or empirical evidence. In Christianity, prophetic words often predict future outcomes even before the preceding event has occurred. Prophecy is God-given insight into the future. It is not guesswork.

To walk by faith is to have access to the results of a game that has not yet been played. It is the ability to see into the future with unerring accuracy and call out results that you couldn't have known about without some form of insider dealing. In fact, that is what it is – it is insider dealing. You know stuff that you couldn't possibly have known except it was revealed to you. However, how can we distinguish those who claim to have some prophetic gift from those who are the real deal?

The Bible has a lot to say on this issue. Moses, one of the greatest prophets in the Bible, in fact someone who could be referred to as the pre-eminent prophet because of his contribution to Bible history and prophecy, explains the surest way to know who a prophet is. According to Moses, when a prophet speaks in the name of the Lord if what the prophet proclaims in the name of the Lord does not come to pass, such a prophet has spoken presumptuously [Deuteronomy 18:21-22]. Now some prophets will speak of things to come in the distant future even when their viewpoint is discredited.

Jeremiah was one such prophet. Prior to God sending Israel and Judah into exile in Babylon for seventy years due to their rebellion, he sent various prophets to warn them; one of these prophets was Jeremiah. When the people refused to repent, and the time for exile drew near, Jeremiah prophesied that God had placed the nation under the dominion of King Nebuchadnezzar of Babylon [Jeremiah 27:6-11]. Through Jeremiah, God warned the people about listening to prophets who were prophesying that Israel would not serve the king of Babylon because those prophets were lying to them. God made clear that the prophets were not sent by Him and that they were lying in His name [Jeremiah 27:14-15]. One of the false prophets was a man named Hananiah who prophesied that rather than Israel going into exile, God was going to break the yoke of King Nebuchadnezzar from the neck of all the nations within the space of two years [Jeremiah 28:9-17]. Jeremiah however told Hananiah that he had not been sent by God and because he was making the people trust in a lie, he would die that same year. Later that year Hananiah died. It was not coincidence. As we know, the Israelites were ultimately exiled just as Jeremiah had predicted.

Before David confronted Goliath [1 Samuel 17] he informed King Saul that he would kill him. King Saul admired his courage but didn't give him much of a chance because of the facts. The facts indicated that David would be killed. When Goliath saw David, he was even more scornful and felt insulted by Israel's choice of a warrior to fight him. Goliath was looking forward to a tournament with a formidable opponent that he could subdue and kill. His reputation depended on it. If the fight was too easy, he wouldn't be commended or rewarded by his Philistine masters. The Bible records that he despised David and cursed him by his gods. In the hope of intimidating him, Goliath boasted that he would give David's flesh to the birds and wild animals.

Undeterred, David stood his ground and prophesied that the Lord would deliver Goliath into his hands. David declared that he would strike Goliath down and cut off his head and then give the carcasses of the Philistine army to the birds and the wild animals. This was a battle of words by two men whose confidence was in their abilities. Goliath's confidence was in his size, experience, and training but David's was in his God-given anointing. We all know the outcome of that encounter. David had correctly called out the results before the fight because of his relationship with God.

Because the future is a mystery that belongs to God, those who are in close relationship with Him are granted insight [Psalm 25:14]. That insight is prophetic. The substance of prophecy is revelation. Now this gift of prophecy is not reserved for a select few but it is expected that anyone who walks by faith will operate to some extent in that gift. Apostle Paul urges us to aspire for the prophetic gift because the one who prophesies edifies the church [1 Corinthians 14:1-4]. How do we edify the church? By bringing spiritual enlightenment to our fellowship so that we function in the way God intended. Jesus operated in the prophetic and we are called to function like him [Romans 8:29]. When God calls us to arise and shine in the midst of the pervading darkness [Isaiah 60] in the world around us, prophecy is a critical element in our capacity to glow.

The way Paul describes the operation of the gift makes clear that it is one that God bestows generously on the body of believers known as the church. It is not merely desirable but essential; a must-have rather than a would like-to-have.

At the very least each of us who claim to walk by faith should be our own prophet. We should not seek a prophet to speak into our lives but should speak prophetically over our own lives in accordance with God's revelation to us. As God reveals things to us about ourselves, we should declare them prophetically – calling those things which are not as though they actually exist [Romans 4:17]. Beyond ourselves we should yearn to speak prophetically into the lives of others as the Holy Spirit directs. God speaks to us through revelation which often comes as a result of meditation on His word or from just spending time in His presence praying. It is through this medium that He shares with us the results of a game that we have not yet participated in as a means of boosting our faith. If we know the outcome, we are less bothered about the game or our opponents. We can simply focus on performing to the best of our ability in the assurance that God has already given us victory.

True faith calls out the results before the game because it operates in the realm of the prophetic.

71

Sleeping in a storm

Faith is sleeping in a storm. To sleep in a storm is a reflection of one's state of mind. Most people will pace around in a storm either trying to figure out a solution or giving in to worry and anxiety about the outcome. A storm represents disruption and potential devastation. It may be short-lived or long-lasting, and it is designed to alter a state of affairs.

The exodus of the children of Israel from Egypt was the fulfilment of a prophecy that was over 400 years old [Genesis 15:13-14]. God had promised Abraham that his descendants would be delivered from their captivity in a foreign nation and come out with great possessions. As the children of Israel eventually marched out of Egypt after 430 years, laden with the wealth they had dispossessed their former masters of, it was a moment of joy [Exodus 12:31-42]. However, that joy was soon turned to sorrow and panic when the newly liberated people found out that Pharaoh and his army were in pursuit [Exodus 14]. On one side of their camp was the Red Sea and on the other the Egyptian army. Terror gripped the people as they visualised the horror awaiting them, and many turned on Moses blaming him for bringing them out to the desert to die. However, Moses did not lose his focus.

As the army approached, Moses urged them to be still and that they would see the deliverance of God. He assured them that the Egyptians pursing them would soon be no more because God would fight for them. As we know, God made a way for them through the Red Sea – a humanly impossible solution. Because Moses trusted in God, he was able to be His instrument of deliverance. At the end of the day, the Red Sea created a way of escape for the Israelites but became a grave for the pursuing Egyptians. In the midst of a storm, we need to be still to see God's deliverance. Being still is sleeping or being calm. Speaking through Prophet Isaiah [Isaiah 30:15], God cautioned the Israelites for seeking the help of the Egyptians in their hour of need. What He said applies to us. God said that if we come back to Him, we will be saved and by remaining calm and trusting in Him we will be strong. This is our response to storms.

This reaction is aptly captured by Jesus during His earthly ministry [Mark 4:35-41]. Jesus and His disciples were crossing a body of water in a boat with the intention of getting to the other side. At the start of the journey, as with all journeys of this nature, the waters were calm and gave no hint of what lay ahead. And then suddenly with no warning they strayed into turbulent weather – a great storm comprising of strong winds and chaotic waves. The combination of powerful forces rocked the boat about until it was filled with water. Emphatically, the Bible records that Jesus was asleep, lying on a pillow, in the boat at the hindermost part. One can only presume that the hindermost part of the boat was the least affected area as it is hard to imagine even Jesus sleeping beneath water. Bearing in mind their training, as fishermen from a fishing community, most of the disciples began to do what any well-trained fisherman would do – bail water. Water seeping into boats was not uncommon and bailing it out was not beyond the realms of expectation. However, I suspect that the more water they bailed out the more that poured in. At last, at their wits end, they went to rouse Jesus from His deep sleep asking if he wasn't worried that they were perishing.

Jesus woke up and possibly yawned and stretched before coolly rebuking the winds and saying to the choppy waters, "Peace, be still." Instantly the strong winds ceased and there was a great calm. As the disciples tried to process what had just occurred, Jesus asked why they were so fearful and wanted to know why they had no faith. In other words, He was asking why they had to wake Him up to do something they could have done themselves if they were walking by faith.

Some believe that the storm was started by God so Jesus could fulfil scripture. Others believe it was a test for the disciples and that Jesus had foreknowledge. Others believe it was the devil attacking them. However, the origin of the storm is less important than our reaction in it. In every storm of life God expects us to respond by faith. Storms come primarily to stretch us. There are many who have died in storms admittedly but often the real test is for those survivors who have to look beyond the tragedy at the big picture [Job 1:1]. When God sends a storm the objective is never to kill us, but to establish His will [Jonah 1:1-16].

To understand how to function in a storm we need to consider the account of Apostle Paul's trip to Rome that was disrupted by a devastating storm triggered by Euroclydon a tempestuous wind [Acts 27]. This was a storm sent to kill Paul and lasted over a fortnight with the ship's crew losing control of the vessel and for many days there was no sign of either the sun or the stars. However, Paul kept his eyes on Jesus and received assurance from an angel of God that he would survive the journey and fulfil his purpose for going to Rome. As he was sharing his vision with the crew and passengers, Paul told them to be cheerful because he had faith in God and believed that it would happen just as He told him. As the Bible confirms, everyone survived that storm and Paul made it to Rome. They lost the ship and all their goods and possessions but there was no loss of life. Those who walk by faith in the midst of a storm enjoy the peace of God regardless of the conditions. They understand that their attitude in it is more important than surviving it.

72

Remaining upbeat even when there is a cloud over your head

Faith is remaining upbeat even when there is a cloud over your head. You have often heard the expression *every cloud has a silver lining*. There are diverse interpretations, but one of the most commonly accepted ones is that difficult seasons or times are like clouds that block the sun. So, clouds merely present a smokescreen to the real situation. The silver lining around the edges of the cloud is an indication that the sun has never stopped shining and once the cloud has passed over, we will again see the sun. As people of faith, we must see clouds as illusory and fix our eyes on Jesus whose glory never stops shining.

All of us can recall a time when we looked at the clouds and believed that the sun had stopped shining over our lives. However, those who manage to keep their eyes on Jesus through the gloom always remain upbeat. The only way of keeping our eyes on Jesus when we have a cloud overhead is by dwelling on His promises. So, in that gloom, the word becomes a lamp unto our feet and a light unto our path. [Psalm 119:105]. We keep our eyes on the word because the Bible instructs us to fix our eyes on Jesus (the word) who is the author and finisher of faith. As no one has seen Jesus face to face, we focus on His word.

Now Jesus Himself instructs us about the attitude to adopt when we have a cloud over our heads. Towards the end of His earthly ministry, Jesus informed His disciples that in the world they would have tribulation but urged them to be of good cheer because He had overcome the world [John 16:33]. Apostle John informs us that whatsoever is born of God overcomes the world and the victory that overcomes the world is our faith. The Apostle then clarifies that those who overcome the world are the ones who believe that Jesus is the Son of God [1 John 5:4-5]. If we know that clouds are not the evidence of defeat but opportunities to conduct victory parades, we will discover the grace to remain upbeat.

Apostle Paul exemplifies the sort of believer who manages to maintain an upbeat attitude regardless of the density of the cloud overhead. Paul's emphatic instruction on the issue is for us to rejoice in the Lord always [Philippians 4:4]. He does not call us to delight in the circumstance but for us to rejoice in the Lord always regardless of what we are facing. How can we delight ourselves in the Lord when we have a thick cloud hovering over our heads? We delight ourselves in Him by dwelling on His promises and assurances. Paul goes on to advise us not to be anxious about anything, but in every situation, we should present our petitions to God with thanksgiving. The apostle promises that if we do this, the peace of God which surpasses all understanding shall guard our hearts and minds in Christ Jesus [Philippians 4:6-7].

Apostle Paul lived what he preached as many will recall from the account of his imprisonment in the city of Philippi [Acts 16:16-34]. Having been beaten-up and thrown into prison along with his protégé Silas for casting out a demon from a soothsayer, Paul refused to let that cloud dampen his mood. Even though they were bruised and in agony from the beating as well as from the stocks fastened around their feet, they began to pray and sing praises to God. Their voices were loud enough to be heard by the other prisoners and this gives some indication of the gusto with which they worshipped. Their upbeat mood had everything to do with where their minds were located. For even though they were in a depressing situation their focus was on God and His promises. This produced an earthquake as God responded to their worship and this in turn led to many conversions within the prison. I am sure we agree that Paul and Silas couldn't have sung praises if their minds were on the situation.

Hannah was barren and tormented [1 Samuel 1]. Childlessness for a married woman who desires to be a mother is like a cloud over her head. I have never met a woman in those circumstances who didn't desire to experience motherhood above all else. I recall a pastor mentioning how his late aunt had never had children and how she confided in him before she died that she would have given anything to experience pregnancy even if it didn't result in the birth of a child. This may sound extreme, but it was her honest desire to experience what many take for granted. So we can appreciate Hannah's dilemma. Taunted by her husband's other wife, Peninnah, because of her barrenness, Hannah was inconsolable. Not even her husband, Elkanah's words of comfort could reassure her.

However, when Hannah received a word from the Priest Eli, her countenance brightened. Eli saw her pouring out her heart to the Lord, and initially thought she was drunk because no audible words escaped her lips, but when she been praying out her great grief and anguish, he said "Go in peace, and may the God of Israel grant you what you have asked of him." That word was enough to alter her mood. The Bible records that she went her way and ate something, and her face was no longer downcast. Was she still barren at this point? Yes, she was. But the word from God made the difference.

Elsewhere in this book, we have discussed the account of Apostle Paul's voyage to Rome and the difficulties he encountered. During the trip, a turbulent wind called Euroclydon hit them creating treacherous conditions that made steering the vessel almost impossible. Surrendering the vessel's navigation to the powerful waves and doing all they could to keep it on course, for many days they saw neither sun nor stars. Faced with the impossibility of the situation, the ship's crew and passengers despaired and lost all hope of being saved. Noting their dismal countenances, Apostle Paul urged them to be of good cheer (cheerful disposition) as there would be no loss of any life even though a shipwreck was awaiting them. Paul clarified that he had had a visitation from an angel assuring him that he would keep his appointment in Rome and that God had promised His protection to everyone onboard the vessel. He again encouraged them to be of good cheer because he believed God and knew that events would occur exactly as God had told him. Noting that the men had abstained from food for over a fortnight, he urged them to eat for the sake of their health. After Paul had given thanks, broken bread, and started eating, the others became of good cheer and also ate.

By keeping his focus on God, Paul was upbeat when there was a cloud over the heads of all the crew and passengers aboard that vessel. Because he was upbeat, he was able to encourage others who in turn became upbeat.

73

Shutting down negative input

Faith is shutting down negative input. Negative input comes in the form of words or imagery that contradicts God's promises. Our ears and eyes are conduits for various sources of information, and they deposit the substance in our minds. However, not everything we hear or see is encouraging which is why we need to be on our guard about what we retain in our minds (hearts). The information we read and see doesn't just drift away and within it are encoded messages like a virus which are programmed to affect our behaviour and wreck our relationship with God. The broadcaster of negative headlines is Satan, and he disseminates his negative reports via his demonic reporters who are also assigned to steal, kill, and destroy. They often wait for us early in the day and before we even open our eyes they have embarked on a campaign of dispensing dark propaganda. Their ultimate objective is to steal the word of God from our hearts, to kill our faith so as to destroy our destiny.

If you wake up and hear a voice in your head comparing your accomplishments with your more prosperous neighbour and then telling you that you are a failure and worthless, that is the agent of darkness assigned to derail you. They tempt you to sin and when you fall for it, they switch roles and start condemning you for being a spiritual let-down and argue why you are not pleasing to God. These demonic minions are the architects of most bouts of depression and the instigators of suicides. We all pray that these voices will go away and stop plaguing us but they're persistent. They accuse God to you and say He doesn't care and then accuse you to

God telling Him why you are not worth the effort [Zechariah 3:1-5; Job 1:9-11, 2:4-5].

So how do you shut down this negative input? Our eyes and ears are gateways for information and unless we place filters before them, we will absorb stuff that is harmful. The world addresses sin from a psychological or psychiatric perspective. So, a person with suicidal ideation is given therapy which may include counselling and medication; the person with addictions is also given therapy and counselling to address this. To an extent these methods bear some results which is why they are still being practised and developed. The methods have become fields of study and created employment for those specialising in those disciplines. However, ultimately, they are ineffective because they are reactionary and do not address the spiritual element of the issue. So, a person can successfully complete a programme but will spend the rest of their lives battling the claw-back from the negative input. Whilst people have been successfully delivered from the consequences of negative input through the power of the Holy Spirit and in the name of Jesus, prevention is always the preferable option.

The ability to shut down negative input comes down to the aforementioned filters which many of us carelessly neglect but which are freely available. Filters are a zero-cost option that will save us grief down the line. These filters are spiritual, and they are found in only one place – God's word. Jesus makes clear that God's word is truth, and His prayer is that we will all be sanctified by it [John 17:17].

Sanctification is about purification. God's word sanctifies us and empowers us to resist the negative input from the devil. Osmosis is a scientific concept often defined in contemporary terms as the process of gradual or subconscious assimilation of knowledge and ideas. This is how the negative input enters in and starts to transform us back into the image of darkness that God delivered us from [Colossians 1:13]. The Apostle Paul says that our minds should be focussed on whatsoever things are true, honest, just, pure, lovely, of good report, virtuous and praiseworthy [Philippians 4:8]. All these things are found in one place – the word of God.

We are called to meditate on the word of God and allow it to renew our minds so that we may be transformed [Romans 12:2]. The word of God is our filter to subject every piece of information to spiritual authentication. The more of God's word we have imbibed through meditation, the more powerful our filters will be when negative information is targeted at our optical and auditory gateways. It has often been said that abstinence is the best way to avoid being infected with the virus contained in negative input, and as commendable as this is, the reality is that many struggle to abstain from the stuff that they desire. Before we even came into this world there were certain negative patterns programmed into our genes. These genes pretty much dictate what we are drawn to auditorily and visually. How many have the willpower to resist the magnetic force exerted by their genes? It is why we have otherwise decent people engaging in secret depravities.

The whole idea of spiritual filters is to create an opposing force in your mind that stands guard in your subconscious but places sentries at your eyes and ears to vet what you expose yourself to. The filters identify all the harmful influences and trigger alarms which place you on notice. The Bible describes Joseph's reaction when invited to have an adulterous affair with his master's wife. [Genesis 39:6-13]. The woman pestered him frequently, but he refused to listen to her, or be with her, and when she eventually cornered him, he fled naked leaving his garment in her hand. Joseph's sharply defined filters were the evidence of a relationship with God built upon the indwelling of God's word. You can contrast this with King David, who was a man after God's heart but had momentarily lapsed in his meditation on God's word when he had an adulterous affair with Bathsheba [2 Samuel 11:1-4].

So, what do we do when negative information sneaks past our filters because they haven't been updated? We repent. Repentance is how we restore our relationship and reinforce our filters. This is what King David did. Thereafter, we resume meditation of the word and don't quit because it's how we receive strength to resist.

The Bible presents the example of the man who is blessed as one who has appropriate filters in place as a result of meditating on the word of God [Psalm 1:1-3]. Such a person we are told does not walk in the counsel of the ungodly, nor stand in the way of sinners, nor sit in the seat of the scornful, because his mind is saturated with the word of God. As a result, everything he does prospers. This is evidence of faith.

74

Recognising and accepting closed doors.

Faith is about recognising and accepting closed doors. The journey of faith, for it is a journey, encompasses closed doors. As much as we desire open doors as a validation of our faith, very often we encounter doors that either slam shut in our face or refuse to respond to our persistent knocking. Learning to recognise and accept closed doors is an emphatic step in our maturity as believers and in our demonstration of faith. Many of us have grown up on a diet of theology that encourages us to ask, seek, and knock [Matthew 7:7-8]. We are assured that if we knock it shall be opened to us. But what do we do when we knock, and the door remains shut?

The Bible makes clear that God controls doors. It says that He opens, and no one can shut, and He shuts, and no one can open [Revelation 3:7]. Therefore, it is important for every believer to know that where closed doors are from Him, it is futile to keep knocking at them. God says that His strength is made perfect in our weakness [2 Corinthians 12:9], and this extends to opening doors; this is because even when we are at our weakest, we are not helpless. God promises that He will set before us an open door which no man can shut if we keep His word and do not deny His name [Revelation 3:8]. So, if we have been keeping His word and have not been denying His name, we can rest easy when a door refuses to open before us.

Recognising and accepting closed doors enables us to eliminate waste; we stop wasting time and energy at closed doors. Hanging around closed doors indefinitely is frustrating. We may be convinced that the door is one that requires our resilience, fortitude, and endurance to open, but if it's a closed one it will be an agonising wait. It is important, however, to be patient just in case it's an open door that requires a season of waiting. The way we know whether a door is open or not is by revelation. It is the work of the Holy Spirit to reveal to us the nature of the doors in front of us. This is why we need to cultivate a close relationship with the Holy Spirit. The voice of God in our ear is our firmest assurance regarding the actions we need to take when confronting a door. Do we stand and keep knocking or do we turn around and walk away without even touching the doorknob?

Joseph, the favoured son of Jacob was sold into slavery in Egypt and ended up as a servant in the house of a man named Potiphar. Falsely accused of attempted rape, he was thrown into prison where his duty was to care for the welfare of other inmates. One day, Pharaoh's butler and baker ended up under his care, having been thrown into prison for some misdemeanour. Both men had dreams and Joseph interpreted their dreams which saw the butler restored to his former post, but the baker executed. Before the butler left prison, Joseph protested his innocence and asked him to put in a good word for him with Pharaoh. The butler however left prison and promptly forgot about Joseph for a space of two years. Two years later, Pharaoh had a dream and the butler recalled Joseph. Joseph was summoned to see Pharaoh and interpreted his dream which resulted in him becoming the number two man in Egypt [Genesis 39; 40; 41]. Now, was the butler a closed door or open door?

The butler was an open door for Joseph, but he got the timing wrong. He knocked in the wrong season.

Sometimes we knock at a door that God intends to open but we do so outside His timing and face frustration when it doesn't yield. There are doors we have knocked at which have remained shut and we have probably given up knocking and walked away but if they are open doors, we will eventually be led back to them in the right season.

King David was anointed by the Prophet Samuel to be the next King over Israel because the current king – Saul had offended God. Following the anointing, David began to perform many audacious feats such as killing a lion and a bear that attacked his father's flocks and then crowning his achievements with the killing of a Philistine giant named Goliath. David was enlisted into Saul's army and fought for Israel, but his popularity soon outgrew Saul's leading to jealousy. Saul tried to kill David several times resulting in David going into exile.

On two separate occasions David had an opportunity to kill King Saul. On the first occasion, Saul went into a cave to relieve himself without knowing that David and some of his men were hiding further back in the cave. David's men urged David to rise up and kill Saul telling him that it was a God given opportunity, but David resisted the temptation because he did not believe that it was God's will for him to kill God's anointed one. David recalled that it was God who had chosen Saul and so David did not take the bait [1 Samuel 24:1-22]. On the second occasion, David was hiding in the wilderness of Ziph when Saul and his men came looking for him. Whilst Saul and his men slept, David came to their camp with one of his men Abishai. On seeing Saul in such a vulnerable position, Abishai informed David that God had given Saul into his hands and urged David to let him slay Saul with his own spear. But David pointed out that no one could slay the Lord's anointed and not be found guilty before God. David said that it was for God to decide the moment and manner of Saul's death but that he would never stretch forth his hand against the Lord's anointed [1 Samuel 26].

On both occasions, David recognised the closed doors and refused to succumb to the devil's temptation. Killing King Saul was not the way that God had opened before him and if he had gone down that route it is possible that he may never have ascended to the throne as Saul's successor. Even if he had become king, he may have found himself embroiled in huge controversy that might have impacted his tenure. However, David recognised and accepted closed doors and did not waste his time with them.

Real faith recognises and accepts closed doors because it knows that God is not the author of confusion [1 Corinthians 14:33]. He is a God of order. He will never lead us to a door He has not opened in that season. This is where having a relationship with the Holy Spirit becomes so critical. With insight, we are not disappointed when doors refuse to open. When our adversary presents a closed door as evidence of our spiritual anaemia, we can fling it back in his face as evidence of our faith.

75

Being still when everything else is mobile

Faith is being still when everything else is mobile. Sometimes it takes great faith to remain still when there is a lot happening around us. The desire to get involved and take control or establish some kind of order is very tempting. However, God may be saying that we should down tools and leave it to Him. At times we may feel that God is not moving as quickly as we desire and become restless, functioning in an observer capacity, but faith empowers us to resist that temptation.

Being still in a spiritual context does not connote inactivity. We might not be involved in tackling the problem, but we may be called to the place of prayer, fasting, praise, or meditating on scripture. All these are activities. Sometimes we may be prompted to engage in all of them. At other times, the instruction for us to be still requires us not to react in line with how we feel on the inside. If we are panicky, stillness requires us not to act on our anxiety or apprehension. If we feel insecure, stillness may require us not to respond to those insecure feelings. The command to be still simply lets us know that this is a battle God will fight on our behalf and that He is moving on our behalf. Scripture is awash with evidence of how God intervenes in our stillness. Being still also enables us to focus on God and not the situation.

We may recall the account in the Bible where the Children of Israel were departing Egypt after over four hundred years in forced servitude and how the Egyptian army pursued them to bring them back [Exodus 14]. The Children of Israel began to panic as soon as they saw the

Egyptian army and they turned on Moses. They bemoaned their fate and accused Moses of leading them out to the wilderness to die. They also said they preferred to go back to Egypt rather than dying in the wilderness [Exodus 14:11-12]. However, Moses told them not to fear but to stand still and see the salvation of the Lord which He would perform in their sight that very day. Moses assured them that the pursuing Egyptians would not be seen again, as God was fighting their battle.

By telling the people to be still, Moses was urging the people not to respond to their impulses or react to how they were feeling. This was a body of people ready to capitulate and submit to the Egyptian army. They were ready to give up on the liberty God had given them and return to captivity. They had begun to see the virtue in being servants to the Egyptians again and seeing no visible way of escape, surrender seemed like the only viable option. As Moses spoke to the people, he was also crying out to God for a solution [Exodus 14:15]. The solution he received required the children of Israel to go forward towards the Red Sea which seemed like an invitation to commit suicide. However, God working through Moses created an escape route for the Children of Israel by parting the Red Sea so that they could walk across on dry ground. God then caused the waters to drown the pursuing Egyptians to reveal Himself as the God who makes a way when there seems to be none [Isaiah 43:19].

When King Jehoshaphat of Judah was confronted with the threat of invasion by a powerful coalition of hostile nations, his immediate reaction was to give in to fear but that drove him to seek God and proclaim a fast throughout the land [2 chronicles 20:1-25]. The whole nation responded to the threat by seeking God. They did not run around helter-skelter trying to respond to the threat by reinforcing their territory. They did not start building walls or gathering an army; they sought God through prayer, fasting, and praise. They reminded God of who He was; His past achievements on their behalf; and His promises to them. They then handed the problem to Him because it was too overwhelming for them [2 Chronicles 20: 6-12]. This is what it means to be still. This is what it means to walk by faith. God responded to their faith by telling them not to be afraid or dismayed because of the proposed invasion because the battle was not their but His. God told them that they would not need to fight in this battle, but they were to stand still and see the salvation of the Lord. We subsequently see Jehoshaphat arrange for a choir to lead the way to the battlefield ahead of the army singing praise to God. And when they began to sing God caused the armies within the coalition to turn on each other until every soldier was dead.

King Hezekiah was in a similar situation to Jehoshaphat in that during his reign over Judah, the Assyrian king – Sennacherib decided to invade the country. The Assyrian king relied heavily on propaganda as part of his battle strategy. He sent a letter to Hezekiah telling him not to trust in God because the gods of other nations had not been able to save them from invasion by the Assyrians [2 Kings 19]. When Hezekiah received the letter from the Assyrians, he presented it before God in the temple. Like Jehoshaphat, Hezekiah reminded God of who He was and then invited Him to get involved. Hezekiah presented the facts about Assyria's track record against other nations whose gods were no gods but the work of men's hands. Hezekiah rounded-up by asking God to deliver the nation out of the hands of the

Assyria so that they may know that there was no God like Him. Hezekiah's prayer caught God's attention and He responded by promising to defend the city and prevent the Assyrian king from setting a foot within it or even shooting an arrow within its boundaries. That same night God sent an angel to destroy one hundred and eighty-five thousand Assyrian soldiers and their king was forced to return to his country where he was murdered by his sons. Again, there was no need for human involvement because God took over the battle. They were still and witnessed God's salvation.

The greatest example of being still in the Bible is reserved for Jesus Christ who became still throughout His trial and execution for our sakes. Prior to Christ's arrest, His disciple Peter cut off the ear of the High priest's servant (Malchus), but Christ restored the man's ear. Christ then made clear that he could have prayed to God for more than twelve legions of angels to rescue Him but if He did, scripture would not be fulfilled. Christ submitted Himself to God's will and was still. Like a lamb led to the slaughter He did not resist arrest or try to escape. He submitted to the unjust process and allowed Himself to be crucified. He could have come down from the cross at any time but chose to hang there so that He could defeat the power of death by dying in our place [Matthew 26:47-75; 27]. To be still sometimes could entail sacrifice as the evidence of our faith in God but ultimately, we will have victory.

76

Believing that the seen was created by the unseen

Faith believes that the seen was created by the unseen. In other words, the invisible is more real than the visible because it emanated from it. A work of creation can never be more real than its source. The source of a thing is the essence of that thing's reality. Put another way, the reality of a thing is embedded in its source. If I appear to be overstating the principle, it's for emphasis. The stance that whatever cannot be perceived by the five senses is not real is made by those who have no access to the unseen realm. Apostle Paul who is one of the leading exponents on this subject says that we do not focus on the things which are seen but on the things which are not seen because the things which are seen are temporary but the things which are not seen are eternal [2 Corinthians 4:18]. A believer fixes their gaze on the unseen realm because this is where eternity dwells. We know that our Promised Land is located within eternity and our desire is to reside there with our Lord and saviour forever.

Therefore, by faith we believe that the worlds were framed by the word of God so that things which are seen were created by things which cannot be seen [Hebrews 11:3]. The worlds in this context refer to the universe and every planet, star, galaxy, and constellation within it. Whatever a scientist discovers through the lens of a telescope was created by an unseen God. This God, who is immortal, dwells in an invisible eternal realm shielded by unapproachable light and no natural eyes have ever seen Him [1 Timothy 6:16]. However, since the creation of the world, God's invisible but divine nature and characteristics such as His eternal power have been made evident to humanity through the things that He made so that people are without excuse [Romans 1:19-20]. Because natural eyes cannot see God, and the human brain cannot compute His nature, it has become convenient for humanity to deny His existence and instead ascribe glory to creative works that can be seen.

One can, therefore, only believe in a God that cannot be seen with natural eyes, by faith. The mind that is open to discovering the truth will ultimately find it. The more such a mind meditates on the works of creation and considers the order in Nature, it becomes difficult for it to deny the existence of a creator. The moment a human mind can submit to the idea of a creator who manufactured every work of Nature including the human, animal and plant life, the mountains, rivers, oceans, forests, jungles, and weather patterns and conditions, it becomes easy to embrace the message of eternal life. God has given us enough evidence of His existence for us to believe.

Without faith it is impossible to please God, those who come to Him must believe that He is and that He rewards those who diligently seek Him [Hebrews 11:6]. So, doubting in God's existence makes it impossible to believe that He created the heavens and the earth. The Bible teaches that in the beginning God created the Heaven and the Earth [Genesis 1:1] and Moses describes step by step how this invisible God created all the evidence we see around us today. However, there is evidence that God did not create the universe alone but was ably assisted by two other members of the entity we call the *Godhead*, namely the Word and the Holy Spirit.

In the beginning we are told there was the Word, and the Word was with God and the Word was God. The same was with God in the beginning [John 1:1-14]. All things were made by Him and there is nothing made that was made without Him. He was born into the world that was made by Him, but the world did not recognise Him. In essence, this Word became flesh and dwelt among us, and His earthly name was Jesus Christ. As part of that Godhead or Trinity, Jesus Christ was with God at the very beginning in His divine embodiment as the Word. So, when God says, "Lets us make man in our own image, after our likeness..." He is speaking to other members of the Trinity – the Word and the Holy Spirit. Apostle Paul concurs with John when he teaches that by Christ were all things created, that are in heaven, and that are in the earth, visible, and invisible, whether they are thrones, dominions, principalities, or powers: all things were created by Him and for Him [Colossians 1:16]. Paul says that He is before all things and by Him all things exist. I believe that God the Father originates, the Word who is His son declares what the Father originates, and the Holy Spirit produces what has been declared by the Word. God thinks, the Word speaks, and the Holy Spirit makes – the Trinity therefore thinks, speaks, and makes.

At the very beginning of creation, Moses tells us about the Holy Spirit who was moving upon the face of the waters [Genesis 1:2], making it clear that He was also present. God is described by Jesus as being a spirit [John 4:24] meaning that the Trinity is spiritual in nature. The Trinity created human beings in their own image so that is why man is a spirit, who lives in a body and has a soul. Scripture confirms this presentation of man's primary parts. King Solomon clarifies that the spirit of man is the lamp of the Lord searching all the man's innermost parts [Proverbs 20:27]. Apostle Paul makes clear that the Holy Spirit bears witness with our spirit that we are children of God and co-heirs with Christ [Romans 8:16]. In his letter to the members of the church at Thessalonica, Apostle Paul prayed that their whole spirit and soul and body would be preserved blameless unto the coming of the Lord Jesus Christ. Anyone who doubts the existence of their spirit and soul cannot walk by faith, because these elements cannot be seen by natural eyes but perceived through the eyes of faith.

Once we scale the hurdle of believing in the existence of an eternal spiritual Trinity, it becomes easier for us to accept the concept of the universe being created by an invisible and all powerful being that precedes time and dwells in eternity. When questioned by Pontius Pilate, the Roman ruler over Palestine, Jesus clarified that His kingdom was not of this world [John 18:36]. This was a mystery to Pilate who struggled to understand the deity of Jesus Christ when all he could see before him was a man he perceived to be under his power. Pilate had no idea that the one standing before him was the Word of God in human form. Even as Jesus' kingdom is not of this world so also is our kingdom not of this world. Our kingdom is in the eternal realm from where everything that can be seen was manufactured and if we believe this then we are walking by faith.

77

Submitting to the unknown

Faith is submitting to the unknown. This is a challenge because the last thing our humanity wants to do is submit to the unknown. It is why man always seeks a god that can be perceived with the five senses. The origin of idols was man's quest for a God that they could relate to with their humanity. Since the fall of Adam and Eve, we have lacked the capacity to see God and not even the resurrection of our dead spirits has been able to achieve this. The problem lies with our flesh which is marked for death and unable to reside in the presence of a Holy and Righteous God without being consumed by the fire of God [Exodus 33:20]. We are saved but our flesh isn't.

Apostle Paul makes clear that those who walk after the flesh (according to a mindset cultivated from information deposited by the five senses) are desirous of earthly things. Those who live like this can be described as being carnally minded but this mindset leads to death because it is the evidence of rebellion against God. Such carnal mindsets do not submit to the law of God and find it impossible to do so. Therefore, those that walk after the flesh cannot please God [Romans 8:3-8]. Paul says that the things of God cannot be received by a naturally minded man because they are foolishness to him, and neither can he discern them because they are spiritually discerned [1 Corinthians 2:14]. These things remain a mystery to those who are carnally minded, and they live their lives with incomplete information. They see facts but cannot discern the truth.

In his message to the Church at Corinth, Paul says that his preaching and teaching were not delivered through enticing words rooted in human wisdom but in demonstration of the Spirit (Holy Spirit) and of power [21 Corinthians 2:4-8]. This was done according to Paul so that their faith should not be based on the wisdom of men but in the power of God. The wisdom Paul preached was not of this world but the divine wisdom of God that was shrouded in mystery – hidden wisdom predetermined by God before the world was created. This is why Paul explains that it was even unknown to the political and religious rulers who could not see the deeper purpose behind the crucifixion. How could they have known that they were carrying out the will of God for the redemption of humanity? The unknown remains a mystery unless it is revealed to those who have the capacity to receive it.

Providing further insight, Paul says that no eye has seen, nor ear heard, neither has it entered into a person's heart the things which God has prepared for those who love Him. But God has revealed them to us by His Holy Spirit who searches the deep things of God. These things of God are only known by the Holy Spirit and not by any man, but because we have received the spirit, which is of God, we know these things that have been freely given to us by God [1 Corinthians 2:9]. In this scripture, Paul reveals that nobody can know the will or plan of God except it is revealed.

Whilst visiting Athens, Apostle Paul's spirit was stirred within him at the sight of a city consumed with idolatry [Acts 17:16-34]. Athenians of that era were superstitious and spent their time seeking new philosophies, doctrines, and practices bordering on mysticism. When Paul addressed them at Mars Hill, he expressed his concern about their practices and mentioned passing an altar dedicated to The Unknown

God whom they ignorantly worshipped. Paul then clarified how God who made the world and all things within it was the Lord of Heaven and Earth and did not dwell in man-made temples; neither is this God served by human hands because He has no needs. Paul explained that God gives life and breath to everything.

From one man, Paul explains that God created all the nations on the face of the earth and decided beforehand the appointed seasons when they would rise up and come to an end as well as their geographical boundaries. According to Paul, God's purpose was for the nations to seek Him and if they searched for Him, they would find Him because He is not far from each of us; for in Him we live and move and have our whole being. Paul made clear that God is not an idol carved out of gold or silver or stone by some skilled craftsman. In times past, God overlooked this ignorance but now commands people everywhere to repent of their sins because He has appointed a day in which He will judge the world in righteousness. That judgment will be by the man He has appointed (Jesus Christ) who was revealed unto all men when God raised Him from the dead.

This passage of scripture contains the most apt description of the unknown that we are called to submit to because this is the heartbeat of faith. The unknown cannot be condensed into a graven image or idol because He created all things and determines the times and boundaries of the kingdoms in the world. He is the life source of all creation and is self-sufficient. There is nothing He requires from us other than our submission. That submission is initially reflected through our repentance.

Submission to the Unknown Creator is ultimately achieved through submission to His will as captured in

His word. However, we cannot submit to His word if we are not in a loving relationship with Him. The two most important commandments are for us to love the Lord with all our heart, soul, strength, and with all our mind; and then to love our neighbour as ourselves [Luke 10:27; Matthew 22:37-40; Mark 12:30-31]. The evidence that we love God is that we keep His commandments [John 14:21 and 23]. The promise from Christ is that those who keep God's commandments will attract His presence. For those privileged to enjoy such an enduring divine presence, God will cease to be unknown.

FINAL WORD

I have confined these faith statements to seventy-seven, but as you dwell on them, I'm sure you could keep on adding to the list. Faith defies boundaries and limitations, and this book is not intended to place restrictions on your revelatory expression. What I hope for is seeds of wisdom to be planted in the soil of your hearts and that you can face life with renewed confidence in a God who honours His words.

Please note that faith is not misplaced confidence in God. Misplaced confidence is when we attempt to superimpose our desires on Him and remain expectant for a favourable outcome. If our desires do not line up with His will, He isn't obliged to grant them. However, He has made it easy for us to know His will, by gifting us His written word – the Holy Bible, and the Holy Spirit who aids our understanding of it. In the development of our faith, there is no substitute for studying His word and meditating on it with the Holy Spirit's assistance.

As you progress along this well-worn pathway of faith, I pray, as Apostle Paul did for the church at Ephesus, [Ephesians 1:18 &19], that the eyes of your heart may be enlightened in order that you may know the hope to which He has called you, the riches of His glorious inheritance in His holy people (us), and His incomparably great power for us who believe.

BEYOND THE PIT

The Story of Joseph

By

JOSEPH AMAEZE

My name is Joseph and I have a story to tell. It may resonate with you. Born into a polygamous family, riddled with conflict, I lost my mother before my tenth birthday. My father tried to compensate, but my sense of loss was never fully appeased. In my teens, at a point when I was finally finding closure, I was trafficked across borders into a life of domestic servitude. Why? Well you need to read my detailed account. Life sometimes throws us curved balls. Betrayed by those I loved, and separated from the only home I ever knew, I was thrust into a darkness I never imagined possible. Stripped of my identity and abused, I discovered the hopelessness and helplessness that lurks within the hearts of those classed as chattels. The only thing that kept me from giving up was the promise I had received in happier times – a promise that provided the only light in a tunnel of uncertainty. A promise of redemption!

Available for Sale at Amazon and other prominent online retailers.

ISBN: 978-0-9935860-2-6